# STANDARDS OF VALUE

# Standards of Value

MONEY, RACE, AND LITERATURE
IN AMERICA

BY *Michael Germana*

UNIVERSITY OF IOWA PRESS, *Iowa City*

University of Iowa Press, Iowa City 52242
Copyright © 2009 by the University of Iowa Press
www.uiowapress.org
Printed in the United States of America

Design by Teresa W. Wingfield

Chapter 2 is reprinted from *Arizona Quarterly* 61.3 (2005) by permission of the Regents of the University of Arizona.

The University of Iowa Press is a member of Green Press Initiative and
is committed to preserving natural resources.

Printed on acid-free paper

LIBRARY OF CONGRESS CATALOGING-IN-PUBLICATION DATA
Germana, Michael, 1971–
Standards of value: money, race, and literature in America / by Michael
Germana.
     p.  cm.
Includes bibliographical references and index.
ISBN-13: 978-1-58729-818-9 (cloth)
ISBN-10: 1-58729-818-x (cloth)
 1. American fiction—19th century—History and criticism.  2. Money
in literature.  3. Race in literature.  4. American fiction—20th centu-
ry—History and criticism.  I. Title.
PS374.M54G47 2009
813'.009'355—dc22     2009005977

*To Alyssa*

# CONTENTS

# ACKNOWLEDGMENTS

This book would not have been possible were it not for Kathleen Diffley, whose guidance, patience, and sagacity enabled *Standards of Value* to come to fruition. I am also indebted to Kathleen's colleagues at the University of Iowa—Bluford Adams, Corey Creekmur, Barbara Eckstein, Tom Lutz, and Kim Marra—with whom I had the great pleasure to collaborate during my tenure there. Thanks also to Sandra Barkan and the University of Iowa Graduate College for funding my archival research on Ralph Ellison at the Library of Congress and providing me precious time to write.

Since joining the faculty at West Virginia University, I have benefited greatly from both the advice of my colleagues in the Department of English and the support of WVU's Eberly College of Arts and Sciences. I am grateful for the thoughtful suggestions I received on an earlier draft of the introduction from the members of the Faculty Research Group of WVU's Department of English: Jonathan Burton, Ryan Claycomb, Pat Conner, Jay Dolmage, Lara Farina, Marilyn Francus, Donald Hall, Tim Sweet, Lisa Weihman, and Scott Wible. I would especially like to thank John Ernest, who, in addition to being a member of this group and a thoughtful reader of the complete manuscript, has buoyed me with his generosity of spirit, encyclopedic knowledge, and unflagging support. Financial assistance has been provided by the Eberly College of Arts and Sciences in two forms: a Riggle Fellowship in the Humanities, which funded trips to the Harvard Theatre Collection and the Boston Public Library, and a generous subvention, which helped defray the cost of producing this book.

In addition to recognizing the librarians and staffs of the Library of Congress, the Boston Public Library, and the Harvard Theatre Collection for all their help, I would like to thank Donald Pease for giving me the opportunity to workshop a draft of chapter 1 at the 2008 Futures of American Studies Institute, where I received invaluable advice from

Gabriel Briggs, Michael Chaney, Lázaro Lima, Alan Nadel, Michele Speitz, and Rachel Watson.

Finally, a special thanks to Alyssa Wright, whose love and friendship have brought me so much joy over the years, and whose keen insight and honest criticism have made this a better book. I dedicate *Standards of Value* to her with much love.

# INTRODUCTION

*Why should the intelligent elements of the South, embittered by a sense of outrage and crushed under negro legislation, care to maintain those standards of value that represent only ruin to themselves?*

C. F. ADAMS, JR., "THE CURRENCY DEBATE OF 1873–74" IN THE *North American Review*

The meaning of words, the value of money, and the significance of race all fluctuate within economies of difference. Words have meaning only in relation to other words; the dollar rises and falls based upon the performance of other commodities; and race appears and disappears based upon perceived differences between body types. The cultural turn of the mid- to late twentieth century made the contingencies of linguistic meaning, monetary value, and racial identification readily apparent, if not commonsensical. But for the cultural turn to run its course the economies of difference that give meaning to language, race, and money had to merge, not merely coexist. *Standards of Value: Money, Race, and Literature in America* shows how American novelists helped realize this merger by promoting commerce between literary, racial, and monetary discourses. It demonstrates how American authors renegotiated the value of racial difference in the United States by drawing analogies between popular arguments over the form American money should take and their own assertions about the form black-white relationships, and thus also the nation, should take. By showing how this narrative strategy changed both public perceptions of racial difference and the arc of the cultural turn, *Standards of Value* introduces a new approach to the study of the American novelistic tradition and reconsiders the role U.S. monetary policy and American popular culture together played in the articulation of racial discourse from the mid-nineteenth to the mid-twentieth century.

It is impossible to talk about race in America without lapsing into double-speak. The reason, to riff on the preacher's chant in the prologue of Ralph Ellison's *Invisible Man* (1952), is that race is . . . an' race ain't. As a lived system of social divisions and cultural practices, race *is*. But as an ideological construct reified by such divisions and practices, race *ain't*. Contemporary cultural historians emphasize the Janus-faced nature of race by calling it a social construction; a concept, fully institutionalized, that signifies and reinforces social cleavages along the lines of real or imagined differences in body type. Because this concept structures American society in the absence of any biological basis for differentiating groups along racial lines, race *is*, even though it *ain't*.

The theory of racial formation explains how the two-ness of race is maintained through an ongoing process of reciprocal determination. According to Michael Omi and Howard Winant, racial categories either coexist in symbolic and institutional forms or they don't exist at all.[1] Racial formation describes the processes by which the ideological linkage between these two forms—between racial signification and racialized social structures—is reinforced. The agents of racial formation are what Omi and Winant call racial projects. Racial projects can be large or small, political or personal, public or private, but each is simultaneously discursive and institutional because each connects the meaning of race to "the ways in which both social structures and everyday experiences are racially *organized*, based upon that meaning" (Omi and Winant, *Racial Formation* 56; italics in original).[2]

While Omi and Winant underscore the irreducible duality of race and the role racial projects play in maintaining it, Henry Louis Gates, Jr., illustrates how racial formations resist subversion by signification alone. In "Writing 'Race' and the Difference It Makes," Gates argues that race was literally written into existence to subordinate peoples along racial lines. Race, therefore, is not and never has been "an objective term of classification," he notes, but has always been "a dangerous trope" (5). The virtual reality of race that Gates describes poses a dilemma for anyone representing racial difference to hold a mirror up to a racialized society, for such writing has the corollary effect of rewriting race, that is, remarking (and thus remaking) racial difference.[3] "Black people, we know, have not been liberated from racism by our writings," Gates observes. "Black writing, and especially the literature of the slave, served not to obliterate the difference of race; rather, the inscription of the black voice in Western literatures has preserved those very cultural differences to be repeated, imitated, and revised in a separate Western literary tradition, a tradition of black difference" (12). The reason the concept of race is so readily and easily reinscribed, notes John Ernest, is that "the formidable manifestations of history continue to define various and interconnected cultural, economic, and political landscapes" (474). In other words, the sociopolitical edifice that race orders and shapes—what David Theo Goldberg calls the racial state—lends significance to a concept of difference that such representation reinforces.[4] Hence Saidiya V. Hartman's observation that the performative has "the power . . . to produce the very subject which it appears to express" (57).

If, as Gates demonstrates, literary texts cannot break the ideological linkages between social structure and cultural signification that make them meaningful, and if, as Omi and Winant argue, texts that reinscribe race constitute racial projects, then works of literary fiction by authors who sought to reform race relations in the United States must be evaluated within, not apart from, the racialized social and cultural contexts they engage in dialectical commerce. Such an evaluation must therefore begin by reevaluating the objectives of both reform-minded authors and the critics who study them. If a cultural economy in which signs are exchanged is, like the society to which it is inextricably linked and into which individuals are inserted as subjects, always already racialized, then the goal of reform-minded authors is to change the *value* of racial difference within that economy. In other words, their objective is not to demystify race itself, but to develop racial counter-projects that destabilize the link between representations of racial difference and the structure of the racial state. The goal of contemporary literary critics, in turn, is to illustrate how this objective is achieved within the discursive systems and structures of power these texts critique.

To these ends, *Standards of Value* argues that from the mid-nineteenth to the mid-twentieth century American novelists effected this destabilization by grafting the value of black-white difference onto another ideology of value metonymically represented by the nation's money. Incorporating the language, logic, and imagery of U.S. monetary policy reforms as they were popularly understood (or misunderstood) into their texts, these authors drew analogies between the monetary projects of the period, which reified the ideological connection between the form and value of U.S. currency, and their own racial counter-projects, which aimed to rewrite the association between ethnicity and human worth. Using money to self-reflexively comment on both the cultural currency of race and his or her own participation in its circulation, each of these authors forged a connection between the cultural politics of race and the rhetoric of political economy—a connection that continues to make its unconscious return in the popular cultural texts of contemporary America.

Narratives that followed this strategy hailed large audiences because from the antebellum years to the post–WWII era Americans of all stripes were preoccupied with two questions of value: the race question, which hinged upon the value of racial difference, and the money question, which pegged the value of the nation's money to the form it took. By inflecting race in the accents of American political economy, authors like Harriet Beecher Stowe, George Washington Cable, Charles Chesnutt, James Weldon Johnson, Walter White, Jessie Redmon Fauset, Nella Larsen, and Ralph Ellison showed readers that the value of racial difference, like the standards of literary and monetary value, is inseparable from the operation of discourse. More importantly, by introducing the rhetoric of political economy into the discourse of racial reform—an articulation facilitated by the inherent dialogism of the genre of the novel—these authors effectively wrote race into the discourse of monetary reform, a move that helped insure that race would follow money as it slouched toward autonomous representation to be (re)born as a sign of purely relational value.[5] So if, as Barbara Herrnstein Smith has argued, literary value is contingent upon "the changing interests and other values of a community" in which literature circulates (10), and if, as Lindon Barrett illustrates, the abstract concepts of race and value are "isomorphic" in U.S. culture (1), then the reconceptualization of monetary value is the principal contingency affecting the cultural currency of American literary texts that took race as their subject.[6]

As this yoking of literary, monetary, and racial discourses illustrates, signs constitutive of racial difference do not acquire their currency in a vacuum. Instead, their value is and always has been overdetermined by interlocking, dynamic cultural processes that, operating together, promote the materialization of racial difference. Consequently, the frameworks through which the body is read intersect in complex and meaningful ways. These frameworks tend to be mutually reinforcing, but they are subject to evolutionary changes. One such transformation began during the 1840s when shifting immigration patterns and American imperialist imperatives led to the expansion and internal fragmentation of blackness and whiteness into broad categories of distinct races.

As Matthew Frye Jacobson has shown, the influx of Irish immigrants to the United States during the 1840s and the subsequent waves of European migration that followed led to "a fracturing of whiteness into a hierarchy of plural and scientifically determined white races" (7). Meanwhile, as Lázaro Lima has illustrated, the annexation of Texas and the ensuing Mexican-American War laid the groundwork for legal processes of racialization that turned many Mexicans "black" and thereby excised them from "an emerging sense of Americanness that, paradoxically, became ever more restrictive in measure with its territorial expansion" (26).[7] The combined result was the subjection of an increasing number and variety of peoples to a black-white racial calculus that helped contain and neutralize the threat of unruly hybridity on multiple fronts.

The expansion during the 1840s of racial descriptors organized around signs of normative whiteness and blackness reflects what Jacobson calls "a shift from one brand of bedrock racism to another—from the unquestioned hegemony of a unified race of 'white persons' to a contest over political 'fitness'" (42–43). Because civil liberties and rights of citizenship—even basic human rights—were granted or denied on the basis of such value judgments, the racial debate in the United States, which spilled onto the pages of American fiction, came progressively to be framed along black-white lines. The authors examined in this book did not reproduce the black-white racial binary because they had faith in its stability or confidence in its inclusiveness. Rather, their particularistic rendering of race reflects a consolidation of investments in black-white difference that radically reshaped the American century that followed the 1840s.

African Americans' quests for self-possession and self-determination were played out against this backdrop of broadening racial categories and expanding racializing practices. It goes without saying that the evolution of race profoundly affected the experiences of African Americans in an era shaped by slavery, the Civil War, Reconstruction, and Jim Crow. Among other things, the gerrymandering of racial categories in the 1840s helped preserve mythologies of race that formed the foundation of the slave system—mythologies that, as Ariela J. Gross has shown, emerge from the mutually constitutive relationship between the legal history of race and the social practices it prescribed and/or proscribed.[8] The perverted logic of racialization after 1848 was therefore an extension of an equally perverted racial calculus that served as justification for the enslavement and/or continued subjection of individuals of African descent. By transforming blackness from a signifier of racial identification to a sign of racialization, the authors examined in this book challenged the racialist economy that gave blackness its significance. Just as the black-white racial calculus racialized those who did not self-identify as either "black" or "white," so too did the decentering of this binary have implications that transcended the narrow channels of black and white racial identities.

## WHY MONEY MARKS THE SPOT WHERE BLACK AND WHITE MEET

Examining race through the lens of political economy is profitable for cultural historians because the value of racial difference, like the value of money, is materialized in the marketplace. As Michael O'Malley has so keenly observed, the very function of markets is to assign value to difference. The process of exchange makes these differences meaningful, and money is the sign of this meaning. The story is the same for race. Ever since the nation was founded a premium has been placed on maintaining black difference, which enabled a system of slavery that transformed black persons into movable property, and later perpetuated the caste structure that slavery prefigured by sanctioning the continued operation of Jim Crow policies and procedures. The value of racial difference has always shaped and been reshaped by market forces, which give meaning to the exchanges this difference makes possible. Race is not an intrinsic quality of the body, but the sign of this meaning. Fortunately for the authors this project examines, the fungibility of signs makes their value negotiable, and as Marc Shell, Walter Benn Michaels, and others have illustrated, literary fiction constitutes a symbolic marketplace wherein such brokering can take place. From the 1850s to the 1950s, activist writers transformed this marketplace and renegotiated the value of racial difference by recalculating the value of its sign—a process facilitated by tying race to money, that is, by treating the race question as germane to the money question.

The success of this narrative strategy depended in large part upon the ubiquity of the money question, which played itself out on the pages and stages of American popular culture for well over a century. Contrary to twenty-first-century practice, monetary policy was once a subject hotly debated by the American public, not just pundits and policymakers. At stake in these debates was the very definition of value, including the nature of its production and the source of its authenticity. Reform-minded American authors capitalized on the popular rhetoric of these debates by drawing analogies between the values of money and race to redirect the class, sectional, ideological, and even philosophical inflections of the money question to their own ends. However, because (d)evolutionary changes in the standards that governed the values of money and race also reformed the cultural currency of literature itself, the ends of literary interventions into the race question gradually merged with the means. This is why nineteenth-century writers like Harriet Beecher Stowe and George Washington Cable could use the language and logic of monetary reform to propose broad changes in government policy that addressed institutionalized racism, while the monetary metaphors of twentieth-century authors like Jessie Redmon Fauset, Nella Larsen, and Ralph Ellison were deployed self-reflexively to show what literature cannot say about race and racialism. In addition to recovering the cultural critiques that the money question made possible, *Standards of Value* illustrates how the progressive reforms that relocated both the value of money and the authenticity of race in performance led to a crisis among authors committed to remedying what W. E. B. Du Bois called the problem of the color line. For as cultural performances of race became race itself, so also did representations of racial difference redraw the color line.

In exploring the cultural currency of currency itself, this project builds upon the work of three New Economic[9] critics: the aforementioned Marc Shell, Michael O'Malley, and Walter Benn Michaels, each of whom examines coinage and currency in relation to other discursive systems within broader cultural contexts. In *Money, Language, and Thought*, Marc Shell argues that language and thought are bound by, as well as expressions of, the economic systems from which they spring. He claims that "money, which refers to a system of tropes, is also an 'internal' participant in the logical or semiological organization of language, which itself refers to a system of tropes. Whether or not a writer mentioned money or was aware of its potentially subversive role in his thinking, the new forms of metaphorization or exchanges of meaning that accompanied the new forms of economic symbolization and production were changing the meaning of meaning itself" (3–4).

In short, as economic models came and went, each relocating value in some way, so also was the logic of representation and its impact upon culture reformed in new ways. This is what Shell refers to as "the tropic interaction between economic and linguistic symbolization and production" (4) that shimmers to the surface of texts like Poe's "The Gold-Bug" (1843) with which he begins his analysis, and which I reread below.[10]

Where Shell concentrates on the tropic interaction between money on the one hand and language and thought on the other, Michael O'Malley examines the rhetorical vocabulary shared by hard money advocates and proponents of essentialist theories of race during the nineteenth century. In his seminal article "Specie and Species: Race and the Money Question in Nineteenth-Century America," O'Malley shows how a ubiquitous analogy whereby the money of the nation was likened to the blood of the body, when paired with hegemonic hard money rhetoric, was used to prop up essentialist definitions of race and thereby support discriminatory social and political policies that relied upon race as a stable system of classification. "Thomas Hobbes understood money as the blood in Leviathan's body," writes O'Malley, "and the metaphor served proslavery Southerner John C. Calhoun equally well nearly two hundred years later" (372).[11] Of particular interest to O'Malley are the shared assumptions of Reconstruction-era monetary policies and racial politics, each of which, as he demonstrates, underwrote the other.

No one to date has examined the evolution of the analogy O'Malley identifies between monetary and racial signification systems to show how the persistence of these shared assumptions facilitated constructionist articulations of race in the twentieth century. And with the exception of Hildegard Hoeller, who examines Zora Neale Hurston's "The Gilded Six-Bits" as a commentary on racial politics informed by and critical of the gold standard debate,[12] no one has filled the critical lacuna that separates Shell's work from O'Malley's—a gap that is flanked by two of Walter Benn Michaels's major works, *The Gold Standard and the Logic of Naturalism* and *Our America*. In the former, Michaels explores the logic shared by naturalist literature and the gold standard without addressing race, and in the latter he explains how racial pluralism, by equating race with culture, grafted racial difference onto nationalist identity, without examining how the tropic interaction between money and literature during the same period contributed to pluralism's unconscious racialism.[13]

Taking at face value (without taking for granted) the similarities between discursive systems that these theorists identify, this project explores the cultural work that this network of tropic interactions made possible for American authors who sought to exchange their revaluations of racial difference for liberating social praxis. It also explains why dollars and cents so frequently mark the spot in the American literary text where black and white bodies literally and/or figuratively meet. Not all of these money-marked contact zones are equally complex in their tropic interactivity, however. In some of these meetings, coinage and currency act merely as metaphors for the class differences onto which racial difference has been grafted, such as in Flannery O'Connor's short story "Everything That Rises Must Converge" (1964), the climax of which is triggered when Julian's mother, a white woman nostalgic for a bygone Southern aristocracy, presents Carver, a black child, with a shiny penny. At other times this meeting-ground is more symbolic, like in chapter 99 of *Moby-Dick* (1851), which portrays members of the *Pequod*'s crew taking turns interpreting the signs embossed on a gold coin nailed to the mainmast by Captain Ahab before putting on a mini minstrel show replete with blackface songs and a stump speech.[14] These two types of black-white convergence themselves converge in Charles Chesnutt's novel *The Marrow of Tradition* (1901) when Tom Delamere blacks himself up with burnt cork, first to win a cakewalk, and later to murder the matriarch Polly Ochiltree for the money in her cedar chest. The clue that simultaneously reveals Tom's racial crossdressing and his guilt for committing the murder is "a five-dollar gold piece of a date back toward the beginning of the century" (638), which Tom's grandfather discovers just in time to save Sandy, his black servant, from being lynched by a white mob for a crime he didn't commit.

These black-white contact zones and the monetary symbols that mark them become a more complex form of symbolism when authors use these symbols to draw analogies between the cultural politics of race, the logic of money, and the hermeneutics of literature. Edgar Allan Poe's short story "The Gold-Bug," which Marc Shell uses to initiate his analysis of the monetary logic of American literature and letters, both exemplifies this three-way analogy and demonstrates the recovery work that remains to be done in this area. Shell correctly notes that "Poe was less concerned with partisan problems of monetary policy than with the implicit ideological relationship between aesthetic and monetary symbolization" (10), but he does not connect this relationship to the subaltern subject of Poe's story: the value of the manumitted slave, Jupiter, whose punning speech reveals how race, like the intrinsic value of gold to which it is likened, is "*no* tin," or no-thing outside of the symbolic, discursive systems that maintain it.

As Shell points out, Poe extends an invitation to his readers to apply the same interpretive methodologies that the story depicts to the story itself. When the reader takes up the author's invitation, Shell argues, it becomes clear that Poe is drawing an analogy between the process of turning marks on paper into meaning (in the case of the treasure map/cipher Legrand finds) and the act of turning marks on paper into value (in the case of paper money with which this map/cipher is associated). But while Shell makes it clear that Poe's short story equates hermeneutics with economics and thereby equates the production of meaning with the production of value, he does not examine how Poe's story also raises the specter of the uncertain meaning or value of black difference—the political economics of race—in the process.

"The Gold-Bug" portrays the interpretive process as a kind of alchemy by which marks on parchment and the scarab beetle that helps Legrand decode them lead to the "gold of which it [the gold bug] is the index" (48). Jupiter, the manumitted slave who remains in Legrand's service, offers a clue to the alchemical logic of the story that contains him when he says of the scarab, "Dey aint *no* tin in him, Massa Will, I keep a tellin' on you . . . de bug is a goole-bug, solid, ebery bit of him, inside and all, sep him wing—neber feel half so hebby a bug in my life" (43). Jupiter's observations are responses to Legrand's recollection that the bug has "two jet black spots near one extremity of the back, and another, somewhat longer, at the other" (43). If Jupiter equates the black marks on the beetle with the tin that adulterates gold in the alchemical process, then his own name, which signifies tin in alchemy,[15] points to an alchemical formula of which the freedman, and in particular the meaning or value of his blackness, is a part.

The central, unanswered question in "The Gold-Bug" is: what keeps Jupiter in Legrand's service? Legally, Jupiter was "manumitted before the reverses of the [Legrand] family," which reduced its members from wealth to want (42–43). Yet Jupiter "could be induced, neither by threats nor by promises, to abandon what he considered his right" to attend to Legrand, around whom he is in constant orbit (43). The answer, Poe implies, has everything to do with Jupiter's racial status, of which his blackness is the index. When the reader applies the alchemical logic of Jupiter's utterance to the formula of which it is a part, Jupiter's blackness becomes nothing more than a mark upon an otherwise solid-gold body. In short, he is just like the gold bug: black/tin on the outside, but gold/"*no* tin" inside. Poe thereby begs the question: what accounts for Jupiter's devaluation? To extend the monetary metaphor, Poe draws an implicit parallel between Jupiter and the "very large and heavy coins" included in the treasure, which are "so worn that we could make nothing of their inscriptions" (57). Gold coins retain their precious metal value when the marks that denote their face value are removed. Poe here suggests that Jupiter, but for the pigment that inscribes his skin—or rather the interpretation of its meaning—is just as valuable.

Again, the clues to solving the story's racial riddle are provided by

Poe himself, who has both Legrand and the narrator mistake the parchment upon which the cipher is printed, a literal skin, with a piece of paper that is placed in Legrand's wallet like paper currency. The key to unlocking the cipher is Legrand's discovery that the document is, in fact, colored skin. And deciphering the meaning of the "chemical preparations" that color the skin is what leads Legrand to the treasure. Neither Legrand's parchment nor the paper money of which it is an analogue nor the written tale to which it is likened has intrinsic value. But each, through a process of signification and interpretation, leads to something of real value. The same is true for the color of Jupiter's skin and its difference from Legrand's, the value of which is not intrinsic, but produced (and reproduced) by the processes of representation and interpretation. It stands to reason, then, that marks on paper, especially in the form of narratives like Poe's, can alter the value of racial difference by helping readers reinterpret the meaning of the optical density of skin. There is real value in this.

William Wells Brown draws a similar three-way parallel between writing, race, and the value of paper money in his introduction to *Clotel* (1853) entitled "Narrative of the Life and Escape of William Wells Brown." In this self-reflexive autobiographical sketch Brown writes of how he turned his fledgling barbershop into a bank by issuing promissory notes and putting them into circulation. When the author's rival, the white barbershop owner across the street, organizes a run on Brown's bank, Brown learns that the way to stay in the banking business is to recycle his debt. A friend instructs him, "When your notes are brought to you, you must redeem them, and then send them out and get other money for them; and, with the latter, you can keep cashing your Shinplasters" (69). Aside from drawing an enticing parallel between the socially constructed values of racial difference and paper money like Poe does before him, Brown also likens the recycling of debt to the perpetual deferral of linguistic meaning. In the process, he hints that race, like any other sign, is an empty cipher whose significance is inseparable from the economy in which it circulates—an economy of differences and the values attributed to them by social contract.

## U.S. MONETARY POLICY AND THE RACIAL LOGIC OF AMERICAN LITERATURE

Authors like Poe and Brown who incorporated money into their texts tapped into popular public sentiment about the form U.S. currency should take, a concept that may seem foreign to contemporary readers for whom economic policy is largely hidden, decided and implemented by government bureaucrats behind closed doors. But monetary policy was once an inseparable part of American popular culture. For example, the "money question" received editorial treatment in just about every magazine from the *Atlantic Monthly* to the *Workingman's Advocate*. Dollars and cents were key props in minstrel shows, and the policies that determined money's value were debated in newspaper columns and other mass circulation media for well over a century.[16] These polices in turn became the subjects of Thomas Nast's cartoons and William A. Croffut's "Bourbon Ballads," which included numbers like "Resumption—Greenbacks at Par" when they were published in the *New York Tribune*. In short, from the 1830s to the mid-twentieth century, U.S. monetary policy *was* popular culture. And, thanks to the authors this book studies, monetary policy became one of the frameworks through which the body was explicitly rather than implicitly read.

What distinguishes the authors this project examines from writers like O'Connor, Melville, Poe, and Brown is that in the process of tying the subject of money's value to both the value of racial difference and the role literature plays in its negotiation they made explicit references to the monetary policies enacted by the U.S. government from 1834 to 1934. In so doing, these authors rendered intelligible the interdependent logics of money, race, and literature during the period. In their texts, coinage and currency act as metaphors for economic and symbolic exchanges while serving as metonyms for the American political-economic movements that overdetermined the meaning of such commerce.

The cultural currency of American currency, upon which these authors' critiques relied, was the product of two overlapping trends: the historical tendency of U.S. monetary policy reforms to reform the nation itself, and the development of new technologies for the reproduction and dissemination of texts, which revolutionized American popular culture and reformed the relationship of individuals to the whole of American society. As for changes in the form of the nation's money changing the nation itself, a cursory glance at American history confirms the thrust of the Greenback Party's motto, "All reform waits for money reform. Then let us get money reform first."[17] Nowhere is the truth of this statement more evident than in the debates over monetary policy that led to Shays's Rebellion of 1786–87, or the process by which Shays's Rebellion led to the formulation and ratification of the U.S. Constitution.

Historian Leonard Richards locates the catalyst of Shays's Rebellion in the Massachusetts State Constitution of 1780, which effectively "consolidated power in the hands of the mercantile elite and the eastern part of the state. It shifted power from the rural backcountry to Boston, from the poor to the rich, and from town meetings to the state senate and the governor's office" (74). Against this backdrop of power consolidation was an issue tied directly to the Revolutionary War debt and the Federalist monetary policies that addressed it. In a nutshell, Massachusetts paid its soldiers with paper money it could not honor at face value. Because most of these soldiers were farmers and other men without means they parted with their notes, often for a tenth of their face value, in exchange for goods, services, or hard money with which to pay taxes. The overwhelming majority of this paper money, around 80 percent, wound up in the hands of speculators who lived in and around Boston. This was the situation when the new state legislature met and, ignoring the market value of these notes, promised to redeem them at face value, that is, for their worth on the day they were issued. In order to pay this burdensome sum to the speculators who now possessed most of these notes the legislature had to raise taxes. Ninety percent of the money needed to pay this debt (at 6 percent interest) came from property taxes, which had to be paid in coin, that is, with gold or silver. Thus the laboring classes, whose members were previously forced to relinquish their notes for a pittance, were now required to pay for their redemption, too.

The uprising that ensued may ultimately have been a failure for the Shaysites, but it had a lasting impact upon the new nation and even played a key role in the form the nation took. For though Shays's Rebellion was ultimately put down, the threat of insurrection it represented was adopted and brandished by nationalists who used it as "Exhibit A" in their case for a stronger national government. This reactionary backlash led directly to the meeting of the governing elite that created the U.S. Constitution. It also accounts for the anti-democratic policies embodied in the Constitution, which further consolidated power in the hands of the elite.[18]

As monetary policy gave rise to the new constitution, the U.S. Constitution reshaped American monetary policy by paving the way for Alexander Hamilton's plan to nationalize the public debt held by individual states. As Richards points out, Hamilton had no plans to actually pay off this debt; rather, he recycled it in order to expand the economy. The effect was to further enrich those speculators who held the notes that embodied the Revolutionary War debt—the notes whose redemption was the root cause of Shays's Rebellion in the first place.

Because reforming the money literally reformed the republic during the Revolutionary Era, monetary reform came to connote national reform. This connotation achieved mythic status during Andrew Jackson's presidency, and remained a key ideological component of national political movements until the mid-twentieth century. It informed Andrew Jackson's war against the Second Bank of the United States during the 1830s, fueled the formation of the Greenback Party after the Civil War, found its expression in William Jennings Bryan's famous "Cross of Gold" speech, which launched his candidacy for president in the election of 1896, and formed the foundation of the New Deal. As was the case with Shays's Rebellion, it was the drive for monetary reform combined with the reforms themselves that reshaped American society by mobilizing and reorganizing persons, sentiments, and resources at a national level.

If the rise of this connotative association accounts for the creation and maintenance of money's cultural currency, then the reformation of American popular culture transformed the economy in which this currency circulated. Over the course of the nineteenth century and the first half of the twentieth century the creation and implementation of new technologies of mechanical reproduction and mass-market distribution led to a reformation of popular culture and with it the creation of new publics. This, in turn, led to a new relationship of subjects to publics by changing the way subjects were reproduced in relation to these publics. As audiences got bigger and media messages became more synchronous, texts that addressed the money question and/or the race question became sites for the articulation of axiological ideologies, both monetary and racial, on a national scale. Monetary policy and its transformative power may have made the issue of value more salient, but the reformation of popular culture made the era's questions of value more immediate while making the ideologies that animated them more hegemonic.

These two threads, the evolution of U.S. monetary policy and the transformation of American popular culture, converge in each of the texts this project examines. Accordingly, each chapter of this project revolves around a different popular cultural manifestation of the money question to explore its redeployment in and/or rearticulation by one or more novels. Because the authors of these novels tied the question of the value of racial difference to the question of monetary value expressed by U.S. popular culture, the reformation of race in American literature cannot be divorced from the revolution in popular culture or the evolution of the money question across the period.

The first chapter, "Jacksonian Abolitionism: Money, Minstrelsy, and *Uncle Tom's Cabin*," examines the minstrel gestures of Stowe's famous novel to show how its monetary metaphors, which were rehearsed on the minstrel stage during the 1830s and 1840s, redirect minstrelsy's class-inflected critiques to abolitionist ends. *Uncle Tom's Cabin* (1852) consolidated antislavery sentiment in the urban North in part by tapping into and then soothing the anxieties of white, working-class men who feared becoming "wage slaves" in a new market-capitalist economy. During the antebellum years, blackface minstrels used American money, and in particular its changing form after the Coinage Act of 1834, to associate the economics of black slavery with those of working-class wage slavery and reinforce Jacksonian beliefs that democracy and wage labor were incompatible. White minstrels "blacked up" to protest their demotion from artisans to wage laborers and used silver dollars, the substance of which was more valuable than their face value after 1834, to express a conviction that they too were devalued in the market and denied their inherent worth as white men. In *Uncle Tom's Cabin*, Stowe borrows this motif and places a silver dollar around Uncle Tom's neck to suggest that slavery denied him his inherent value as a human being, thereby likening him to a working-class minstrel hero victimized by economic forces beyond his control. By incorporating the conventions of minstrelsy—including its self-reflexive monetary references—Stowe redeployed minstrelsy's logic to make the "peculiar institution" of slavery appear antithetical to long-lived Jacksonian Democratic ideals that remained entrenched until the Civil War.

During the Civil War, the Union funded its battles with the Confederacy by creating and putting into circulation a new form of currency called United States Notes or "greenbacks." These paper promises of future payment were not backed by precious metals, but relied solely on the credit of the federal government for their value. Anti-abolitionists lampooned the Union cause by likening the federal legislation of 1862 that turned fiat money into legal tender to Lincoln's Emancipation Proclamation, which promised to turn Southern slaves into free persons. This analogical connection between fiat money and freedmen became a defining characteristic of American popular culture during the postbellum years when the national debt, embodied by $430 million in greenbacks, became the source of the money question, and four million former slaves became the subject of the so-called Negro question of the postwar South. Chapter 2, "Real Change: George Washington Cable's *The Grandissimes* and the Crime of '73," examines the analogies George Washington Cable drew in his novel *The Grandissimes* (1880) between the money question during Reconstruction and the reorganization of the postwar South. As Walter T. K. Nugent has shown, debates surrounding the national debt that remained after the Civil War ended were expressed in the popular Utilitarian rhetoric of the day. Applying the principles of Isaac Newton to political and moral affairs, Utilitarians put their faith in the laws of nature and applied scientific methods to social and legal issues. A testament to the elasticity and ubiquity of Utilitarian terminology, political economists of all stripes, no matter what position they advocated on the national debt, couched their arguments in the language of Newtonian social science. In *The Grandissimes*, Cable applies the Utilitarian rhetoric of postbellum political economy to sociopolitical ends by grafting the moral issues of 1870s monetary reform onto the caste system that had outlived slavery and that he sought to abolish. Mapping the debates surrounding the money question onto the Negro question during Reconstruction, *The Grandissimes* fostered renewed debate about the rights of freedmen by appealing to popular social scientific principles, which shaped postwar monetary policy but had yet to be applied to the laissez-faire social and civil policies of the New South.

As monetary Populists were squaring off against hard money conservatives in the presidential election of 1896, Homer Plessy was using his ability to pass for white to stage an act of civil disobedience. The result in both cases was an essentialist backlash against the remaking of difference. The triumph of "gold bug" William McKinley over the inflationist "free silver" candidate William Jennings Bryan affirmed the public's faith in intrinsic value(s), and the *Plessy* decision (re)defined race as an inherent quality of the body. The third chapter, "The Gold Standard of the Passing Novel: Exploring the Limits of Strategic Essentialism," uses the logic of the gold standard to re-evaluate novels about racial passing and their evolving use of what Gayatri Spivak calls strategic essentialism: the deconstructive strategy of using a reader's investment in essentialism—the belief in intrinsic value and its stability—to critique that investment. Most passing novels employ strategic essentialism to critique racial discrimination in some form or other. But an examination of the gold standard metaphors that anchor these texts reveals how passing novel authors used strategic essentialism first to critique institutionalized racism and later to demonstrate the limits of this narrative strategy. Spanning the years 1900 to 1933, the years the United States was on the gold standard, this chapter examines how pre-WWI passing novels serve strategic essentialist ends by conforming to the logic of the classical gold standard, and shows how the competing logics of the gold standard after WWI mirror the contradictory aims of Harlem Renaissance writers whose consolidation of and investment in race as a commodity forestalled the constructivist objectives of their work. By taking a diachronic approach to the passing novel and its conformity to the logic of an evolving gold standard, this chapter reveals what the individual texts that compose this genre do not. And by reading Harlem Renaissance passing novels in light of the monetary logic of the era—a logic that is incorporated into the novels themselves—this chapter ultimately shows that the relationship of authors like Nella Larsen and Jessie Redmon Fauset to the Harlem Renaissance project of marketing black authenticity championed earlier by Alain Locke was uneasy at best.

With the Depression came the New Deal, and with the New Deal came the abolition of the domestic gold standard. But while U.S. monetary policy shifted dramatically toward a constructivist, managed currency system, the racial state remained segregated as black Americans remained marginalized by the dictates of Jim Crow. Ralph Ellison explores this contradiction—this divergence in the theories of monetary and racial value—in his novel *Invisible Man* (1952). The fourth chapter of this project, "Black Is . . . an' Black Ain't: *Invisible Man* and the Fiat of Race," treats Ralph Ellison's *Invisible Man* as a retrospective history of literary interventions into the race question. Set at a time when the United States was abandoning the gold standard, *Invisible Man* riffs on the language and imagery of New Deal monetary reform to show how race, as a socially constructed trope of difference, continues to circulate at face value even after the essentialist pretenses that anchored the theory of race are abandoned. Drawing an analogy between U.S. currency after the gold standard and contemporary American fiction, Ellison illustrates why novels like his own, which maintain the fiat of race, are limited in their ability to redress the causes of racism. Ellison punctuates this analogy with allusions to L. Frank Baum's *The Wonderful Wizard of Oz* (1900), which is both an allegory for the rise and fall of monetary Populism and a cautionary tale about the "humbug" of fiat money. Using Baum's narrative to reflect upon his own, Ellison draws a parallel analogy between Baumian/Populist ambivalence about fiat money and his own wariness about the relocation of race's authenticity in performance, that is, the fiat of race. The result is a proto-postmodern examination of an epistemological turn that began with the devolution of American money toward simulacra and would eventually encompass race's demotion from essence to metaphor to sign. Tracing the arc of this turn, Ellison anticipates the changing role of literature—itself a form of circulating paper—in the revaluation of racial difference.

In the second half of the twentieth century the selfsame confluence of historical, cultural, and political forces that gave U.S. currency its cultural currency as a metaphor for the value of racial difference transformed dollars and cents into mythic signs of race itself, for as money became the sign of the value it once possessed, so too did race become the sign of the difference it reinscribes. Money still marks the loci of racial difference in contemporary popular cultural texts, but the coincidence of money and race within them now underscores, often ironically, the limited ability of cultural texts to catalyze social reforms. The cultural turn brought about the realization that while hegemonic discourses of race may reify ideologies of racial difference, their reformation is limited by the very racial formations these discourses reinforce. But as the chapters to follow collectively argue, the cultural turn itself could not have occurred, nor could its implications for the evolution of race in America have been realized, had the monetary changes these texts chronicle not taken place.

# 1

## JACKSONIAN ABOLITIONISM

*Money, Minstrelsy, and "Uncle Tom's Cabin"*

*Johnny come down de hollow. Oh, hollow!*
*Johnny come down de hollow. Oh, hollow!*
*De nigger-trader got me. Oh hollow!*
*De speculator bought me. Oh hollow!*
*I'm sold for silver dollars. Oh hollow!*
*Boys, go catch de pony. Oh hollow!*
*Bring him round de corner. Oh hollow!*
*I'm goin' away to Georgia. Oh hollow!*
*Boys, good-bye forever. Oh hollow!*

SOUTH CAROLINA SLAVE SONG

*Good by Chloe, fare well children*
*Poor old Tom you'll see no more*
*Mind be good and hab religion*
*'Twill bare you to the faithful shore*
*Do not weep nor shed tears bout me*
*Suffering's over in de grave,*
*But at de glorious resurrection,*
*We'll meet with him, who died to save.*

GEORGE C. HOWARD, "UNCLE TOM'S RELIGION"

Before it was changed to "Life among the Lowly," the subtitle of Harriet Beecher Stowe's *Uncle Tom's Cabin* was "The Man Who Was a Thing." Besides introducing Stowe's critique of slavery as an institution that commodified black bodies, the original subtitle describes the waking nightmare of Northern, white, working-class men in antebellum America, who found it increasingly difficult to avoid becoming wage slaves in an emergent market capitalist economy. Stowe's original subtitle, which appeared in an announcement for the novel on May 8, 1851, may have been revised before serialization of her novel began in the *National Era* on June 5, 1851. But the novel, which Stowe had only begun to write when its first installments went to press, would continue to address the anxieties of white men who feared becoming things, and would, in its finished form, redirect these anxieties to abolitionist ends in revolutionary ways.

It is fitting that Stowe would, from the onset, seek to mobilize attitudes toward market forces that gave rise to wage labor's dominance since, as John Ashworth has shown, the rise of wage labor was a precondition for the ascendance of abolitionist thought in the urban North and thus also for the acceleration of sectional antagonisms that led to the Civil War. In Northern cities, wage labor transformed the home from a microcosm of the community into a refuge from work, thereby invigorating the ideology of separate spheres and its proscription of marketplace intrusions into the home. Because slavery not only brought the market into the home but also entangled the family in it, the "peculiar institution" came under new scrutiny and abolitionist sentiment was able to grow.[1]

This shift and the concomitant association between antislavery agitation and a nascent free labor movement brought abolitionist ideology into opposition with a prevailing Jacksonian philosophy that revised Jeffersonian agrarianism and declared democracy and wage labor to be incompatible.[2] In Jacksonian rhetoric, wage labor was wage slavery. By the start of the Civil War these Jacksonian sentiments remained firmly entrenched in much of the agrarian South, but a tectonic shift had taken place in the urban North, and wage labor no longer signified a lack of freedom but an expression of freedom as the antithesis of Southern slavery.[3]

Stowe is often cited as a catalyst for this consolidation of antislavery sentiment in the North. But how did Stowe address white, working-class Northerners who resisted wage labor's ascendance and continued to adhere to a Jacksonian social philosophy forged in the 1830s and 1840s? How did she bring these individuals into the free labor/antislavery fold? The short answer is that Stowe wrote *Uncle Tom's Cabin* in a way that made slavery appear antithetical not only to Christian doctrine, but also to long-held Jacksonian ideals. The long answer concerns Stowe's redeployment of two expressions of classical Jacksonian social philosophy, namely the monetary policy this philosophy dictated, and the popular cultural form that articulated its core values, blackface minstrelsy.

As Marvin Meyers and his successors have shown, Andrew Jackson responded to the emergence of modern capitalism and the uncertainty it produced with a nostalgic utopianism that reified the ideology of American exceptionalism and turned a deaf ear to the death knell of the yeoman republic. Jackson's hard money policy and his war against the Second Bank of the United States were expressions of this anxiety as well as attempts to stem the tide of a new economy that threatened to turn (yeo)men into things (that is, wage laborers). To those of Jacksonian persuasion, the erosion of the yeoman republic was a function of economic processes that unfairly favored moneyed aristocrats, and could be slowed if not reversed by regulating the form of the nation's money. For Jackson and other hard money advocates, this meant replacing as much paper currency as possible with gold coinage that had real value, which, unlike paper money's face value, could not be manipulated by creditors at the expense of laborers.[4]

As the cultural expression of Jackson's social and economic policies, early minstrelsy was also preoccupied with the slippage between inherent value and face value—between form and content—and used money along with burnt cork to underscore the constitutive difference between men and things. In early minstrel shows, which were put on primarily in the antebellum urban North, white minstrels blacked up to protest their demotion from artisans to wage laborers, and used silver dollars, the substance of which was more valuable than their face value after the Coinage Act of 1834, to express the conviction that they too were devalued in the market and denied their inherent value as white men. Paper money also played a role in early minstrelsy. Having only a commodity value that was established and maintained by social contract, dollar bills often stood in for and/or accompanied black characters that sought to possess themselves, and mocked these characters for their pretensions to intrinsic value—a value that, from the racialist, white supremacist point of view, blacks either did not have (as the property of slave owners) or did not deserve (as an inferior race). Paper money therefore mirrored the black mask of dispossession in that it was another thing used by white men on the minstrel stage to differentially define what they believed to be their inherent value, and to protest market forces that were erasing the differences between white laborers and black slaves.

Stowe brought these monetary and minstrel metaphors together in *Uncle Tom's Cabin* to tap into and then soothe lingering anxieties about work and independence and to direct them to abolitionist ends. In the novel, George Harris and Uncle Tom perform minstrel gestures and carry the forms of money that were featured in early minstrel shows. But rather than simply reinforce traditional Jacksonian ideologies, Stowe's protagonists adopt minstrelsy's formal conventions to break negative associations between wage labor and slavery that prevented abolitionist entrée into working-class circles in the urban North. Transforming her protagonists into minstrel heroes, Stowe uses their stories to launch a two-pronged attack upon the anti–wage labor, proslavery and/or laissez-faire sentiments of many working-class Northerners. Specifically, George Harris's story decouples wage labor from wage slavery by promoting an association between wage labor and self-possession, while Uncle Tom takes center stage in a Jacksonian Passion play that joins Christian theology to hard money ideology, and portrays slavery as the enemy of both.

Scholars like Michael D. Pierson have already analyzed the gender, labor, and slavery politics of Stowe's novel to show how they support an ascendant Republican ideology.[5] What remains to be explored is how the novel's racial and monetary politics inform one another, and how they worked in tandem to appeal to Northern working-class Democrats at a time when Democratic allegiances were in flux. By the time Stowe's novel began appearing in the *National Era*, a Free-Soil newspaper, the debate over slavery—particularly the threat of slavery's unchecked expansion to the West—had already produced a sectional split among Democrats. A key consequence of this split was the formation of the Free-Soil Party by a radical faction of New York Democrats known as the Barnburners, who were joined by antislavery Whigs and members of the abolitionist Liberty Party in opposing slavery's expansion. The Free-Soil Party built a political platform upon the core concepts of "free soil, free speech, free labor, and free men," conjoining the issues of white labor and black slavery. The champion of the former, they argued, was the enemy of the latter.

Not all Democrats were willing to join the free-soil movement, however. As Eric Foner notes, "Most Jacksonians could not bring themselves to abandon their party," even in the 1850s (150). And as Jonathan H. Earle has convincingly shown, the radicals who became free-soil Democrats remained committed to traditional Jacksonian ideas, not the least of which was an unwavering commitment to egalitarianism in general and to hard money in particular. Earle keenly observes that "not every radical, hard-money Democrat" reached the same "conclusions about slavery and slaveholders" (8). Instead, Democrats remained divided over the issues of slavery and western expansion, even in the urban Northeast. "Obviously," concludes Earle, "opposing centralized authority and the paper economy was not, in and of itself, enough to prompt a Democrat to become a Free Soiler" (10).

The Democratic Party's identity crisis and fraught relationship to its Jacksonian past accounts for the classical Jacksonian appeals of Stowe's novel, specifically its overtures to the heirs of Jackson's legacy who had not yet defected to the free labor/free-soil cause. By mapping out common ground between free-soil Democrats and the Jacksonians of yore, Stowe encourages her Democratic readers to believe they too can join the free-soil cause without selling their Jacksonian souls. It would not have been sufficient, however, for Stowe merely to portray the promise of free labor as the antithesis of Southern slavery. To succeed at turning old Jacksonian Democrats into new Free-Soilers she also had to assuage what Pierson calls "Democratic fears about social change" (6).[6] This meant, among other things, making her free labor/antislavery appeals without radically challenging traditional racial hierarchies. Incorporating the conventions of blackface minstrelsy therefore served two rhetorical purposes: it enabled Stowe to pay lip service to a racialist status quo, and provided her with a Jacksonian vehicle for yoking the Money Power, Jackson's hydra-headed mortal enemy, to the Slave Power, the political organization of southern slaveholders.[7]

## THE SUBLIMATION OF UNCLE TOM'S DOLLAR

*Uncle Tom's Cabin* begins with a conversation between Kentucky farmer and slaveholder Arthur Shelby and the slave trader Dan Haley in the parlor of the Shelby home. Mr. Shelby, whose financial speculations have put him in Haley's debt, reluctantly agrees to give his servants Uncle Tom and young Harry Harris, son of George and Eliza Harris, to the trader as payment. Soon thereafter Harry flees in the arms of his mother, and together they complete the miraculous (and oft restaged) crossing of the frozen Ohio River by jumping from ice floe to ice floe. But Tom submits to his fate, accompanying Haley first to Washington, Kentucky, where Haley purchases more slaves, before boarding a boat headed downriver to be sold with Haley's newly-purchased slaves at another auction. Before the slave trader has taken Tom any further than the local blacksmith's shop, however, young George Shelby, son of Arthur and Emily Shelby, overtakes their wagon and jumps aboard for a brief farewell. With Haley busy having Tom's fetters fitted, George takes the opportunity to offer the slave a parting gift:

> "Look here, Uncle Tom," said he, turning his back to the shop, and speaking in a mysterious tone, "*I've brought you my dollar!*"

"O! I couldn't think o' takin' on 't, Mas'r George, no ways in the world!" said Tom, quite moved.

"But you *shall* take it!" said George; "look here—I told Aunt Chloe I'd do it, and she advised me just to make a hole in it, and put a string through so you could hang it round your neck, and keep it out of sight; else this mean scamp would take it away." (87)

The dollar, explains George, is a promise and a reminder to Tom that he will eventually find him and buy his freedom so he may one day return to the Shelby farm and his wife and children. As George Shelby's horse speeds the boy from Tom's view, the dollar assumes greater significance for the slave. For though Tom knows he is watching "the last sound or sight of his home" disappear over the horizon, "over his heart there seemed to be a warm spot, where those young hands had placed that precious dollar" (88).

At first glance the dollar coin's symbolism is layered but transparent. As a commodity in the process of being exchanged himself, Tom is a lot like the dollar he carries. And like the specie whose form it takes, Tom embodies the value(s) he espouses—he practices what he preaches. Furthermore, while the coin warms his heart, Tom warms the reader's heart as part of the novel's sentimental economy. Uncle Tom's dollar thus critiques the ordinariness of his own purchase, signifies his inherent value as a human being, and self-reflexively comments upon his own circulation as the tragic hero of an abolitionist text that seeks to affect change by changing affect.

Upon closer inspection, however, the shifting shape of Uncle Tom's dollar suggests a more complex form of symbolism. Disappearing and later reappearing in a different form, the dollar undergoes an elemental transformation that complicates its interpretation. Even though the narrator does not specify one way or another, contemporary readers of *Uncle Tom's Cabin* would have assumed George Shelby gives Tom a *gold* dollar, not a silver one. There are two reasons for this. First, following the Coinage Act of 1834, which changed the ratio of silver's value relative to gold from 15:1 to 16:1, silver dollars became more valuable as bullion than as money and therefore circulated poorly.[8] In fact, after 1834 most silver dollars were exported as soon as they were minted and melted back into bullion by the nations that received them as payment. And second, following the discovery of gold in California in 1848, gold dollar coins appeared in great quantities and circulated widely. Coinage records from the United States Mint underscore the degree to which gold had replaced silver as the money metal of choice. In 1851, the year Stowe began writing and serializing *Uncle Tom's Cabin*, 3,568,820 gold dollars were minted compared to only 1,300 silver dollars. In 1852 even fewer of the undervalued coins were minted: 1,100 (*CoinFacts.com*). Considering that George Shelby has to bore a hole through the coin on short notice and that Tom is now "in circulation" himself, a gold dollar would have made monetary, metallic, and metaphoric sense.[9] But two events that occur later in the novel complicate this interpretation.

The first is the apparent pocketing of the dollar by Simon Legree. After Tom rescues young Eva St. Clare, who has fallen overboard from the ship taking Tom downriver to be sold, he is bought by Eva's father, the benevolent but apathetic Augustine St. Clare. But after Eva and her father die in quick succession, Tom is sent once more to the auction block and purchased by Legree. Aboard the steamer that will take Tom to Legree's plantation the slave owner confronts the slave:

> "Stand up."
> Tom stood up.
> "Take off that stock!" and, as Tom, encumbered by his fetters, proceeded to do it, he assisted him, by pulling it, with no gentle hand, from his neck, and putting it in his pocket. (292)

Stowe's reader has every reason to believe that "stock" refers here to movable property, not a neckcloth. Tom was, after all, referred to as Haley's stock after he was sold to the trader earlier in the novel (88). In fact, Tom is described by the narrator as stock immediately after George Shelby gives him the dollar and departs, further cementing the reader's association of the slave, another form of movable property, with the dollar he carries. Emily Shelby's lamentation just prior to Tom's departure that she would give Tom money to take with him but it would only be taken from him, coupled with young George Shelby's prediction that Legree would take the coin away if he saw it, strengthens the reader's belief that Legree has just pocketed Tom's own stock: the precious dollar in which he has invested so much hope.

It therefore comes to everyone's surprise—especially Legree's—when Sambo brings the "witch thing" to him after Tom's first flogging and "a silver dollar, and a long, shining curl of fair hair" that Eva cut for Tom on her deathbed come tumbling out of it (322). The lock of hair, of course, marks the return of the repressed for Legree, reminding him of his mother and of his choice to abandon both her faith and her forgiveness. As for the silver dollar, Legree "sent it smashing through the window-pane, out into the darkness" where Sambo flees to escape Legree's rage (322).

The plural noun in the title of the chapter that contains this scene, "The Tokens," indicates that the coin has as much significance as the lock of hair in the novel's symbolic economy. But while Eva's golden curls play an immediate role in the plot by catching the conscience of Legree, the sublimation of the golden dollar into its silver counterpart is, to most present-day readers, thrown out the window. The first step to recovering the symbolic potential and significance of this sublimated specie is to recognize how the dollar coin's miraculous transformation not only parallels Tom's own transfiguration from slave to Christian martyr, but also reflects the shifting shape of United States money during the antebellum years. Because minstrelsy's monetary metaphors hinged upon these selfsame changes, the formal transformation of Uncle Tom's dollar is the key to unlocking Stowe's formal transformation of minstrelsy.

## MONEY, MINSTRELSY, AND JACKSONIAN AMERICA

*Uncle Tom's Cabin* implies a connection between money and minstrelsy in its opening chapter, where the novel's first minstrel gestures occur amidst discussions of debt and demonstrations of speculation and its risks. As Arthur Shelby and Dan Haley are negotiating payment of Mr. Shelby's debt, young Harry Harris makes a fateful appearance on the scene. "Hulloa, Jim Crow!" says Shelby to the boy, invoking the name of Thomas Dartmouth Rice's famous blackface alter ego before asking Harry to perform what is essentially a mini minstrel show for Haley.

> "Come here, Jim Crow," said he. The child came up, and the master patted the curly head, and chucked him under the chin.
>
> "Now, Jim, show this gentleman how you can dance and sing." The boy commenced one of those wild, grotesque songs common among the negroes, in a rich, clear voice, accompanying his singing with many comic evolutions of the hands, feet, and whole body, all in perfect time to the music.
>
> "Bravo!" said Haley, throwing him a quarter of an orange.
>
> "Now, Jim, walk like old Uncle Cudjoe, when he has the rheumatism," said his master.
>
> Instantly the flexible limbs of the child assumed the appearance of

deformity and distortion, as, with his back humped up, and his master's stick in his hand, he hobbled around the room, his childish face drawn into a doleful pucker, and spitting from right to left, in imitation of an old man.

Both gentlemen laughed uproariously.

"Now, Jim," said his master, "show us how old Elder Robbins leads the psalm." The boy drew his chubby face down to a formidable length, and commenced toning a psalm tune through his nose, with imperturbable gravity. (3)

Here, Stowe has Harry reproduce the codified, three-part minstrel show of the 1840s and 1850s right down to the stump speech.[10] She even incorporates the popular myth of how T. D. Rice drew Jim Crow from a real-life rheumatic black man (Wittke 24–25). Harry's capers demonstrate that Stowe had a firm grasp upon the formal conventions and even the history of minstrelsy, even though she probably never saw a minstrel show. And the routine coincidence of minstrel gestures and monetary matters in Stowe's novel is a reminder to contemporary readers that money and minstrelsy went hand in hand in the antebellum popular cultural imagination. But what did minstrelsy and money have to do with one another? The answer is that, from its inception, minstrelsy incorporated money in various forms in order to reflect upon its own shifting conventions and the Jacksonian logic that made them meaningful.

Blackface minstrelsy was born when T. D. Rice first "jumped Jim Crow" in or around 1830, and it flourished during the years of Andrew Jackson's presidency. As a Democratic popular cultural form par excellence, early minstrelsy was unequivocal in its praise for Jackson, and took up subjects near and dear to audiences of Jacksonian persuasion. Minstrel songs of the 1830s thus routinely relived the glory of Jackson's 1814 victory over General Pakenham in the Battle of New Orleans,[11] took offense at South Carolina's threats to secede from the Union in 1832,[12] and rehearsed Jackson's personal disdain for the privileges of class in American life. But none of these subjects were treated more often in early minstrel compositions than Jackson's war against the Second Bank of the United States.

The Bank War, as it came to be known, pitted U.S. president Jackson against U.S. Bank president Nicholas Biddle. Jackson, who had long believed that the Bank had too much power and influence, expressed his desire to dismantle the financial colossus soon after his inauguration in 1829. Because he was unable to propose an alternative to the institution, however, it seemed that Biddle's bank would be spared Old Hickory's wrath. But when Biddle applied to Congress for renewal of the Bank's charter in 1832 even though it wasn't scheduled to expire until 1836, Jackson felt provoked, and he vowed to fight Biddle and his Bank to the last. Biddle's strategy in submitting the application early was to turn renewal of the Bank's charter into an election issue, betting that Jackson would be unwilling to stake his political clout on it and risk reelection. But Biddle's gambit backfired. Once Congress approved the recharter, Jackson vetoed the bill and left it to the American people to judge his actions at the ballot box that November. When Jackson was reelected, he took his victory as an endorsement by the people of his anti-Bank policy, and he proceeded to dismantle the Second Bank of the United States in the people's name by removing the federal deposits from its vaults and placing the government's money in state banks friendly to the Democrats.[13]

Early minstrel sketches not only lauded Jackson for his experiment in deposit banking, they also scourged critics like Daniel Webster and Horace Binney who opposed Jackson's veto. This is apparent in an 1835 fictional autobiography of Jim Crow handed out at the Walnut Street Theatre in Philadelphia, which states, "Guess de folks tink I gwan to do like ole Dan Webster, when he spit him great speech 'bout de Bank,— begin to talk 'bout one ting and end wid anoder, for all de world like de sea sarpint, de head or tail ob which nebber found yet, nor ebber will be, 'cording to my notion of noseology, or whigology, its all de same to a rale Kaintuck 'bacco nigger" (qtd. in Lhamon, *Jump* 387). This same autobiography invokes and critiques another pro-Bank, anti-Jackson speech when Jim Crow weaves a tale about how "I hab to go out on de balcony and make dem [the people of Cincinnati] a speech, jis like Mr. [Horace] Binney did to the bank folks in Baltimore, only I got ten times more plause, doe I did'nt say half as much as him did, do I spec mine war more to de parpose" (393). Likewise, in the Atwill edition of "Jump Jim Crow" entitled "Jimmy Crow," the narrator goes to Washington and takes on Nicholas Biddle, whom Jim Crow calls "Ole Nick," that is, the devil.[14] Jim Crow goes on to imply that it was he who suggested the veto of the charter renewal bill to Jackson:

I den go to de Presiden,
He ax me wat I do;
I put de veto on de boot,
An nullefy de shoe.

He laff most harty tink how smart,
I spick so mighty big;
He tole me for go to de house,
And call dem all a pig. ("Jimmy Crow")

Perhaps the most revealing example of minstrelsy's articulation of Jacksonian monetary ideology, however, is an 1834 version of "Zip Coon" published by George Willig, Jr.,[15] that contains these verses:

I tell you what's a goine to happen now very soon,
De United States bank will be blown to de moon,
Den all de oder bank notes will be mighty plenty,
An one silver dollar will be worth ten or twenty.

O glory be to Jackson, for he blow up de Banks,
An glory be to Jackson, for he many funny pranks,
An glory be to Jackson, for de battle of Orleans,
For dere he gib de enemy de hot butter beans. (qtd. in Lott 179)

As the narrator of "Zip Coon" intimates, Jackson's position against the Second Bank of the United States was, at bottom, an expression of his beliefs about the form money should take (hence the observation that, once the Bank was "blown to de moon," hard money would no longer be devalued by fiat paper money circulating alongside it). Jackson was no different from many of his nineteenth-century counterparts in believing that the form American money took determined the form American society took. To Jackson, only hard money, gold and silver specie, was sound money. Paper money and the debts it represented was, by contrast, the tool of the privileged—the "aristocrats" in his rhetoric—and the bane of the laboring classes when in overabundance. According to hard money advocates like Jackson, a paper-based economy was prone to cycles of boom and bust. When the economy boomed, creditors—not laborers—reaped the benefits. But when boom turned to bust, credit became scarce and working-class people were left without money to pay their debts. Because the Second Bank of the United States represented a monopoly of credit and flooded the market with paper, Jackson accused the institution of failing to provide the nation with a sound currency. Because the U.S. Constitution charges the federal government to provide sound currency, argued Jackson, the Bank itself was unconstitutional. In addition to leveling this charge against the Bank, Jackson's veto message of July 10, 1832 blamed the institution for skewing the distribution of wealth. "Distinctions in society will always exist under every just government," he wrote—

> Equality of talents, of education, or of wealth can not [*sic*] be produced by human institutions. In the full enjoyment of the gifts of Heaven and the fruits of superior industry, economy, and virtue, every man is equally entitled to protection by law; but when the laws undertake to add to these natural and just advantages artificial distinctions, to grant titles, gratuities, and exclusive privileges, to make the rich richer and the potent more powerful, the humble members of society—the farmers, mechanics, and laborers—who have neither the time nor the means of securing like favors to themselves, have a right to complain of the injustice of the Government.[16]

To replace as much of the offending paper money as possible and thereby rectify the anomalies it produced in the distribution of wealth, Jackson proposed eliminating all denominations of banknotes under twenty dollars once the federal deposits were safely relocated to his pet banks.[17] The reason, as William Gouge's popular and influential 1833 treatise *A Short History of Paper Money and Banking in the United States* explains, is that when banknotes circulate in a country no more specie can be retained in that country than is necessary for transactions of a smaller amount than the least denomination of paper (107). Jackson took his hard money policy further than this. He presided over the Coinage Act of 1834, which revised gold's value relative to silver from 15:1 to 16:1. Pushing gold's money value above its precious metal value, this legislation brought gold coins back into circulation, albeit at the expense of driving silver dollars, which instantly became more valuable for their form (grains of silver) than for their face value (one dollar), out of circulation. Furthermore, after a period of rampant land speculation in America, Jackson issued the so-called Specie Circular in July 1836, which decreed that only gold and silver were acceptable for the purchase of public lands.

At the core of Jacksonian monetary ideology was the belief that remedying the class conflicts that threatened the republican way of life depended upon restoring congruity between the form and content of U.S. currency. As Jackson himself argued, members of the working classes would not be able to possess themselves so long as American money could not possess its own value. But as Marvin Meyers has shown, the real catalyst for the class animosities that Jackson loathed was the rise of modern capitalism, not U.S. monetary policy. In fact, the Bank's policies were reactions to, not the causes of, wage labor's ascendance and the class divisions it produced. But because the dissolution of the yeoman republic (or the dispelling of its myth) caused no small amount of anxiety during the Age of Jackson, a scapegoat became necessary. The U.S. Bank became that scapegoat, and the Bank War was an expression of Jacksonian anxiety waged by Democrats to assuage fears of those attached to or associated with the old republican order. Andrew Jackson may have been in denial, but his denial was a popular cultural sensation, as early minstrelsy's preoccupation with the Bank War illustrates.

Early minstrel performers found in the Bank War and the monetary meditations it engendered more than just another way to pay homage to Jacksonian ideology or riff upon class antagonisms; they also discovered a way to comment, ironically and self-reflexively, upon the friction between minstrelsy's formal conventions and its subject matter. References to the Bank War and, by extension, to Jackson's hard money policy were, like the medium that incorporated them, contradictory and complex. For while early minstrelsy's messages were Jacksonian celebrations of American lumpen culture, the medium itself relied upon an incongruity between form and content.

Minstrelsy's contemporary critics, most notably Alexander Saxton, W. T. Lhamon, Jr., and Eric Lott, have all examined the ways antebellum minstrelsy's form informed its content and explained how the medium capitalized upon its own contradictions. Saxton, for example, observes that minstrelsy's racist medium masked and therefore enabled its class-inflected ideological messages. Lhamon goes a step further in his 2003 book *Jump Jim Crow* by portraying Rice's seminal blackface character as a border-crossing incendiary who invited marginalized members of the working classes to recognize their exclusion from the dominant culture via identification with Rice's blacked-up protagonist. And Eric Lott, like Lhamon, echoes minstrelsy's own preoccupations with money when describing minstrelsy's constitutive incongruities, noting that minstrelsy circulates as cultural capital, not in spite of its counterfeit form but because of it. Lott and Lhamon may have contributed more to our understanding and appreciation of minstrelsy and its meaningful contradictions than any of their contemporaries, but as the following examples show, they did not "coin" these monetary metaphors themselves so much as reproduce early minstrelsy's own playful recognition of them.

Early minstrel songs were filled with tongue-in-cheek references to minstrelsy's own formal conventions in general and its own artifice in particular. For example, in the version of T. D. Rice's "Jim Crow" published by E. Riley at 29 Chatham Street circa 1832, the narrator—a white man in blackface—claims to be "jist about as sassy, / As if I was half white." This self-referential humor belies the song's serious subject matter, the erosion of artisan culture and the rise of modern capitalism. "O by trade I am a carpenter," sings Jim Crow, "But be it understood, / De way I get my liben is, / By sawing de tick oh wood." Jim Crow's transformation from tradesman to pieceworker is no isolated incident, as the song goes on to point out. Instead, many working-class white men are occupying jobs formerly held by slaves:

I'm berry much afraid of late
Dis jumping will be no good.
For while de Crow are dancing,
De Wites will saw de wood.

Because this song, like so many other early minstrel tunes, rails against an emergent economic system that was turning white workers into wage slaves, the formal irruption informs rather than conceals the song's content. For working-class audiences didn't identify so much with white entertainers like T. D. Rice or the black characters they portrayed; they identified with white men who became black, that is, they identified with laborers who were still white men but whose distinction from black slaves was eroding in a new economy. Early minstrelsy's white audiences thus identified with the white performer's desire to associate himself with, and simultaneously disassociate himself from, the black mask he wore. Michael Rogin describes this performative double-gesture when he writes, "Whites who black up call attention to the gap between role and ascribed identity by playing what, in the essentialist view, they cannot be" (34). In early minstrelsy, this double-gesture was a matter of class and race. Early minstrels promoted class affiliation between whites and blacks, likening white working-class disenfranchisement to black dispossession, while simultaneously reinforcing racial division. "We are becoming slaves," was early minstrelsy's message, "and this shouldn't happen to white people."[18]

Money and the forms it took were often incorporated into early minstrel texts because, aside from facilitating commentary on economic issues, money mirrored minstrelsy's complex dialectic of form and content. Money served both as a metonym for economics in minstrelsy's critiques of modern capitalism and as a metaphor for the vexed relationship between the minstrel performer's black face and his white body. This is exemplified by the aforementioned verses of Willig's "Zip Coon," which praise Jackson's Bank War and by extension Jackson's hard money policy for restoring the primacy of inherent value, hence the reference to the silver dollar's valued status over "de oder bank notes." By lauding a hard money system that Jackson believed could prevent wage slavery, the song articulates Jacksonian sentiments about the form money should take and the role monetary policy played in determining the form society took. And because silver dollars became more valuable for their substance than for their face value following the Coinage Act of 1834—the same year "Zip Coon" was published—the silver dollar was a productive mirror in the text for minstrel performers who wore the mask of the dispossessed slave to express a belief in the inherent value of white bodies. The silver dollar in "Zip Coon" is thus both a synecdoche for Jackson's monetary policies—policies that working-class Jacksonians believed might ameliorate their unwelcome role as white slaves—and a symbol for early minstrelsy's formal conventions deployed in the name of white privilege.

Rice's Faustian burlesque *Bone Squash Diavolo* extends this self-reflexive monetary play. In this dramatic farce, Bone Squash, who was played by Rice himself, sells his soul to the devil, but balks temporarily when Mephistopheles offers to pay for it with paper rather than specie:

DEVIL: There's the rhino [money].
BONE SQUASH: What's dis? A check?
DEVIL: Yes, and any of the brokers will cash it.
BONE SQUASH: I doesn't deal in paper. I want de real buttons. Isn't you got any of de hard cash? Come, dump up. (qtd. in Lhamon, *Jump* 186)

Like in "Zip Coon," the implied connection between the blackface character and the money with which he appears is both a self-referential gag and the hinge upon which the text's Jacksonian critique turns. Zip Coon, the urban dandy, mocks his own counterfeit appearance by praising Jackson's hard money policy, which sought correspondence between actual value and face value. Bone Squash does likewise by insisting he be paid with hard cash when he himself is a counterfeit, a white man in black drag. And, once again, playful self-mockery gives rise to social commentary. Considering that Rice's Jim Crow likened Nicholas Biddle to the devil and Andrew Jackson believed hard money to be the key to self-possession, this financial transaction between Bone Squash and the devil takes on allegorical significance. An object lesson in Jacksonian monetary ideology, paper money proves to be the agent of dispossession: Bone Squash literally loses his soul in the deal. As a consequence, he comes to resemble the paper for which he has exchanged himself: an empty shell, a body without a soul. For white, working-class audiences feeling dispossessed of their own inherent value, the pleasure of the play consists of Bone Squash outwitting the devil and thereby deferring payment on his debt forever.

As these examples of the popular cultural form illustrate, early minstrelsy was both a vehicle for the production of the self in the marketplace and a locus of constitutive desire. The desire for the black body that minstrelsy put on display was in fact a demonstration of how this object cause of desire could not—or should not—be attained.[19] As the mirror in the minstrel text, money was therefore always either overvalued or undervalued. Undervalued coins like silver dollars mirrored white men's claims to a tentative and exclusive self-possession on the grounds of racial inheritance (read: white supremacy). Within the economy of the hegemonic rigid racialism of the period, whiteness was, like the value of a silver dollar, more than just skin color, transcending face value to script social standing and even moral superiority. Overvalued paper money and/or counterfeit currency, by contrast, mocked the inability of blacks to possess themselves, especially after the emergence of the codified minstrel show in the winter of 1842. Whereas undervalued silver dollars symbolized the inherent value of white men underappreciated in a new marketplace, overvalued paper money and counterfeit currency, which do not possess the value for which they stand, represented black desire for self-possession and, by extension, the futility of this desire.

This monetary symbolism is clearly visible in Dan Emmett's banjo tune "Elam Moore—Jig," which tells the story of "Ole Dandy Cox" who "hasn't got a red cent" and cannot recognize the intrinsic value, let alone the surplus value, of a silver dollar. The song describes Cox in the traditional minstrel costume of the urban black dandy: a "Ruffle shirt wid standin' collar, / Fit so tight he couldn't swaller." His attempt to dress like a white man is entirely transparent, like the stereotype he reproduces would have been in the minstrel show, and his attempts to counterfeit himself as a white man are further parodied when "All de time de nigger holler, / Go way wid your pewter dollar" (qtd. in Nathan, *Dan* 345–46). Dandy Cox forfeits real value by dismissing it as counterfeit, all the while counterfeiting himself to pass for a real white man. Given the racial dynamics of money in minstrelsy, Dandy Cox's mistaking the undervalued silver dollar for an overvalued counterfeit parodies his attempts to locate the authenticity of race. A reassurance to audience members invested in white supremacy, Cox's performance of whiteness doesn't bring him any closer to becoming white or any nearer to possessing himself—black desire for the racial inheritance of whites is, in the racialist economy of minstrelsy, a lost cause.

Paper monies of dubious value like "shinplasters" were used in antebellum minstrel performances to comment, with tongue-in-cheek irony, upon the artifice of the form itself and to mock the aspirations of those characters on display who sought recognition for their humanity and intellect. J. B. Harper's "New Jim Brown, 'Bout de Sputed Territory" collates such monetary references into a stump speech describing the dispute between Great Britain and the United States over the location of the border between Maine and New Brunswick—a dispute that came to a head during Martin Van Buren's presidency. "Well, well, dars no use talking any furder pon dis subjec," announces Jim Brown—

> Had Jon Bull persulted Mr. Brown on de rassion, I'd settled dat in three minutes less dan no time; but Massa Buren got so hipervious on de rassion, dat I didn't hab de plauseability to konsuade ob de inconsistency ob de hessication; but I merely wanced my pinion dat de only way to settle dat spute, had be, to let John Harvy pick out a Canady Nigger, and Martin Van Buren pick out a Long Island Nigger, and step dat land off wid de size ob dar foot, and settle dat question by de rule ob treezology. De State ob Maine needn't concarn demself, but she will gain all de sputed territory, and three or four acres ob dat wot aint 'sputed territory; to de tune ob de New York shinplasters has specie. (qtd. in Harper, *Jim Along Josey Roarer* n.p.)

Jim Brown, of course, doesn't possess any more political clout than the shinplasters he describes possess specie or the value it represents. The final couplet, "Sub-treasury note dar all in my eye, / Good by white folks till I cum agin," both cements the association between Jim Brown and worthless paper money and allows the white performer in the guise of Jim Brown to wink to the white folks in the audience who are no different from himself. But there is also an anti-abolitionist subtext to this tune. In a skit called "The Rival Darkies," Jim Brown is a black abo-

Sheet music by Dan Emmett and E. Bowers for Bryant's Minstrels. "Greenbacks!
New Song for the Times" and "How Are You Green-Backs!" Courtesy of the Harvard
Theatre Collection, Houghton Library.

litionist who has been "'pointed trabblin' agent fur de Bobolition Society" (Christy 12).[20] Predictably, the skit lampoons Jim Brown's desires
for liberation and integration into white society. Because "shinplasters"
stands in for "nigger" in "New Jim Brown" and Jim Brown is "the New
York nigger," then Jim Brown's desire to possess himself by way of his
abolitionism is likened, in Harper's text, to the failure of paper money
to possess the value for which it stands. Harper's song and the speech it
contains may chronicle a dispute over a border between two territories,
but its monetary metaphors articulate a racialist ideology in which the
boundary separating black from white is non-negotiable and the desire
of blacks to possess themselves is unprofitable.[21]

While black desire for self-possession was being played out on a national stage during the Civil War, minstrels of Jacksonian Democratic
persuasion lampooned this desire with satires on Lincoln's greenbacks,
which not only had no intrinsic value, but were not even backed by
precious metals. For example, in *Rose Dale*, Griffin and Christy's Minstrels' burlesque of Lester Wallack's 1863 smash *Rosedale; or, The Rifle*

*Ball*, Aunt Rose Dale and Ragley—played by Christy and Griffin themselves—comment on the United States Notes or greenbacks, punning
on the name of Salmon P. Chase, then Secretary of the Treasury:

> AUNT R. Ragley, hast gold?
> RAG. I hast none—not even greenbacks.
> AUNT R. Greenbacks! *Chased* greenbacks! I want none of such things
> as they! I have had enough of your *promises to pay* already! (qtd. in
> Engle 114)

Paper money in general and greenbacks in particular were ideal symbols
for slaves in the minstrel shows performed during the Civil War—ideal
to proslavery white supremacists, anyhow.[22] To these critics of abolitionism, the U.S. government's decree that greenbacks were themselves legal
tender despite having no intrinsic value or precious metal backing was
analogous to the 1863 Emancipation Proclamation's award of freedom
and citizenship—the perceived birthright of white men—to Southern
slaves. A song with lyrics by E. Bowers and performed by Dan Bryant
exemplifies this sentiment. Entitled "How Are You Green-Backs!" Bowers's minstrel tune likens the republican cause to the paper money used
to finance it, and lampoons the futility of both:

> We're coming, Father Abram, one hundred thousand more.
> Five hundred presses printing us from morn till night is o'er . . .
> To line the fat contractor's purse, or purchase transport craft
> Whose rotten hulks shall sink before the winds begin to waft.[23]

As these Civil War–era examples of early minstrelsy illustrate, Jacksonian desire—along with the monetary metaphors that articulated it—
was still around long after Stowe's novel was published. But Stowe was
able to redirect enough of this desire to consolidate antislavery sentiment in the urban North and thereby become, in Abraham Lincoln's
famous (if apocryphal) turn of phrase, the author whose book started
the great war between the states. She did this in part by following the
practice of early minstrel authors and drawing analogies between the
value of money and the value of racial difference. Only in *Uncle Tom's
Cabin*, Stowe uses money and minstrelsy to portray slavery as the antithesis of Jacksonian virtue.

The role blackface plays in *Uncle Tom's Cabin* is inseparable from the part money plays in the novel. For while Stowe incorporated the language and imagery of minstrelsy to appeal to readers who were hailed by minstrel shows, she tweaked the genre's monetary metaphors to redirect minstrelsy's class-inflected critiques toward abolitionist ends. *Uncle Tom's Cabin* therefore enacts a Jacksonian double gesture, riffing upon the class, racial, and sectional tensions that blackface articulated, while undermining the foundations upon which Jacksonian ideology was erected.

Critics who have examined Stowe's use of minstrel tropes have rightly claimed that blackface signifies subversively in *Uncle Tom's Cabin*. Christina Zwarg, for example, argues that Stowe uses conventions of blackface to investigate alternatives to the rhetoric of patriarchy in her own feminist poetics.[24] As for the degree to which *Uncle Tom's Cabin* depends upon the minstrel forms and gestures it incorporates, scholars like Eric Lott and W. T. Lhamon, Jr., observe that the novel's blackface base is coextensive with the bounds of Stowe's abolitionist text. Lhamon not only claims that minstrelsy "profoundly shaped her [Stowe's] writing" (*Raising* 97), but he goes so far as to suggest that Stowe may have subconsciously named her protagonist after T. D. Rice, whose friends and family called him "Tom" (*Jump* 90). There is something to recommend this reading. The character of Jim Crow was, like his creator, Rice, born in Kentucky. Of course, Jim Crow was *figuratively* born there, newspaper accounts showing that Rice probably first jumped Jim Crow in Louisville in or around 1830 (Cockrell 64). What might be more profound, however, is not how Uncle Tom was drawn from Rice or from Jim Crow, but what Rice may have picked up from Stowe when he began playing Uncle Tom at the Bowery Theatre in 1854. For it was around this time that Rice, the father of blackface minstrelsy, developed the eccentric habit of using five- and ten-dollar gold coins for buttons on his coat and vest (Wittke 32).[25]

Minstrelsy's symbolic potential is realized over the course of Stowe's novel. Accordingly, black characters like Sam and Andy, who appear at the beginning of the novel and who seem largely unconscious of their own buffoonery, are gradually replaced by characters like Sambo who self-consciously wear the mask of servitude. The capers of Harry Harris and "the summersets of Sam" thus give way to the "cunning glances" of Topsy (207) and the "trick and grimace" of Sambo (284).[26] As minstrelized figures become increasingly aware of the roles they play, so also does the novel become more self-reflexive in its deployment of minstrelsy's conventions. Sam may perform "the most ludicrous burlesques and imitations" (64), and express himself "by all sorts of supernatural howls and ejaculations" early in the novel (62), but Stowe's editorial intrusions, one of which reminds the reader that "the dealers in the human article make scrupulous and systematic efforts to promote noisy mirth among them, as a means of drowning reflection, and rendering them insensible to their condition" (283), collectively deconstruct the myth of the happy darky as the novel approaches its conclusion.

As Stowe gradually reveals the performances of black slaves to be conscious efforts at preventing white intrusions, she transforms her mulatto characters into minstrel heroes. Stowe accomplishes this transformation in part by drawing analogies between her mulatto characters and the paper money with which they are associated—a strategy that conforms to the logic of antebellum minstrelsy. The story of George Harris is the novel's most perfect example of this transformation and accompanying monetary self-reflection. George plays the part of a working-class hero in the early minstrel tradition, bringing together racial masquerade, the desire for self-possession, and the paper money that connects them.

George Harris's story is told in mechanic accents, incorporating the dominant narrative of working-class life in antebellum America. When George and Eliza are first introduced in the novel, the reader learns that George recently lost his position at the bagging factory where he was working with his master's permission. While at this factory, George invented a machine that cleaned hemp and "displayed quite as much mechanical genius as Whitney's cotton-gin" (10). But when Mr. Harris, his master, became aware of George's successes and began to feel inferior as a result, he decided he would "take him back, and put him to hoeing and digging, and 'see if he'd step about so smart'" (10). George's demotion from inventor to "dray-horse" (13), or from tradesman to slave, would have struck a chord with working-class readers of the period, just as it would have with minstrel audiences who imagined themselves wage slaves who deserved much better.

If these audiences could sympathize with George Harris's labor crisis, so too could they embrace the steps he takes after declaring his independence—steps that include blacking up. After bidding goodbye to his wife and setting off for Canada, George darkens his skin with walnut bark and dyes his hair black (94). Thus when George encounters Mr. Wilson, the owner of the bagging factory at which he used to work, at a small country hotel, Mr. Wilson doesn't immediately recognize his former employee. But once George reveals his identity and his plan to his former boss, Mr. Wilson responds by offering the fugitive "a roll of bills from his pocket-book" to assist him in his quest for freedom (98). George refuses the money at first, but later accepts it as a loan, saying, "On condition, sir, that I may repay it at some future time" (98). George's masquerade helps him escape to Canada, and his happy ending includes "constant occupation in the shop of a worth machinist" where he earns "a competent support for his family" (371).

George Harris is an abolitionist hero to which Stowe's working-class readers could relate. His laboring life mimics a working-class white man's during the Age of Jackson, and he rectifies the social injustices that oppress him by playing a part that working-class white men played on the early minstrel stage. But because he is not a white man, paper money appears in place of specie when George Harris enacts his minstrel performance and symbolically occupies the position of a white performer on the minstrel stage. Joining minstrelsy's themes of white displacement and black dispossession, George seeks recognition of his intrinsic value while striking out to possess himself. Hence the substitution of paper money for specie, for like the bills he accepts from Mr. Wilson (and unlike a white minstrel performer) George does not legally own his body any more than the bills he carries possess their own value. Instead, like the paper money with which he is associated, George is recognized only for his exchange value. The appeal to Jacksonian hard money sentiment is therefore great, for Stowe effectively likens legislation that perpetuates slavery—in particular the Fugitive Slave Law of 1850, which forced the urban North to participate more directly in the perpetuation of slavery—to soft money legislation that favored capitalists at the expense of laborers, and which early minstrelsy lampooned.

The logic of minstrelsy that gives shape to George Harris's blackface performance also erupts into his role as co-protagonist of *Uncle Tom's Cabin*. Simultaneously playing the part of working-class white man and his blacked-up alter ego, George calls attention to the symbolic minstrel role he plays in Stowe's text—a role that his blackface masquerade announces. For even when he's not blacking up, George is visually as well as legally half-white and half-black. Stowe's description of his physical features underscores this by characterizing George as a white man with black skin: George's European features, which constitute the *structure* of his face, are inherited from his white father, but "from his mother he had received only a slight mulatto tinge" (94). Like a minstrel performer onstage, and like Rice's Jim Crow in particular, he is, according to Stowe's description, a white body in black skin. George Harris thus promotes an association between mulattoes under slavery and white working men after the proverbial fall from artisanal grace. But as George Harris's minstrel gestures redeploy the tropes of Jacksonian ideology, his story also promotes an association between wage labor and freedom by representing wage labor as the antithesis of Southern slavery. When he arrives in Canada, George Harris gains possession of his body, but he doesn't regain his tradesman status. Instead, he spends five years as a wage laborer. Rather than enslave him, however, his labor is an expression of his freedom; his labor power is his own to sell because his body is finally his own.

Because George attains one of early minstrelsy's ends—recognition of his intrinsic value—by not only mimicking but also embodying the form's means, Stowe invites her readers to associate her mulatto hero with a minstrel hero. The chain of economic minstrel signification extends when Stowe invites these same readers to associate her remaining mixed-race characters with George Harris by way of the common currency that connects them, namely the paper money with which they are all associated. Minstrelizing all her mulatto characters, Stowe turns their actual mixed-race ethnic and legal status into symbolic blackface, prefiguring stage adaptations of the novel that were performed by white men and women in burnt cork until the twentieth century.

For example, after Eliza crosses the Ohio in a series of wild gestures that W. T. Lhamon, Jr., likens to a minstrel dance,[27] she accepts a ride from Senator Bird to the home of John Van Trompe where another piece of paper money trades hands. As he is leaving Eliza with "honest John," the senator puts a ten-dollar bill into his hand and says, "It's for her" (80). Likewise, when Cassy and Emmeline are hiding in Legree's garret and effecting a different kind of cross-dressing by wearing sheets and "playing ghost" for Legree, Cassy takes from Legree's desk "a roll of bills, which she counted over rapidly" before taking it on the lam (353). It's no coincidence that each of the novel's mulatto characters is associated with paper money, is a fugitive of some sort, or succeeds in achieving self-possession through some form of masquerade. Cassy and Emmeline perform as "the *sheeted* dead" (366; emphasis in original), while Eliza holds a mirror up to the minstrel wench by cross-dressing as a man. Her son does likewise when he is transformed from Harry into Harriet during the last leg of their journey to Canada. The fact that Harry is explicitly likened to Jim Crow in the novel's first chapter only reinforces his resemblance to a heroic minstrel character.

But for the novel's ethnically black characters paper money signifies differently, such as when Aunt Chloe attempts to "redeem" her husband, Uncle Tom, with the paper money she saves while working for a confectioner in, of all places, Louisville. Chloe doesn't just save money to buy her husband out of slavery, she "pertinaciously insisted that the very bills in which her wages had been paid should be preserved, to show to her husband, in memorial of her capability" (378). By hoarding the dollar bills she earns as if they had intrinsic value, Chloe appears to conform to, rather than redirect, the minstrel stereotype of the inept "darky" whose belief in paper money's intrinsic value mocks his or her own devaluation under the system of slavery. When George Shelby returns home and tells Chloe of Tom's death and his own inability to redeem the slave as he had promised, this mockery seems complete. But the reason Chloe's dollar bills cannot redeem Uncle Tom has less to do with Chloe's racial status (or Stowe's racialism) and more to do with the novel's ultimate minstrel transformation and a different kind of redemption.

Like George Harris, Uncle Tom desires to possess himself. This becomes readily apparent when, after being promised his freedom by Augustine St. Clare, Tom "felt the muscles of his brawny arms with a sort of joy, as he thought they would soon belong to himself, and how much they could do to work out the freedom of his family" (274). Unlike George Harris, however, Tom expresses his desire for self-possession in strictly physical terms, and for good reason, for whoever owns Tom's body does not own his soul. His soul, as he so often remarks, is the property of Christ. Stowe describes this divine ownership and the sacrifice that made it possible in financial terms. God is "the great Paymaster" in her economy (291), and when Tom is sent to the slave warehouse after St. Clare's sudden death, Stowe surrounds him with

> an abundance of husbands, wives, brothers, sisters, fathers, mothers, and young children, to be "sold separately, or in lots to suit the convenience of the purchaser;" and that soul immortal, once bought with blood and anguish by the Son of God, when the earth shook, and the rocks rent, and the graves were opened, can be sold, leased, mortgaged, exchanged for groceries or dry goods, to suit the phases of trade, or the fancy of the purchaser. (283)

This financial metaphor, that Christ literally purchased Tom's and everyone else's soul with his blood, is reprised when Tom tells Legree, "No!

no! no! my soul an't yours, Mas'r! You haven't bought it,—ye can't buy it! It's been bought and paid for, by one that is able to keep it" (309).

Like George Harris, whose symbolic white body is differentially valued against his black skin, Tom's white soul, the possession of Christ, is differentially valued against his black body—his "black shell" to use Legree's words (309). The character of Uncle Tom thus conforms to the logic of blackface as much as George Harris's does. But while George dons the blackface mask in order to flee the country, Tom steps into a minstrel role in order to become the martyr resurrected in the system of signs called *Uncle Tom's Cabin*. These differences are marked by a shift in the novel's monetary metaphors. Where paper money reflected George Harris's desire for self-possession in defiance of the laws of the state, the sublimation of Tom's dollar from gold to silver signals his transformation from slave to martyr, and demonstrates a disjunction between natural law and the law of the land—a disjunction that also gave the silver dollar greater value for its substance than for the value minted on its face, and thereby gave Stowe a way to show, in Jacksonian terms, how slavery was out of step with prevailing notions of natural justice. If George Harris is like the paper money he carries because he circulates as a commodity within a state whose laws do not recognize his selfhood or his rights as a citizen, then Tom finds his analogue in a coin whose essential value, the product of divine providence, is greater than the value the government has placed upon it.

Tom's transformation from slave to martyr—the Passion of *Uncle Tom's Cabin*—gets underway once Tom is purchased by Legree. After taking the gold dollar from around Tom's neck, thereby removing the sign of his ordinary circulation, the first thing Legree does is exchange Tom's wardrobe, which includes "his best broadcloth suit" (292), for what is essentially the costume of the plantation slave in the minstrel show. Then, during the ride home to Legree's dilapidated plantation, there occurs a very curious minstrel reference. Angered at the sallow faces of the slaves he has just purchased, Legree tells them to strike up a song. He is even more angered when Tom responds by singing a Methodist hymn. "Shut up, you black cuss!" yells Legree, "did ye think I wanted any o' yer infernal old Methodism? I say, tune up, now, something real rowdy,—quick!" (297). One of the other men in the wagon then strikes up a minstrel song:

Mas'r see'd me cotch a coon,
    High boys, high!

He laughted to split,—d'ye see the moon,
   Ho! ho! ho! boys, ho!
Ho! yo! hie—e! oh! (297)

Legree roars when Tom gives him Methodism instead of minstrelsy, but Stowe then describes the chorus of the minstrel song, which all the slaves in the wagon sing, as a type of Methodist prayer. "It was sung very boisterously," she writes, "and with a forced attempt at merriment; but no wail of despair, no words of impassioned prayer, could have had such a depth of woe in them as the wild notes of the chorus. . . . There was a prayer in it, which Simon could not hear" (297).

What are we to make of this connection between minstrelsy and Christianity? How are we to interpret the appearance of Uncle Tom dressed in plantation garb and singing along to plantation melodies, which Stowe then likens to prayers? More perplexing still: why does Tom assume this minstrel role en route to playing his part as a Christian martyr? It is no mere coincidence that Tom blacks up to play Christ, or that Tom's dollar is resurrected in sublimated form once he steps into this role. For while George Harris calls attention to the symbolic black-face role he plays in the economy of Stowe's text by blacking up, Uncle Tom assumes the minstrel guise to self-reflexively reveal his role as both blackface Christ and Jacksonian hard money martyr.

To claim that Tom assumes a messianic role as the end of the novel approaches is to restate the obvious. Stowe makes a number of explicit references that liken the slave and his death to Christ and the cruci-fixion. For example, after Tom's crisis of faith is over and Legree discovers him singing in his cabin, Stowe writes, "That submissive and silent man, whom taunts, nor threats, nor stripes, nor cruelties, could disturb, roused a voice within him, such as of old his Master roused in the demoniac soul, saying, 'What have we to do with thee, thou Jesus of Nazareth?—art thou come to torment us before the time?'" (342). Legree's sarcastic comment that Tom is a saint "let down among us sinners . . . to talk to us . . . about our sins" only strengthens the like-ness (309). The more pressing question, however—the more perplexing problem—is what does Stowe have to gain by presenting the Passion of Christ as a minstrel performance? The answer, in a nutshell, is that Stowe is once again appealing to Jacksonian audiences, and Uncle Tom is therefore not only martyred on the cross of slavery, but he dies for the sins that Andrew Jackson sought to remedy. By so doing, Stowe shows how slavery is antithetical not only to Christian law, but to the Jacksonian Democratic ideal, effectively driving a wedge between the issue of slavery and others near and dear to the Democrats.

This demonstration hinges upon the overlapping redeemer roles that Tom plays. As a messianic figure he resembles Christ, the redeemer of souls. But Tom simultaneously plays the part of hard money in a Jacksonian allegory, redeeming the paper debts of others and rectifying imbalances of trade. Hence the hard money symbol to which he is literally as well as figuratively tied. As long as Uncle Tom continues to circulate and is entrusted to manage the economic affairs of others, both Tom and the people who put their trust in him thrive. When he arrives at Legree's plantation and is taken out of circulation, however, he becomes a mere cog in the economic machine. The resulting message is an overt appeal to Jacksonian sentiment: take specie out of the economy and the result is a corrupted system. More to the point, a system characterized by gainful employment is transformed into one of debased slavery. Given this recapitulation of Jacksonian hard money rhetoric and working-class displacement expressed by early minstrels, it should come as no surprise that Uncle Tom blacks up to signify his debasement or to play a redemptive role. Only here the monetary metaphor does double duty: the Savior not only makes Tom like specie by giving his soul transcendent value, specie itself is portrayed as a kind of savior. Standing in for both coin and Christ, Uncle Tom takes center stage in a Jacksonian Passion play in which hard money ideology and Christian theology go hand in hand.

At both the Shelby farm and the St. Clare mansion Tom plays the role of financial redeemer, and his contributions are described in the same language that hard money advocates used when describing specie as honest money for an honest economy. Arthur Shelby tells Dan Haley that he's "trusted him [Tom] . . . with everything I have,—money, house, horses,—and let him come and go round the country; and I always found him true and square in everything" (2). And Augustine St. Clare, who was "indolent and careless of money" (176), finds it worth his while to put Tom in charge of his family's finances. "St. Clare at first employed him occasionally," writes Stowe, "but, struck with his soundness of mind and good business capacity, he confided in him more and more, till gradually all the marketing and providing for the family were intrusted [sic] to him" (176). Tom thereby rectifies "the wasteful expenditure" of the St. Clare establishment (176), just as he managed Shelby's farm "like a clock" (2).

The complicating forces that drive Uncle Tom's migration and ultimate demise are likewise informed by Jacksonian ideology, with each of Tom's owners embodying one or more anti-Jacksonian principles. The reader already knows that Arthur Shelby sold Tom in the first place to get out of debt. Here, Tom is like specie redeeming the paper debts held by Haley. But the nature and the scope of Shelby's debt damns him in the eyes of those of Jacksonian stripe, for he didn't just speculate, but "speculated largely and quite loosely," and "involved himself deeply" (8). The sale of Uncle Tom and Harry Harris cancels his debts, but only temporarily, and when the narration returns to the Shelby farm later in the novel the reader discovers that Mr. Shelby is once again in over his head. This is why, when Emily Shelby tells her husband that Tom has been asking "when the money for his redemption is to be raised" (219), Arthur Shelby can only chant a litany about the perpetuation of debt. "It's like jumping from one bog to another, all through the swamp," he observes, "borrow of one to pay another, and then borrow of another to pay one,—and these confounded notes falling due before a man has time to smoke a cigar and turn round,—dunning letters and dunning messages,—all scamper and hurry-scurry" (219). The problem, of course, is that Arthur Shelby is no fiscal conservative. When Mrs. Shelby suggests such a financial policy by asking, "Suppose we sell off all the horses, and sell one of your farms, and pay up square?" he skirts the issue and exclaims, "O, ridiculous, Emily! You are the finest woman in Kentucky; but still you haven't sense to know that you don't understand business;—women never do, and never can" (220).

Uncle Tom's next owner, Augustine St. Clare, embodies another cardinal sin decried by Jackson and his adherents. St. Clare's problem is that, while he fancies himself a democrat, he is really no less of an aristocrat than his brother Alfred. Ophelia and Alfred both expose the hypocrisy of St. Clare's self-aggrandizement by noting that, although he is no longer a planter like his brother, he still hasn't freed his slaves. St. Clare is also an aristocrat in the Jacksonian sense, living off his father's inheritance and taking up residence in "the New Orleans family mansion" (201). In short, he's not a member of the laboring classes that Andrew Jackson considered real Americans. The corrupting influence of wealth without work is demonstrated by St. Clare, for though "he was well versed in the forms of law" and could easily write out the deeds to free his slaves (268), he never gets around to freeing Uncle Tom before it is too late, even though he has all the leisure time in the world in which to do it.

Consistently portrayed as the antithesis of the speculators and aristocrats who own him, Tom eventually arrives at Legree's plantation where he ceases to circulate. Which finally brings us back to the dollar George Shelby gave to Tom and the significance of its evolution. When Legree opens the "witch thing" and the dollar emerges from it in sublimated silver form, Legree's gesture of tossing it out the window signifies a rejection not only of Uncle Tom's Christianity, to which the silver dollar holds a mirror, but also the hard money system this specie metonymically represents. More precisely, it is a rejection of Jackson's hard money policies, which made the silver dollar more valuable for its silver content than for its dollar form in 1834, and thereby made its messianic symbolism in Stowe's text possible. Legree, and by extension the system of slavery for which he is a metonym, is thereby portrayed by Stowe as both anti-Christian and anti-Jacksonian.

The disappearance and reappearance of the dollar in undervalued form is likened to the crucifixion and resurrection of Christ as well as the ascendance of Uncle Tom, who is transformed from a Christian slave in Stowe's novel to an abolitionist martyr resurrected in the popular cultural imagination. It is therefore also symbolic of Stowe's transformation of minstrelsy itself. White minstrel performers blacked up to proclaim the superiority of their white content—their so-called white blood—over the black form they assumed while onstage, and used silver dollars as symbols for this introjective logic. By playing a minstrel part in Stowe's novel, Uncle Tom underscores the value of his immortal soul—his content—over the form his black body assumes on earth, using the self-same silver dollar as mirror in the text. Stowe thereby changes minstrelsy's dialectic of race and class to which George Harris conformed into a dialectic of race and religion. The minstrel form, however, replete with its monetary metaphors, enabled Stowe to express this dialectic in Jacksonian accents. Returning to George Harris, then, we can see how paper money not only connotes his desire for selfhood and citizenship, but also underscores the fact that he's not yet a Christian. He hasn't yet given himself to Christ in order to gain his soul the way Uncle Tom has.

TOM SHOWS, THE VALUE OF DIFFERENCE, AND
THE UNCONSCIOUS RETURN OF *Uncle Tom's Cabin*

Stowe's romantic racialism, as George M. Fredrickson called it, may have been essentialist, but it was a challenge to the status quo nonetheless.[28] Contemporary readers mustn't forget that Stowe was working within accepted, if not dominant, parameters regarding race and its significance. Or should I say Stowe was operating within parameters established by and expected of white authors of the period, African American writers having pioneered unique approaches to the deconstruction of the concept of race. As Stowe's comments in *A Key to Uncle Tom's Cabin* (1853) illustrate, her novel's critique hinged upon the pleasure it brought to (white) readers.[29] This need to please not only kept Stowe from depicting slavery "strictly as it is" (5), it also led her to encourage her readers to accept race as an intrinsic quality of the body. Hence Stowe's incorporation of the language and logic of monetary reform, which gave her the vocabulary she needed to renegotiate the value of racial difference, or at least show how the value of difference was negotiable, while maintaining race as a stable system of classification. In her economy, God may have made people of different races, but the value attributed to this difference—like the value of silver relative to gold—is and always has been the product of the laws of man.[30]

To overlook Stowe's monetary maneuvers, then, is to miss the distinction Stowe drew between race and racial difference. And to miss this distinction is to fall into the same trap that the creators of the Tom shows did. Like Stowe's novel, the rhetoric of which is reflected in the money it incorporates, the Tom shows used dollars and cents self-reflexively. But in the Tom shows, the mirror that money provided did not signal a transformation of the monetary logic of minstrelsy, but reflected instead the degree to which these shows reified the ideology of non-negotiable difference that Stowe knew enabled the system of slavery.

According to W. T. Lhamon, Jr., when T. D. Rice took on the role of Uncle Tom in 1854, he "was inhabiting a part Harriet Beecher Stowe had tamed from the unsettling stances he had translated into white view two decades before her novel. With his lively inventiveness now reduced, the meaning of Jim Crow passed into the hands of the very salesmen the figure initially challenged" (*Jump* 31). Stowe may have been indebted to Rice for pioneering the popular cultural form her text so deeply engages, but the fact is that, rather than reproduce Stowe's co-opting of blackface forms and gestures, the Tom shows failed to live up to Stowe's deployment of early blackface's associative power, even when Rice was the star. This failure, like Stowe's success, can be measured by the use— or abuse—of monetary symbols both in and around the Tom shows. For unlike Stowe, who used money to reflect upon her redeployment of minstrel forms and gestures, the Tom shows underscored their conformity to, rather than reformation of, minstrel stereotypes when they mimicked Stowe's monetary strategy.

The antebellum Tom shows (re)turned Stowe's symbolic minstrelsy (in)to actual minstrel performances with white actors in blackface playing the novel's black and mulatto characters. Tom show producers also understood that money played a key role in Stowe's novel. But the monetary play in and around the Tom shows was disconnected from the critical content of the text these shows purported to dramatize. This disconnection is illustrated by the example of George Kunkel, manager of the Nightingale Minstrels, who, upon reading *Uncle Tom's Cabin* for the first time, knew he had to perform it. Moreover, he knew he had to play Uncle Tom himself and stage the play as a one-act epilogue to his own minstrel show as it toured the South in 1853. As part of the festivities, Kunkel had a die made that read "Kunkel's Nightingale Minstrels," and he instructed his treasurer to stamp the company's name on a bunch of old Spanish quarters to be handed out as change at the box office.[31] The tour turned out to be a disaster, and by the time Kunkel reached Savannah the heat applied by proslavery Southerners became too much and he gave up the show. As he fled, he left in his wake a trail of defaced quarters (Birdoff 139–40). His incorporation of silver coins without face value into his act proves that Kunkel had minstrelsy and its monetary component down pat, but he just couldn't sell *Uncle Tom's Cabin* to audiences who expected a gross parody of it. In other words, he couldn't account for Southern investments in minstrelsy's cultural currency. Dotting the trail of his flight from the Deep South, Kunkel's defaced quarters reflect his inability to redirect these investments to alternate ends, and trace the path of his exit.

This disconnection also characterizes the two major stage productions of Stowe's story by George L. Aiken and Henry J. Conway, each of which featured minstrel performances and monetary metaphors, but neither of which could connect them in any meaningful way. In Aiken's play, Uncle Tom's dollar is always silver—it is silver when George Shelby gives it to the slave and it is still silver when it tumbles out of the "witch thing" onto the stage. Uncle Tom's dollar never sublimates in Aiken's play. Accordingly, Aiken's play never transcends minstrel stereotypes. Gone from Topsy's repertoire, for example, are the "cunning glances" which mark the self-awareness of her use of minstrelsy's conventions as they mark Stowe's self-awareness of these conventions in her creation of Topsy. Instead, Topsy lists "dancing breakdowns" among her job duties. Similarly, Aiken incorporates Stephen Foster's minstrel hit "Old Folks at Home," whose narrator is "still longing for de old plantation," into the play (Aiken). Actors who performed Aiken's play apparently realized the disconnection between monetary metaphors and minstrel conventions that characterizes Aiken's script. Of the four prompt books housed in the Harvard Theatre Collection, only two preserve Aiken's references to the silver dollar. Of the remaining two scripts, one deletes the entire "witch thing" scene (TS 2696.300), and another selectively deletes the silver dollar as a prop (TS 2696.302), drawing a line through all references to the coin to make the "witch thing" contain only the lock of Eva's hair.

Whereas in Aiken's play the non-sublimating dollar mirrors the playwright's failure to transcend minstrel stereotypes, another non-sublimating silver dollar reflects Conway's inability to harness Uncle Tom's transformative power. In Conway's pro-Compromise play, Uncle Tom, like the dollar to which he is symbolically linked, doesn't undergo any transformation whatsoever. Furthermore, the auction at which Tom is sold is rigged by Legree, the "witch thing" is actually a prop made by Cassy and Emmeline as they "play ghost" for Legree, and rather than have Tom become a martyr, Conway has young George Shelby arrive to take Tom home after Legree spontaneously drops dead. Gone from Conway's version of Stowe's text, then, is any critique of the ordinariness of Uncle Tom's purchase, any critique of slavery's social evils and their perpetuation, and any critique of slavery as anti-Christian, much less anti-Jacksonian.

The three-way connection between minstrelsy, money, and *Uncle Tom's Cabin* continues to make its unconscious return in the twenty-first century, and one need look no further than his or her pocket change for proof. On the reverse of the Kentucky State commemorative quarter issued in 2001 there is a captioned picture of "My Old Kentucky Home." "My Old Kentucky Home, Good-Night!" was, of course, an 1853 hit of Stephen Foster's that eventually became the official song of the state of Kentucky. While Foster is known for his minstrel songs, "My Old Kentucky Home" signals a departure for the composer as it tells the tale of a woeful slave who must soon leave his cabin—his Kentucky home—having been sold downriver to harvest sugarcane. Foster, like many of his contemporaries, was influenced by *Uncle Tom's Cabin*; so much so, in fact, that his original draft of the song was titled "Poor Uncle Tom, Good Night" and contained the chorus, "Oh, good night, good night, Poor Uncle Tom Grieve not for your old Kentucky home Your [*sic*] bound for a better land Old Uncle Tom" (Birdoff 137). Foster's old Kentucky home, then, *is* Uncle Tom's cabin, not the big house depicted on the reverse of the Kentucky State quarter.[32]

2001 Kentucky State commemorative quarter reverse design. United States Mint image.

That Stowe's tale could transform Foster's minstrel songs into more sympathetic ballads is not surprising since Stowe's novel does its rhetorical work by transforming—even sublimating—minstrelsy's conventions to abolitionist ends. But as the coin that riffs on the title of Foster's ballad realizes anew a connection between *Uncle Tom's Cabin*, the reformation of the minstrel tradition, and American money in the twenty-first century, the Kentucky State commemorative quarter also reveals a contemporary desire to whitewash America's racialized history and its bearing upon the present.

Just as minted money reflects the transformative powers of Stowe's novel from within, and holds a mirror up to the failures of the Tom shows, the 2001 Kentucky commemorative quarter symbolizes contemporary American culture's relationship with *Uncle Tom's Cabin* as well as our fraught formulations of race and the value of racial difference. Like Stowe's own monetary symbolism, which has been obscured by more than 150 years of American history and the changes in monetary policy they brought, the role Stowe's text played in creating the nation that minted our money is not as readily apparent as it once was. If Uncle Tom's dollar is a mirror in Stowe's text reflecting the author's incorporation and redirection of minstrelsy's conventions, then the Kentucky State commemorative quarter is a reflective reminder of how Stowe's text forever changed the American cultural landscape. But it is also a reminder of how the racial stereotypes and racialist ideologies upon which minstrelsy depended retain their cultural currency and continue to circulate in contemporary society in simulacral form.

Unlike the silver dollar of Stowe's day, which was more valuable as bullion than as specie, twenty-first-century coins like the Kentucky commemorative quarter have only face value—they are token currency. The differences between these two coins and the locations of their value parallel the differences between nineteenth-century investments in the reality of race, which was symbolically located in the blood, and present-day formulations of race as a social construction—a simulacrum that has value only because of the social contracts that keep it circulating. Decoding the mythic sign(s) on the reverse of the Kentucky commemorative quarter demonstrates that the meaning of race is often lurking behind and/or encoded in the most banal images. More to the point, the caption on the quarter, whose original meaning was forged in debates over the value of racial difference but occluded by a veneer of post-racial ideology, holds a mirror up to contemporary American culture, which was forged through the reproduction of racialized subjects—a fact that informs, but often hides behind, the circulating simulacra of contemporary cultural texts that whitewash American history and satisfy a widespread cultural desire to repress memories of a racist past whose heritage is, as William Faulkner wrote, not even past, but is, instead, the living present.

# 2

## REAL CHANGE

*George Washington Cable's "The Grandissimes"
and the Crime of '73*

*Speech may be silvern and silence golden; but if a lump of
gold is only big enough, it can drag us to the bottom of the
sea and hold us there while all the world sails over us.*

GEORGE WASHINGTON CABLE,
"THE FREEDMAN'S CASE IN EQUITY"

To say George Washington Cable's *The Grandissimes* (1880) is set in
New Orleans at the time of the Louisiana Purchase but grapples
with the problems of Reconstruction is to repeat old news. Replete with
an unwelcome new "Yankee government" (161), carpetbaggers arriving
to establish new businesses, and resistant Creoles lamenting Louisiana's
"trampled rights" while swearing she "will rise again" (326), Cable's first
novel contains so many references to Union occupation and post–Civil
War rhetoric that only a handful of contemporary reviewers and even
fewer modern critics have treated *The Grandissimes* as anything other
than a parable for Southern culture's struggles after the fall of the Confederacy. True, many who read the novel serially in *Scribner's Monthly*
(November 1879–October 1880) or in book form prior to Cable's emergence as an advocate for civil rights in the mid-1880s failed to see how
its critiques of slavery applied to postbellum America.[1] But once Cable
became a household name publishing polemical works like "The Freedman's Case in Equity" (1885) and hitting the lecture circuit as a social
reformer rather than a local colorist, few had any trouble detecting Cable's allusions to Reconstruction or critiques of its shortcomings in *The
Grandissimes*.

But while Cable's politics became clearer over time, their relationship
to the convictions of his protagonist, the American immigrant-turned-
apothecary Joseph Frowenfeld, did not. In fact, few readers seem to
know quite what to make of Frowenfeld, whose arrival in Louisiana at

the beginning of the novel coincides with a yellow fever epidemic that wipes out his entire family, and who, upon recovering from the fever himself, suddenly becomes the axis upon which all of New Orleans society turns. Given the biblical proportion of the plague that smites his family and the miraculous nature of his own resurrection as New Orleans's chosen one, it's no wonder that Cable's critics react to his protagonist with incredulity. In fact, there's even an ongoing debate amongst scholars to decide whether the well-intentioned but overzealous apothecary is a protagonist at all, or if he's just a chorus giving voice to and thus becoming the conscience of the novel's real hero, the white Honoré Grandissime.[2] To make the waters surrounding Frowenfeld even murkier, no one has satisfactorily explained the significance of the apothecary's hobbies of astronomy and meteorology to Cable's tale of American encroachment and Creole resistance aside from observing that Frowenfeld, like his father before him, believes in an ordered universe.[3]

The critics' lack of success in deciphering Frowenfeld's character is, on the one hand, a testament to the apothecary's enigmatic status. But it is also symptomatic of a broader shortcoming in *Grandissimes* criticism, which has yet to adequately analyze Cable's narrative strategy much less Frowenfeld's role in it. For while Cable's critics have had no trouble recognizing that *The Grandissimes* critiques Reconstruction and its failures, few have satisfactorily explained how the novel does its rhetorical work. As a result, extant scholarship has yet to describe how the novel's form and content inform one another, what Frowenfeld's role in this hermeneutical play is exactly, or how the novel's critique of postwar American politics emerges from the resulting fold.

An investigation into the shifting monetary policies of the United States during Reconstruction facilitates a new reading of *The Grandissimes* that addresses all of these shortcomings. Such an examination makes it clear that Cable's novel not only restages the drama of Reconstruction-era monetary reform at every turn, but conforms to the self-same monetary logic it describes—a logic whose critical import is rendered intelligible by none other than Joseph Frowenfeld, and which is ultimately articulated by the novel's centerpiece, "The Story of Bras-Coupé." Drawing analogies between the so-called money question of Reconstruction and the reorganization of the postwar South, Cable applies the rhetoric of Reconstruction-era political economy to his own sociopolitical ends, grafting the moral issues of 1870s monetary reform onto the caste system that had long outlived slavery and that Cable sought to abolish. By tapping into the popular discourse that surrounded the money question, itself an ongoing debate concerning the form U.S. money should take and how changes to it affected American society, Cable deployed its class inflections, sectional feelings, and moral sentiments in his own critique of postwar American politics, which he knew prolonged rather than remedied the disenfranchisement of the freedman. Incorporating the language and imagery of the money question also helped Cable's novel resonate with contemporary readers, who were probably well versed in the events *The Grandissimes* mirrors, even if they were but occasional consumers of American periodicals. Readers of *Scribner's Monthly*, the journal in which *The Grandissimes* first appeared, had all the information they needed at their fingertips, since they were regularly treated to discussions of the money question by the editors themselves.[4] But even if none of Cable's readers ever read the editorials in *Scribner's*, it is hard to believe that anyone in America literate enough to read *The Grandissimes* when it was published could be oblivious to an issue so large and with such far-reaching implications that it was taken up by nearly every press in the United States, from the working-class *Workingman's Advocate* to the more leisured *Harper's Weekly*. Taking advantage of the democratic vocabulary that the money question engendered, Cable found in its rhetoric a way to appeal to readers who might otherwise have turned a deaf ear to his political platform of civil rights for African Americans.

A comparative study of *The Grandissimes* and the money question that shaped American popular culture as Cable was writing his first novel reveals the degree to which the plot of *The Grandissimes* parallels the story of American money across the same period. A compelling narrative in and of itself, the money question of Reconstruction found its principal plot complication in the Coinage Act of 1873, which demonetized the silver dollar and placed the nation on the gold standard. Though this piece of legislation was motivated by real economic conditions, the demonetization of silver provoked a backlash in the American popular imagination, and the Coinage Act of 1873, which removed the 412.5-grain silver dollar as a standard of value, thus became commonly known among monetary populists as the "Crime of '73." The class-inflected debate that ensued between gold monometallists, gold-and-silver bimetallists, and supporters of non-redeemable paper money and other soft moneys took the form of moral, ethical, and even theological arguments over how best to order the nation's money so as to bring order to the nation. *The Grandissimes*, in allegorizing the symbolic return of the bimetallic standard following the passage of the Bland-Allison Act of 1878, maps onto the post-Reconstruction South the principles that shaped these debates. Cable's point was not to argue for the inherent value of precious metal bullion or to canvass for the return of the silver dollar to full legal tender status, but to present his radical reformist ideas about black civil rights in consonant terms. In short, Cable sought to demonstrate how the Utilitarian logic that informed the rightness of the bimetallic standard, itself a compromise of sorts, also dictated the extension of civil rights to African Americans.

The allegorical framework of *The Grandissimes* is established by its romantic subplot, the love affair between Aurora Nancanou and Honoré Grandissime. As they stand in for silver and gold, respectively, the two lovers' pledged union that concludes the novel represents the nation's return to the bimetallic standard—a happy ending that is not only fitting of a romance, but true to the classical Utilitarian logic shared by the novel and the money question it traces. "The Story of Bras-Coupé," however, while functioning as the return of slavery's repressed on one level, likens slavery's legacy to the Civil War debt embodied by the greenbacks on another. The novel's centerpiece thus complicates Cable's contrived happy ending by removing slavery from the imagined past and repositioning it as a circulating debt. Since the circulating debt of the greenbacks was the very catalyst of the money question during Reconstruction, *The Grandissimes* in effect begs the question of the money question, and in the process creates a discursive space for a renewed debate about freedmen's rights in the New South.

## UTILITARIANISM AND THE CRIME OF '73

The money question of Reconstruction that Cable's novel restages was really a debate over the debt that remained when the smoke from the Civil War cleared. During the war the federal government funded its battles with the Confederacy in part by holding onto its gold and silver reserves, suspending specie payment on existing notes, and putting into circulation a new currency called United States Notes or greenbacks, which were not backed by precious metals but based solely on the credit of the federal government. Declared legal tender in 1862, greenbacks were intended to be a temporary expedient for offsetting the Union's wartime expenses. But the sheer magnitude of the federal deficit by the war's end coupled with rising inflation made it impossible to resume specie payments until the $430 million of greenbacks then in circulation were worth their face value.[5] A greenback dollar was worth only sixty-seven cents when the war ended in April of 1865, so to allow the redemption of greenbacks for specie at face value would have quickly bankrupt the Treasury by depleting it of all its precious metal bullion. To put greenbacks on par with the dollar, government legislators had to choose: they could either devalue the dollar by decreasing its gold or silver content, or they could deflate the greenbacks by contracting the money supply to bring wholesale prices down. The Johnson and Grant administrations chose deflation, and they put the nation on a course toward resumption first by pulling a portion of the greenbacks out of circulation to make prices fall, and later redefining the dollar itself by demonetizing silver to further contract the money supply.[6]

The decision in 1873 to abandon the silver dollar and embrace gold monometallism was precipitated by silver's steadily declining market value during the first years of Reconstruction. In the United States, the price of silver was falling because silver production was on the rise and the railroads had penetrated into the principal western mining states, making it easier to bring mined silver to market. This domestic increase in silver production was compounded by the conversion of several nations to the gold standard, since these nations then exported their devalued silver to countries that would still accept it, including the United States. Cheap silver was a novelty to most Americans in the early 1870s and had been ever since 1834 when the official ratio of silver's value to gold was changed from 15:1 to 16:1; sixteen times as many grains of silver as grains of gold being needed to make a dollar. Pushing silver's market value above its money value, the Coinage Act of 1834 (also known as the Gold Coin Act) made it unprofitable to use silver dollars, which became more valuable as bullion than as specie. Silver ceased to circulate, and gold became the money metal of choice. The gold rush of the 1840s drove the market value of gold even lower and made silver's return to circulation seem even more unlikely.

But as early as 1870, the architects of the Coinage Act of 1873 realized that if silver's market value were to continue its steady decline, Americans everywhere would begin spending the silver dollars they had been hoarding, and start bringing their silver to the mint to be coined, since the 412.5 grains needed to make a silver dollar would then be worth less than the dollar into which they were minted, that is, their silver would become more valuable as money than as bullion. Senator John Sherman, chairman of the Senate Finance Committee, Secretary of the Treasury George S. Boutwell, and Henry Linderman, a leading mint official and special advisor to Secretary Boutwell, recognized that silver production would only continue to rise, and they began searching for a way to prevent a deluge of silver that threatened to offset the deflationary trend by dramatically increasing the money supply and thereby deferring further the resumption of specie payments. Their solution was to slice through the Gordian knot and demonetize silver, a move that took the nation off the bimetallic standard for the first time since its instatement by Alexander Hamilton in 1792. Writing the bill that became the Coinage Act of 1873, Linderman and John Jay Knox, Boutwell's Deputy Comptroller of the Currency, effectively rewrote the coinage laws. The dollar was redefined as 25.8 grains of gold exclusively, and the silver dollar was abandoned altogether.

Pursuing a gold monometallist course made it possible for greenbacks to be redeemed for their face value in coin (that is, gold) by the beginning of 1879 as per the Resumption Act of 1875, but for many this end simply didn't justify the means. In fact, the Coinage Act of 1873 galvanized animosity between classes of Americans like few events before it, because it not only widened further the gulf between capitalists and laborers, it also picked at the proverbial scabs of sectionalist enmity left over from the late war—antagonisms whose sentiments Cable articulated in *The Grandissimes*.

Standing in opposition to the gold monometallists were the monetary populists, who knew that lower prices hurt farmers and other producers because deflation made mortgages and debts increasingly more costly, the dollar paid back being more valuable than the dollar borrowed. The populists also believed that decreasing the nation's money supply only stifled production and thus hurt both laborers and manufacturers. Against the gold monometallist position of the Johnson and Grant administrations, these inflationist "producerites" believed that the money supply could and should be increased to meet demand, not reduced to drive down need.

The most radical of these inflationists were the greenbackers, who didn't want resumption at all, but preferred instead the permanent issue and circulation of inconvertible paper money. Represented politically by the Greenback Party they formed in 1874, greenbackers included labor groups, farmers, and other members of the self-proclaimed producing class. Greenbackism's class inflection stood in stark contrast to that of gold monometallism, whose supporters were predominantly moneyed or at least middle-class. The "gold bugs" were university presidents and professors, professional reformers, bankers, merchants, industrialists, and members of the literary establishment.[7] But to the greenbackers, gold monometallists were simply *the* establishment.

The class conflict over the money question was reflected in the ideological underpinnings of its primary antagonists. Gold bugs were strictly laissez-faire when it came to economic matters, and they supported policies that benefited people of entrenched capital and higher social status. Greenbackers, by contrast, decried as unjust any interest rate higher than the rate of increase of national productivity per year because interest *produced* nothing, and aggravated the debts of borrowers while lenders reaped the profits.[8] This class polarization was expressed geographically with the gold monometallists concentrated in the Northeast, and most greenbackers hailing from the agrarian South and Midwest. The class dynamics of the money question and its dueling rhetorics provided Cable with a type of shorthand for addressing the sectional preoccupations he hoped the nation could transcend. At the same time, these monetary debates offered a unique framework for just such a compromise in the form of contemporary social science, the logic of which drove the money question's temporary resolution just as it drives the resolution of *The Grandissimes*.

Despite the obvious differences in their class and sectional self-interests, gold bugs and greenbackers both believed that the money question was a moral matter. And as Walter T. K. Nugent has shown, both sides shared the same rhetorical vocabulary as each attempted to take the moral high ground in the name of social science, or, more precisely, Utilitarianism.[9] Applying the principles of Isaac Newton to political and moral affairs, Utilitarians put their faith in the laws of nature and applied scientific methods to social and legal issues.[10] Accordingly, Utilitarian political economists sought to tie issues of monetary reform to the natural and the universal as well as to the principles of utility and association. For gold monometallists this meant underscoring the intrinsic value of gold, arguing that gold was the natural basis of money, and proclaiming that inconvertible paper money was a prime example of government interference with the mechanistic laws of nature. For greenbackers, connecting their agenda to Utilitarianism meant noting that the natural objective of human behavior was harmonious association, the perfection of which was the object of society, and claiming it was the duty of a just government to increase the money supply in order to stimulate production and trade (Nugent, *Money Question* 59). And for both sides it meant claiming the work of Utilitarian thinkers like John Stuart Mill as their own.[11]

The debate between the gold bugs and the greenbackers took a decisive turn in 1876 when, as the architects of the Coinage Act of 1873 had predicted, silver's market value plummeted and the metal began to appeal to monetary inflationists. But when these soft money advocates discovered that the authors of the Coinage Act of 1873 beat them to the punch and prevented silver from increasing the money supply, the agrarian myth of the Crime of '73 was born, and with it the free silver movement.[12] Greenbackers had always been a minority in the fight against the deflationist establishment, but the nascent free silver movement's demand for the unrestricted and unlimited coinage of silver at the old 16:1 ratio appealed to moderate inflationists, who greatly outnumbered a shrinking greenback faction. A pro-greenback minority thus became a bimetallist majority in the producerite crusade against the gold standard.

But moderates of the fiscally conservative variety were also attracted to silver, namely in the form of limited or international bimetallism, which allowed for silver's return, but only in limited quantities under strict control of the government. Those sandwiched between the moderates and the diehard gold bugs, who found themselves on the defensive against a new coalition of producerites, began to rationalize a return to bimetallism by noting that at least silver was part of the same bullionist establishment as gold. Compromise was in the air, and Cable saw in its promise a model for a Utilitarian alternative to the Compromise of 1877, referred to by Southern blacks as "the Great Betrayal."

Driven in no small part by a desire to put the class and sectional antagonisms born of the Civil War to rest, the push to restore the bimetallic standard became a popular third alternative to gold monometallism and greenbackism that attracted hard money bullionists and soft money advocates alike. Allen Weinstein writes of the ideological investment that was made in silver, noting that "the drive to restore silver as a monetary standard derived [its] broad appeal not from economics alone but from its compelling moral symbolism" (55). This moral symbolism was inseparable from the Utilitarian ideals that shaped the money question. Bimetallism appealed to the Utilitarian sentiments of gold bugs and producerites alike by adhering to the bullionist belief in the inherent (read: natural, universal) value of precious metals on the one hand, while addressing the producerist conviction that, since the utility of money was to promote association in the form of trade and production, new silver discoveries such as the Comstock Lode in Nevada should be allowed to increase the money supply. As such, bimetallism meant more than restoring "the dollar of the daddies." It meant adhering to the first principle of Utilitarianism: what is right is what brings the greatest happiness to the most people.[13]

The battle of the standards was in full force when George Washington Cable began working on *The Grandissimes*. A close reading of the novel reveals the influence the money question had upon the author, who found in its rhetoric a type of shorthand for deploying class and sectional animosities and classical Utilitarian sentiments. The nuances of the money question would not have been lost on Cable, who was no stranger to the world of finance and trade. He worked on an off as a cashier and a bookkeeper throughout his young adulthood, his longest stint being in the employ of Wm. C. Black & Co. For eight years beginning in 1871 Cable worked first as bookkeeper and later as manager in the counting-room of this firm. He eventually became the private secretary of Mr. Black, and then treasurer's clerk and secretary of the finance committee of the New Orleans Cotton Exchange. It's no coincidence that *The Grandissimes* was written during this period of Cable's life when the language of the market and the "science" of trade, as he called it, surrounded him (Bikle 31).[14] Nor should it come as any surprise that Cable used the Utilitarian buzzword "science" to describe the business of trade, as the following reading of *The Grandissimes* demonstrates; for Cable not only had his finger on the proverbial pulse of American political economy, he was also a bit of a Utilitarian himself.

Utilitarianism was the guiding force behind nineteenth-century social science, providing a normative ethical framework as well as a working vocabulary to cultural reformers of the day. It is unclear if Cable read the works of classical Utilitarian philosophers and economists like Jeremy Bentham and John Stuart Mill, but his frequent references to "social science" and his brief affiliation with the Social Science Association show that Cable internalized the rhetoric of a Utilitarian zeitgeist, even if he never read the classics of the Utilitarian canon.[15] Utilitarian social reformers *were* aware of Cable's work, however, and he was invited by the president of the Social Science Association to speak on the subject of freedmen's rights in 1883, which Cable did during the Association's annual meeting in Saratoga in September of 1884. The piece he read at this gathering was published in the January 1885 issue of the *Century* as "The Freedman's Case in Equity," one of Cable's most enduring and controversial essays, in which Cable argued that Southern blacks were being denied the rights and freedoms of citizenship that the amended Constitution was supposed to guarantee ("My Politics" 21–23).

The money question and the Negro question converge in *The Grandissimes*, which examines the Utilitarian principles shared by monetary and social reformers of the period. But Cable's monetary allegory and the Utilitarian logic it follows highlight the disparity between the ends of these two reform movements despite the similarity of their means. Using the resolution of the money question as a benchmark for Utilitarianism's promise, Cable's novel invites its readers to consider why social reformers were failing while monetary reformers were succeeding, and to realize that the freedman's cause was consistent with the Utilitarian principles that shaped the money question.

Just as greenbacks complicated the proverbial plot of Reconstruction, the plot of *The Grandissimes* is complicated by inflated paper. With the Cession coming to pass and the United States assuming ownership of Louisiana, the land titles held by the Grandissime family start losing value . . . if they had any value to begin with. And, just as they did during the 1870s, silver and gold play a central role in the redemption of this inflated paper. Only, in the novel these precious metals are represented allegorically by Aurora Nancanou and Honoré Grandissime, star-crossed lovers from rival houses whose pledged union marks the resolution of the plot.

Honoré's association with gold is hard to miss. His very look is described as possessing "a somewhat golden radiance" (35), and when Aurora mistakenly leaves her purse behind at Frowenfeld's, Honoré fills it "with gold" (55). Honoré is even likened to a gold coin in the heading to chapter 43 where he is referred to as the Eagle, another name for a United States ten-dollar gold piece. But more importantly, Honoré's character conforms to the logic of the gold standard—he *is* as good as he appears. His intrinsic value within the economy of the novel is emphasized when Aurora says of the man she thinks is her landlord, "we shall never be turned out of this house by Honoré Grandissime" because "a man with that noble face could never *do such a thing!*" (131). Furthermore, as the family member in charge of the Grandissimes' land holdings, Honoré proves time and again that he can transform paper into money by selling land titles of uncertain value to speculators. Cable all but spells it out for the reader when, describing Honoré's foresight, he observes that Honoré "seemed to have struck the right *standard*, and while those titles which he still held on to remained unimpeached, those that he had parted with to purchasers . . . could be bought back now for half what he had got for it" (311; emphasis added).

While embodying the gold standard, Honoré gives voice to the laissez-faire ideology of its adherents. Accordingly, he eschews taking any sort of public stand against the inequities of a social hierarchy overdetermined by slavery because doing so would affect the bottom line of his family's business. "Mr. Frowenfeld," he tells the apothecary during their first meeting at the gravesides of Joseph Frowenfeld's family, "my habit is to buy cheap and sell at a profit. My condemnation? My-de'-seh, there is no sa-a-ale for it! it spoils the sale of other goods, my-de'-seh. It is not to condemn that you want; you want to suc-*ceed*. Ha, ha, ha! you see I am a merchant, eh? My-de'-seh, can *you* afford not to succeed?" (38). Privately agreeing with Frowenfeld's convictions, Honoré notes, "Your principle is the best, I cannot dispute that; but whether you can act it out—reformers do not make money, you know" (38). Besides drawing an enticing connection between money and reform that resonates with the money question of Reconstruction, this admission establishes the starting point of Honoré's transformation from self-proclaimed dilettante (154) to payer of debts for the wrongs of the past.

Aurora Nancanou, meanwhile, is associated with devalued silver. But unlike Honoré who is compared to all things golden, Aurora is almost always connected specifically to silver coinage. Accordingly, Aurora's intrinsic value is likened to that of her golden counterpart, Honoré. Charlie Keene speaks of this value when he tells Frowenfeld that Aurora has the "best blood of the Province; good as the Grandissimes" (15). But long before the reader first encounters her a signed document has taken her out of circulation, bringing with it the hard times that drove her to New Orleans, where she lives in poverty with her daughter, Clotilde. The first of many coincident references to Aurora and to silver coinage occurs during her third visit to Frowenfeld's shop, where she has been buying trivial things hoping to make the apothecary's acquaintance. While Aurora stands across the counter from Frowenfeld the narrator-observer is careful to note that Aurora "still had in her hand the small silver which Frowenfeld had given her in change" before she asks him if his basil is for sale (45). The coin is a pistareen, a silver coin of the late colony, and the only money Aurora had in her purse when she left it behind, an oversight that gives the love-struck Honoré his chance to fill the purse with gold. Yet another silver coin connotes Aurora's wisdom as a housekeeper. "On the day they moved into Number 19," the narrator reminisces, "she had been seen to enter in advance of all her

Two silver dollars of the 1870s. The seated Liberty dollar on the left is a trade dollar minted for export. The coin on the right is an example of the Morgan dollars minted after the Bland-Allison Act was passed, which would have been legal tender when *The Grandissimes* was published. Courtesy of Heritageauctions.com.

other movables, carrying into the empty house a new broom, a looking-glass, and a silver coin" (63). As the narrative progresses the silver coin references begin adding up. In a voodoo ceremony she hopes will snare Honoré's heart, Aurora makes an "offering of silver" to pay the floor (74), and when she is just about out of money the reader is told that Aurora is down to her "last picayune," another silver coin (218). Aurora and her daughter even resemble the allegorical visages of Liberty on many nineteenth-century American silver dollars, with their "half-Gallic, half-classic beauty" that makes Frowenfeld believe "they had just bounded into life from the garlanded procession of some old fresco" (139–40). This resemblance, notes the narrator, "was not a little helped on by the costume of the late Revolution (most acceptably chastened and belated by the distance from Paris). Their black hair, somewhat heavier on Clotilde's head, where it rippled once or twice, was knotted *en Grecque*, and adorned only with the spoils of a nosegay given to Clotilde by a chivalric small boy in the home of her music scholar" (140).

The coinage connection is further strengthened by Aurora in one of her free indirect interior monologues during which she expresses her desire to wed Honoré amid concerns for the well-being of her daughter. "This is a world that allows nothing without its obverse and reverse," she pontificates—"Strange differences are often seen between the two sides; and one of the strangest and most inharmonious in this world of human relationships is that coinage which a mother sometimes finds herself offering to a daughter, and which reads on one side, Bridegroom, and on the other, Step-father" (215–16). In her continued musings Aurora also strengthens the connection of Honoré to gold by expressing her "faith that the rent would be paid—a faith which was only a vapor, but a vapor *gilded* by the sun—that is, by Apollo, or, to be still more explicit, by Honoré Grandissime" (217; emphasis added).

The metaphorical marriage between gold and silver to which Aurora's desires allude is informed by Clotilde's commentary on the gender politics of matrimony under patriarchy. Beginning with the assertion "It is not so hard to live . . . but it is hard to be ladies," Clotilde's lamentation is teeming with producerist rhetoric: "We are compelled not to make a living. Look at me: I can cook, but I must not cook; I am skillful with the needle, but I must not take in sewing; I could keep accounts; I could nurse the sick; but I must not. I could be a confectioner, a milliner, a dressmaker, a vest-maker, a cleaner of gloves and laces, a dyer, a bird-seller, a mattress-maker, an upholsterer, a dancing-teacher, a florist—" (255).

Her mother's double and thus another figure for devalued silver, Clotilde speaks of her prohibition from the public sphere the way producerites spoke of the demonetization of silver for which she stands. The Nancanous' reduced class status, itself the result of a contractual agreement beyond their control, only strengthens their resemblance to the populists of the 1870s, who were stung when the Coinage Act of 1873 was passed and the Panic of 1873 kicked off a six-year depression that added insult to injury. So, like Honoré who both embodies the gold standard and recapitulates the rhetoric of its adherents, the Nancanous are the symbolic condensation of both demonetized silver and the ideology of producerites who championed its return as a standard of value. Hence Aurora's love/hate relationship with Honoré: as a member of the Grandissime family he represents the moneyed establishment against which she must fight, but as a potential partner he has the ability to uplift her and her daughter from poverty. To be pro-silver during the 1870s, after all, was to be pro-bimetallism.

The reason Aurora and her daughter are poor in the first place is the hinge upon which both the plot and the monetary allegory turn. Seventeen years ago, we learn, Aurora's husband lost their plantation, Fausse Rivière, to Honoré's uncle Agricola Fusilier in a card game, and then lost his life in a duel after accusing Agricola of cheating.[16] At that time Agricola, in a rare moment of subdued hubris, wrote to Aurora stating that he'd give back the deed to the estate if she would only claim in writing that he'd won it fair and square. But Aurora refused, choosing instead to leave her home and live with her father, who died some months before the novel begins.

To Honoré Grandissime, who inherits the title to Fausse Rivière from Agricola along with the rest of his family's land holdings, the deed is a debt in the form of paper. As for how he's to pay this debt Honoré finds himself in a quandary, for while he knows he should sell the estate and give the money to the Nancanous, the uncertain value of the remaining Grandissime family titles could make such largesse too costly for his family.

This debt of Honoré's and his dilemma over how to pay it serve as reminders of the Civil War deficit and the money question of Reconstruction, respectively. For if the novel chronicles the events of 1878—a suggestion reinforced by Cable's otherwise anachronistic depiction of the yellow fever epidemic that claims Joseph Frowenfeld's family just as it claimed Cable's own son, George, that year—then Aurora's refusal to back Agricola's note coincides with the suspension of specie payments seventeen years earlier in 1861, the very catalyst of the money question. The title to Fausse Rivière, then, is put in Honoré's trust just as the greenbacks were put in the trust of the gold standard. And, as was the case during Reconstruction, there is a premium that would make too premature an attempt at redemption too costly.

In trying to make up his mind about what to do with the Nancanou plantation, Honoré repeats to himself and for the reader the Reconstruction-era question of whether to refund the debt represented by the greenbacks, or to keep inconvertible paper as legal tender. In short, he weighs the sacrifices of hard money redemption (selling the title to the plantation and giving the Nancanous the money) against soft money speculation (retaining the title to Fausse Rivière as collateral to secure his family's remaining land holdings, whose value remains uncertain). He chooses, of course, to pay the debt, eschewing paper's promise to toe the hard money line just like the United States did during Reconstruction. Honoré sells the plantation and gives Aurora and Clotilde a statement saying they have a balance at credit of $105,000 at the Grandissimes' counting room, which is later paid in the form of "two mighty drafts of equal amount on Philadelphia" (280).

Corresponding to the erasure of the gold premium that made both specie resumption and the remonetization of silver possible, Honoré's decision to pay restitution to the Nancanous is likewise driven by moral as well as monetary concerns. For Honoré's redemption of the title to

Fausse Rivière doesn't just balance the books, it rights the wrongs of the past. As the note he scrawls to himself but mistakenly delivers to Aurora says, Honoré acts "not for love of woman, but in the name of justice and the fear of God" (262). The coming together of Aurora and Honoré at the end of the novel is, as Honoré's note announces, informed by but distinct from the debt that Honoré repays, just as the monetary policies that deflated the greenback and allowed for the resumption of specie payments influenced but were separate from the remonetization of silver in 1878. To the gold monometallist establishment of the 1870s, resuming specie payments was the right thing to do because it put the nation's money back into alignment with the laws of nature. Remonetizing silver, however, was a gesture of reconciliation to the political left and the people it represented, made possible by the deflation of the greenback.

The promised union of Aurora and Honoré that concludes the novel thus allegorically demonstrates how the Bland-Allison Act that brought back the silver dollar and the bimetallic standard (albeit a weakened one) in 1878 was driven less by the pressures of national debt than by Utilitarian compromise. The gold standard, after all, had already put the nation back on course, and could have continued to go it alone. Greenbacks were finally worth their face value by the end of 1878, and resumption of specie payments, or "redemption," officially took place without a hitch on January 2, 1879. But a return to bimetallism was, according to the logic shared by the novel and the popular sentiment it rearticulates, the most Utilitarian and therefore best solution.

Each of the participants in the money debates of the 1870s tapped into popular Utilitarian sentiment, using moral Newtonian rhetoric in an effort to make their case. In fact, gold bugs and greenbackers alike claimed that Newton himself would have approved of their policies. But Cable plays the bimetallist trump card by invoking Newton in the form of another astronomer and student of the physical sciences, Joseph Frowenfeld. It was not uncommon for astronomers like Simon Newcomb, Harvard astronomy professor and finance guru, to be quoted as authorities on political economy during Reconstruction, notes Walter T. K. Nugent, who writes, "The age that could tie coinage questions to the metric system and thus, it thought, to the eternal dimensions of the earth, could easily believe economics and finance to possess the same degree of scientific certainty as astrophysics, and give ear to astronomers when they talked of it" (*Money Question* 56). Frowenfeld's hobbies and the role they play in Cable's allegory thus become clear at last. For Frowenfeld isn't so much Newtonian as he resembles Newton himself, and Newton wasn't just the father of Utilitarianism (according to the Utilitarians), he was also the father of modern bimetallism and one-time Master of the Royal Mint.[17]

So when Frowenfeld encourages a union between Honoré and Aurora, it is a statement about the accordance of bimetallism with Newtonian sensibilities. The fact that Honoré and Frowenfeld are each betrothed to one of the two Nancanou women by novel's end underscores this, literally wedding bimetallism with Utilitarianism. But how does Frowenfeld's Utilitarianism square with his (and by extension, Cable's) social agenda? Frowenfeld, as the voice of Newtonian reason, mobilizes popular Utilitarian sentiment, and through him Cable naturalizes his case for the extension of human and civil rights to African Americans. For Frowenfeld, in a move fitting of a latter-day Isaac Newton, invites the reader to *associate* the bimetallist allegory he engineers with the egalitarian society he champions, and recognize that each is in harmony with the laws of nature.

But while Frowenfeld may be the embodiment of Utilitarian idealism, he struggles to express his political views to anyone other than Honoré Grandissime, who shares the immigrant's convictions, if not his zeal for advocating them. The rest of the Creole population, by contrast, finds Frowenfeld's platform of civil and universal human rights anathema—a fact that changes little as the narrative unfolds. Cable suggests, however, that this impasse isn't produced by the apothecary's beliefs so much as by his inability to present them to his detractors. Editorial asides to this effect often accompany instances of Frowenfeld's convictions butting up against his lack of rhetorical savvy, which can be found throughout the text. For example, following his first attempt to spar with the "doctors" that loiter outside of his shop we are told, "Somehow, Frowenfeld's really excellent arguments seemed to give out more heat than light. They were merciless; their principles were not only lofty to dizziness, but precipitous, and their heights unoccupied, and—to the common sight—unattainable. In consequence, they provoked hostility and even resentment" (46–47). Recognizing this, Honoré asks his friend, "Mr. Frowenfeld, you never make pills with eight corners, eh? . . . No, you make them round; cannot you make your doctrines the same way?" (153).

Frowenfeld's struggles and Cable's commentaries upon them play a significant role in the novel's own rhetorical work. For, when taken out of the regionalist context in which they appear, Frowenfeld's arguments bear striking resemblance to Cable's own polemical essays of the mid-1880s. In fact, Cable's position is succinctly summarized by Frowenfeld en bloc when he says to Aurora and Clotilde during a conversation in their parlor,

> One great general subject of thought now is human rights,—universal human rights. The entire literature of the world is becoming tinctured with contradictions of the dogmas upon which society in this section is built. Human rights is, of all subjects, the one upon which this community is most violently determined to hear no discussion. It has pronounced that slavery and caste are right, and sealed up the whole subject. What, then, will they do with the world's literature? They will coldly decline to look at it, and will become, more and more as the world moves on, a comparatively illiterate people. (143)

As Frowenfeld rehearses the arguments Cable himself would later make in essays like "The Silent South" (1885), the cool reaction of the Creoles to the apothecary's sentiments mirrors the rhetorical demands Cable sought to meet, and even anticipates the vitriolic backlash his social commentaries would receive in the post-Reconstruction South. But in *The Grandissimes*, if not in his nonfiction, Cable proved that he could round the corners off the proverbial pill of his philosophy by appealing to popular sentiment, connecting his social agenda to a model of truth that transcended sectionalism, and self-reflexively commenting on his own work via the novel's centerpiece, "The Story of Bras-Coupé."

The story behind "The Story of Bras-Coupé," like the money question of Reconstruction, is a narrative about paper and redemption. Originally conceived and written under the title "Bibi" in the early 1870s, Cable's first Bras-Coupé story about a rebellious African prince-turned-slave never appeared in print. In fact, an extant manuscript of "Bibi" has yet to be found. But a look at Cable's correspondence shows that he sent "Bibi" first to *Scribner's Monthly* in March of 1873, then to *Appletons' Journal* in June of the same year, to the *Atlantic Monthly* shortly thereafter, and to *Scribner's* again in January of 1874, only to receive rejection letters from each, with the reviewer from the *Atlantic*, George Parsons Lathrop, citing "the unmitigatedly distressful effect of the story" as justification for its return (Bikle 48).

These attempts to publish "Bibi" are caricatured by 'Sieur George in Cable's story of the same name, whose efforts to find the winning combination to the Havana Lottery net him only a trunk full of losing tickets. And, like the unfortunate protagonist of his story, Cable kept on stuffing the mailbox with requests for "one more chance" only to receive more rejection letters for his collection. "'Sieur George" (1873) may have struck gold with the editors of *Scribner's Monthly* when it arrived at their office in spring of 1873, but "Bibi" was never published as a story in its own right. Instead, manuscripts of the story circulated only among Cable's friends and colleagues, whose comments demonstrate that "Bibi" was every bit as powerful and disturbing as its revision at the heart of *The Grandissimes*. Edward King, one of Cable's early supporters and author of *Scribner's Monthly*'s "Great South" series from July 1873 to December 1874, wrote "that he had read the manuscript over three evenings in succession and had encountered him [Bras-Coupé] in three successive nightmares" (Bikle 51).

What was sublime for King, however, was *unheimlich* for others, as the paper trail left by "Bibi" testifies. Yet when "The Story of Bras-Coupé" appeared in *The Grandissimes* four years later, it was praised by the same editors who had rejected "Bibi" earlier, even though "Bibi" was incorporated into the novel as "The Story of Bras-Coupé" with apparently few changes.[18] William Dean Howells, the *Atlantic* editor for whom George Parsons Lathrop rejected "Bibi" for its "distressful effect," wrote Cable a letter in 1881 hailing the Bras-Coupé episode in *The Grandissimes* as "most powerful" (qtd. in Stephens 396). Frank H. Scott of *Scribner's* also raved about the revision, writing that "Bras-Coupé has taken hold of our memories with a much more tenacious grip than ever did Uncle Tom," and Robert Underwood Johnson, reminiscing about *The Grandissimes* near the end of his career at *Scribner's*, wrote of the novel's "powerful Victor Hugo-like episode of the death of the slave Bras-Coupé" (qtd. in Stephens 396). If "Bibi" was a pill too hard to swallow, especially for those eager to put slavery or the Negro question behind them after the Compromise of 1877, then the narrative's incorporation into *The Grandissimes* clearly rounded the corners from the Bras-Coupé episode, inviting readers to confront what they formerly could not, thereby thwarting a cultural desire to ignore the legacy of slavery, or to revise slavery's past like so many other Reconstruction-era romances had done. This was no small accomplishment, given Cable's belief that society keeps "the flimsy false bottoms in its social errors only by incessant reiteration" (*Grandissimes* 126). This confrontation, along with the novel's critique, is an emergent property of the interplay between the novel's form and content, which turns upon "The Story of Bras-Coupé," and adheres to the logic of 1870s monetary reform.

Although it appears at the center of *The Grandissimes*, to refer to the Bras-Coupé story as a text separate from the novel that contains it is somewhat misleading, for "Bibi," restyled as "The Story of Bras-Coupé," wasn't simply inserted into *The Grandissimes*. Rather, *The Grandissimes* was written as a vehicle for "Bibi." Cable's own description of the novel as "an expansion of the Bras-Coupé story" (Bikle 180) reinforces this, revealing in the process the novel's inherent potential for self-reflexivity. Invitations to realize this potential and take part in the novel's hermeneutical play are offered by Cable throughout the text, most visibly in the form of the Creole caricature Raoul Innerarity's painting "Louisiana Refusing to Enter the Union," which Frowenfeld correctly identifies as "allegorical" (114). A clearly self-referential double gesture, this anecdote points both to the novel's plot and to its allegorical possibilities: Louisiana is in fact resisting incorporation into the United States in *The Grandissimes*, most notably in the form of the patriarch Agricola Fusilier, and the novel is, as it is becoming clearer to us, allegorical too. The chapter that contains this anecdote also lampoons Cable's efforts to peddle "Bibi," not only because Raoul, like Cable, must rely on Frowenfeld to provide a vehicle for his work (the painting hangs in the window of Frowenfeld's shop), but also because Raoul progresses from dreaming about the picture he could paint of Bras-Coupé to finally painting that picture as the principal narrator of "The Story of Bras-Coupé."

Taking up Cable's invitation and examining "The Story of Bras-Coupé" as a mirror in the text of *The Grandissimes* reveals the story's inherence in the monetary/allegorical logic of the text that surrounds it. Specifically, mapping the novel's self-reflexive network makes it clear that the Bras-Coupé story at the center of *The Grandissimes* is an inextricable part of the novel's paper/debt/redemption theme, mimicking a greenback in both form and content. The formal mimicry of the novel's centerpiece is described by the evolution of the Bras-Coupé story itself: what was paper of uncertain value to Cable as "Bibi" in 1873 finds redemption within the bimetallic context of *The Grandissimes* as "The Story of Bras-Coupé" in 1879. More importantly, however, this greenback logic extends to inform the content of "The Story of Bras-Coupé," which not only tallies the cost of slavery but reminds those among whom it circulates of the debt owed to the inheritors of its legacy.

Recording the enslavement and gruesome death of an African prince, "The Story of Bras-Coupé" is a memory of slavery's past shared by the characters of Cable's allegorical Reconstruction. Captured by his enemies in Africa and traded to slave merchants for a looking glass, another invitation for the reader to think self-reflexively, Bras-Coupé is brought to Louisiana, purchased by Agricola, and sold once more to

José Martínez, an in-law of the Grandissimes. Refusing at first to work, Bras-Coupé falls in love with Palmyre Philosophe who, while indentured to Agricola, is first required to translate for the fallen prince, and then forced to marry him against her will. After drinking too much at the sham of a wedding given to him and Palmyre—a kind of sideshow attraction to José Martínez's own wedding to Honoré's sister—Bras-Coupé strikes his fellow groom and master and then flees, returning from his hiding place in the swamps only to put a voodoo curse on Don José's plantation. Soon thereafter the crops wither and die and the Don begins to do likewise from yellow fever, lending urgency to the search for the fugitive whose "words . . . found fulfillment on every side" (187). When Bras-Coupé is finally caught months later, he is shorn of his ears, hamstrung, branded, and whipped until his back is galled. He dies of his injuries the next morning, but not before lifting his curse from the land, which he does after learning that his master died of the fever, and while holding Martínez's baby in his arms.

Both a synecdoche for all slaves and a metonym for slavery itself, Bras-Coupé's life proves "the truth that all Slavery is maiming" (171), and his death symbolizes the end of the "peculiar institution" he represents. But while slavery might be over, albeit symbolically, for the cast of the novel that contains "The Story of Bras-Coupé" its cost still remains. For Bras-Coupé, of course, slavery costs him his life. In losing her husband, Palmyre loses the "mighty arm" for the dagger in her heart (178), and thus also loses her hopes to lead an insurrection. But the cost of slavery spills over the boundaries of the text of "The Story of Bras-Coupé," and takes its most lasting form in the caste system produced by slavery and maintained by the racism that enabled it—a debt whose inheritance shapes the lives of all peoples of African descent, and which is commented upon most lucidly by Honoré Grandissime's quadroon half-brother, Honoré Grandissime free man of color, or f.m.c.

If "The Story of Bras-Coupé" is a greenback circulating within the narrative economy of *The Grandissimes*, then the debt it represents is embodied by Honoré Grandissime f.m.c., upon whom the dialectic interplay of the novel and "The Story of Bras-Coupé" depends. At first the f.m.c. appears to be but an allegorical figure for the last of the three Reconstruction-era standards of value, the greenbacks themselves. He is, after all, the "other" Honoré Grandissime, and while his half-brother "was like the sun's warmth wherever he went," the f.m.c. "was like his shadow" (185), a description that evokes contemporary references to specie and greenbacks as the substance and shadow of money, re-

A SHADOW IS NOT A SUBSTANCE.

Thomas Nast cartoon, from David A. Wells, *Robinson Crusoe's Money*, 58.

spectively. He even has an "olive complexion" (41), and communicates almost exclusively via circulating paper. But the f.m.c.'s resemblance to the greenbacks is, like Bras-Coupé's role as "a type of all Slavery" (171), metonymic, for the free man of color in fact stands in for the greenback debt itself. Frowenfeld confirms this when describing how the f.m.c. makes his living via paper promises of future payment, or "the unceasing droppings of coupons, rents, and like receivables" (42). The resulting analogy Cable draws between the greenback debt and the inherited cost of slavery, or between the money question and the Negro question, is held together by the shadow metaphor above, for if both the f.m.c. and the greenbacks are shadows of their golden brothers, then Frowenfeld's description of slavery's legacy as "the shadow of the Ethiopian" (156) deploys the pro-resumption rhetoric of Reconstruction, and with it the moral obligation to erase the nation's debts.

Up to this point Cable's monetary allegory follows history turn for turn. And with the addition of the f.m.c. to the cast of allegorical characters the novel once again appears to hold a mirror up to 1878 America. But this close correspondence starts to unravel as the novel approaches its climax. To be more precise, the novel's allegory doesn't break down so much as deviate from the actual resolution of Reconstruction's money question to make a powerful statement. For as the allegory diverges from the historical facts, the novel's call to action emerges from the resulting gap.

It is easy to see how Honoré's settling of the Fausse Rivière account corresponds to the erasure of the premium that put greenbacks on par with gold and made specie resumption possible. Accordingly, this erasure is accompanied by the pairing up of the two Honorés, who finally join ranks to form the mercantile house Grandissime Brothers. But rather than settle the debt the f.m.c. embodies by putting him on par with his brother, this gesture only underscores the fact that something is still owed him. Honoré himself realizes this, admitting "he had come out the beneficiary of this restitution, extricated from bankruptcy by an agreement which gave the f.m.c. only a public recognition of kinship which had always been his due" (279). Some reduction does occur—the f.m.c. becomes "emaciated" shortly after this deal is struck (299)—but he does not disappear. Even after the f.m.c. exacts his revenge, supplying agency to both the symbolically severed arm of Bras-Coupé and the dirk in Palmyre's heart when he mortally stabs Agricola in Frowenfeld's shop, he becomes "thinner than ever" (330), but still he remains, along with the debt he represents.

Cable includes this account of the f.m.c.'s persistence to suggest that while the Civil War debt represented by the greenbacks may have been erased along with the sense of moral indignation that drove resumption, the debt of slavery recorded by "The Story of Bras-Coupé" remains in the form of the caste system that Frowenfeld denounces and the f.m.c. feels powerless to combat. This is why the f.m.c.'s final demise, instead of symbolizing the cancellation of this debt, connotes only another deferral; his last will and testament—another paper promise of future payment—diverts his wealth from "a friendless people" to the object of his unrequited love, Palmyre (331).

The f.m.c.'s belief that there was nothing he could do for "the downtrodden race" to which he belonged is itself symptomatic of the caste system so vociferously denounced by Frowenfeld, who tells the darker Honoré before his death that freemen such as himself "for a paltry bait of sham freedom have consented to endure a tyrannous contumely which flattens them into the dirt like grass under a slab," and that he himself "would rather be a runaway in the swamps than content myself with such a freedom" (195–96). With characteristic straightforwardness (or bombast) Frowenfeld alludes here to yet another paper promise of future payment, the Fourteenth Amendment, which extended civil rights to African Americans and guaranteed equal protection under the law when it was ratified in 1868, but had yet to achieve its face value (that is, it was more inflated paper).[19] The fact that Frowenfeld makes reference to "The Story of Bras-Coupé" by invoking the "runaway in the swamps" only strengthens the paper/debt/redemption theme, since what he's really saying is that he'd rather live with the debt of slavery than operate under the delusion that this debt has already been paid—the very message that Cable is trying to communicate to his readers via the interplay between "The Story of Bras-Coupé" and the demise of the f.m.c. To believe that American society has paid its debt to former slaves or their descendants is to believe Clemence's pretty lie, described by the former plantation slave–cum–*marchande des calas* in the chapter appropriately titled "An Inheritance of Wrong" as a counterfeit gold coin from the devil. To believe the plantation tradition's revisionist history, for example, is to exchange grossly inflated paper for fool's gold. True redemption can only come from meaningful action, and in Cable's narrative economy the catalyst of meaningful action is awakened sentiment.

Just as Cable used Frowenfeld to associate his politics with bimetallism and its self-proclaimed accordance with the laws of nature, "The Story of Bras-Coupé" and the f.m.c. together invite the reader to associate the debt owed to the inheritors of slavery's legacy with the greenback debt, and to react with the same moral indignation over its persistence. In short, Cable invites the reader to consider the contradiction of having been outraged about the greenback debt but remaining blasé about the caste system. The fairer Honoré Grandissime, meanwhile, provides the reader with a model for channeling this indignation in productive ways. For as Honoré exchanges the paper promise of the Nancanou plantation for cold hard cash and redeems himself in the process, the reader is invited to redeem the nation by exchanging Cable's own circulating paper, "The Story of Bras-Coupé," for some real change.

Real change, however, does not mean revolution, insurrection, or even social equality—the three great fears of white supremacist Southerners during Reconstruction—but a change of heart. Why else would a novel whose principal subject matter is slavery and its legacy be anchored entirely by a love story? Recognizing that "sentiments . . . are the real laws" (160), *The Grandissimes* pays homage to the sentimental tradition in general and Harriet Beecher Stowe's *Uncle Tom's Cabin* in particular by using the emotional as a means to the political. *Uncle Tom's Cabin* helped launch the Civil War by galvanizing the feelings of Americans not yet opposed to slavery; *The Grandissimes* awakens sentiments calloused by Reconstruction and hopes thereby to succeed where

Union occupation failed. Cable knew that the Reconstruction-era backlash against African Americans began in earnest when "our sentiment went blind" ("Freedman" 7). He also knew that the blinding of sentiment was aided by the silence of a Southern majority who deplored the hegemonic practices of white supremacists but said nothing.

Silence is golden, as the epigraph that begins this chapter observes, unless it is construed as a quiet endorsement of the status quo. Honoré Grandissime learns this lesson over the course of the novel, and thus by its end remains golden but no longer silent, exchanging his opinion that "condemnation. . . . spoils the sale of other goods" (38) for the practice of "breaking [the] silence" (268)—a particularly meaningful transformation, especially considering that Honoré's own silence was indirectly responsible for the death of Bras-Coupé, and that Cable himself was once an unquestioning Confederate soldier.[20] Honoré thereby prefigures Cable's appeal to readers of "The Freedman's Case in Equity," which charges the "silent South" to speak out against the caste system in the press, proclaiming, "There is but one right thing to do: it is to pour in upon them our reiterations of the truth without malice and without stint" (30).

In Cable's economy, to use writing to move people is to exchange printed paper for something real. And, just as he exchanged the first letter he ever wrote for a gold dollar from his father (Bikle 9), Cable hoped to redeem the pages of *The Grandissimes* in a literary marketplace where silver and gold—speech and silence—worked together. In a letter to novelist and literature professor Hjalmar Hjorth Boyesen dated January 3, 1878, Cable responded to Boyesen's suggestion that he end his literary hiatus and begin writing *The Grandissimes* with a bimetallic reference to speech and to silence: "I ought to be writing," Cable admits. "A man ought to keep invested the talents of gold that God has given him as well as the talents of silver" (qtd. in Turner, *George W. Cable* 80). Aside from providing further proof that Cable was in a bimetallic frame of mind when he began *The Grandissimes*, this letter announces the rhetorical predicament in which the author found himself. To force the issue of civil rights for African Americans would be to invite a knee-jerk backlash from its opponents; to say nothing would be to endorse the status quo of institutionalized racism.

This is why, in another letter to Boyesen, Cable observed that the novel does best "that teaches without telling" (qtd. in Turner, *George W. Cable* 80). Recognizing that Southern society was "sore to the touch," to use Honoré's words (153), Cable used "The Story of Bras-Coupé" and the money question together as mirrors in the text of *The Grandissimes*, enabling him to say without saying what needed to be said, and to thereby mobilize sentiment for the freedman's plight without telling sensitized Southerners what to do. As Cable later wrote in an essay entitled "My Politics," his intention in writing the novel was not to offend Southerners, but to write "upon questions that I saw must be settled by calm debate and cannot be settled by force or silence" (16). The gap that opens between the monetary allegory and the historical record from which it deviates is the space Cable creates for this debate, a space that is expanded by the divide between the realism of "The Story of Bras-Coupé" and the romance of the narrative that contains it. It is a space between force and silence.

The mirror in the text, or *mise en abyme,* is a literary device often used in the literatures of trauma and disaster to self-reflexively transcend the boundaries of the texts that contain them and reveal what these works do not, and in many cases can not, say. In Holocaust literature, for example, authors use *mises en abyme* to gesture toward and thereby make readers aware of an event that defies description, differentially defining the real of the Shoah against its representation. Cable makes a similar move when writing about the holocaust of slavery. "The Story of Bras-Coupé," as a mirror in the text of *The Grandissimes,* reveals what the narrative that contains it conceals, differentially defining the limits of romance. Aurora Nancanou, as a romantic heroine, cannot even speak of Bras-Coupé without breaking down. "Ah! 'Sieur Frowenfel," she says to the apothecary during his visit to her parlor, "iv I tra to tell de sto'y of Bras-Coupé, I goin' to cry lag a lill bebby" (145). When this silence is broken by "The Story of Bras-Coupé" the romance of the narrative that contains it is exposed as a contrivance. The Bras-Coupé episode is, in other words, the return of romance's repressed, and its inclusion in *The Grandissimes* critiques the genteel tradition's inability to address social issues Cable knew could no longer be ignored.

That *The Grandissimes* is a romance that subverts itself should come as no surprise, since Cable had grown to admire the unaffected style of Turgenev, whose fiction was recommended to the author by Richard Watson Gilder and H. H. Boyesen, among others. Boyesen found in Turgenev's work a model for dealing with social issues without contrivances, and when he suggested that Cable read him, Cable replied that he had already read *Smoke* (1867) and was planning on reading other novels by the Russian novelist (Turner, *George W. Cable* 80). Whether Cable's decision to incorporate the Bras-Coupé episode as a mirror in the text of *The Grandissimes* was influenced by Turgenev or not, it allowed Cable to explore a third possibility between the *unheimlich* nature of "Bibi" and the pleasing fiction—the pretty lie—of romance, just as bimetallism introduced a third term between greenbackism and the gold standard. Deploying the rhetoric and imagery of the money question, meanwhile, enabled Cable to intermediate the class differences of gold bugs and greenbackers and the sectional antagonisms this class division connoted, and bring the two sides together into the discursive space he created.

Cable's collapsing of class and sectional differences in *The Grandissimes* represents a kind of social and political wish fulfillment on the author's behalf. The posthumously published essay "My Politics" connects these differences to the Negro question, portraying them as symptoms if not causes of the continued disenfranchisement of African Americans. Here, Cable argues that he was "against the rule of any race over any other, simply and arbitrarily race by race, or even class by class," since such rule was "hopelessly at variance with the national scheme" (10). Southern Democrats, meanwhile, were ensuring that the African American population remained a "black peasantry" (7). Cable called this "a new phase of revolutionary disloyalty" to the United States (8). In short, the political subjugation of blacks was un-American, being feudal rather than democratic.

As for sectionalism, Cable longed for its erasure altogether. Speaking to the graduating class of the University of Mississippi in 1882, Cable argued that slavery made the southern states into "the South," and that when this happened "we broke with human progress. We broke with the world's thought" ("My Politics" 17). He continued his critique of Southern provincialism, noting: "We have not entirely in all things joined hands with it again. When we have done so we shall know it by this—there will be no South. We shall be Virginians, Texians [*sic*], Louisianians [*sic*], Mississippians, and we shall at the same time and over and above all be Americans. But we shall no more be Southerners than we shall be Northerners" (17).

Four years after *The Grandissimes* was first published in *Scribner's* the U.S. Supreme Court decided the Civil Rights Cases of 1883. Declaring the Civil Rights Act of 1875 unconstitutional and holding that the Fourteenth Amendment did not prohibit racial discrimination by individuals, the Civil Rights Cases decision opened the door to Jim Crow segregation, and sanctioned the continued denial of civil rights to African Americans. When the protections offered by the Fourteenth Amendment were effectively invalidated by the Supreme Court, Cable recognized that his imaginative strategy could only do so much and stepped out from behind the proverbial mask of his fiction.[21] Cable thus became more like Frowenfeld, who "decline[d] to be shielded by a fiction" (229). But as a result he also suffered a fate similar to the apothecary, becoming a scapegoat for the community he criticized and in which he lived. Cable's move from his native Louisiana to New England in 1885 only increased the resemblance to his protagonist, and with it the scorn of native Southerners in general and New Orleans Creoles in particular who dismissed Cable as they would have any another Yankee interloper.

As the politics of post-Reconstruction America were thwarting Cable's efforts, the return of bimetallism was also failing to live up to its egalitarian promises. The Bland-Allison Act of 1878 did remonetize silver, but forbade Americans from bringing their own silver to the mint to be made into coins. Instead of offering free silver as the producerites had hoped, the federal government agreed only to buy between two million and four million dollars of silver at market prices from silver producers every month and coin it for use. This kept inflation in check, and kept the nation on a de facto gold standard. So when wholesale prices plummeted again in the 1880s and inflationists once more began to agitate, up went the cry for free silver and the Populist movement was born. The "gold versus greenbacks" debate of the 1860s and 1870s thereby became the "bimetallism versus the gold standard" battles that culminated in the 1896 presidential race between William Jennings Bryan and William McKinley. And rather than settle the class and sectional animosities that characterized the money question during Reconstruction, the Populist movement only exacerbated them.[22]

When bimetallism became the new banner of a nascent Populist movement, it no longer symbolized Utilitarian compromise but widening class differences. As a result, the Utilitarian promise of Cable's bimetallic allegory lost its immediacy very soon after *The Grandissimes* was published. This is, perhaps, why we remember Cable's first novel for its deft grafting of race onto class and its depictions of a growing antagonism between "the people" and "the ruling class" (144), but forget that Cable hoped to reconcile these differences for the benefit of all. *The Grandissimes* stands as a testament to Cable's Utilitarianism, bringing narrative pleasure to the many rather than the few and attempting to effect the social changes that would bring freedom from pain to "a down-trodden race" (195). The novel was, in Cable's own estimation, "as truly a political work as it has ever been called" ("My Politics" 15). And though the cultural currency of its bimetallic allegory was made ephemeral by the events following its publication, Cable's oeuvre was fortunately not so short-lived.

# 3

## THE GOLD STANDARD OF THE PASSING NOVEL

*Exploring the Limits of Strategic Essentialism*

*Meantime there was feverish activity in Harlem's financial institutions. At the Douglass Bank the tellers were busier than bootleggers on Christmas Eve. . . . A long queue of Negroes extended down one side of the bank, out of the front door and around the corner, while bank attendants struggled to keep them in line. Everybody was drawing out money; no one was depositing. In vain the bank officials pleaded with them not to withdraw their funds. The Negroes were adamant: they wanted their money and wanted it quick. Day after day this had gone on ever since Black-No-More, Incorporated, had started turning Negroes white.*

GEORGE S. SCHUYLER, *Black No More*

The Coinage Act of 1834 initiated a slippage between the face value and material worth of silver dollars that minstrel performers riffed upon and Reconstruction-era politicians sought to resolve. This slippage eventually became the subject of the money question of the 1890s, which, like its antecedent during Reconstruction, pitted free silver Populists against gold bug fiscal conservatives and corporate liberals. The Populists, who hoped to capitalize on the disparity between the face value and material worth of silver currency, fought to lift restrictions upon the coinage of silver imposed by the Bland-Allison Act. Fiscal conservatives, meanwhile, sought to eliminate the slippage upon which the Populists' platform depended by abandoning bimetallism altogether. The Gold Standard Act of 1900 marked the consolidation of the conservatives' power, and effectively ended the Populist revolt by abolishing the double standard that made it possible.

The monetary politics that gave rise to the gold standard era share an evolutionary path with the racial politics of the same period. A close resemblance therefore exists between the struggle to define the source of money's value and the ideological contest over the meaning of ra-

Allegorical cartoon depicting the monetary platforms of presidential candidates William Jennings Bryan and William McKinley titled "The Rival Circuses," from the *Overland Monthly*.

cial difference. As the former hinged upon the inflationary disparity between face value and material worth, the latter pivoted upon the slippage between racial signifiers and the inherent qualities or essences they supposedly signified. Racial progressives, like their Populist counterparts, sought to capitalize on what this slippage afforded, namely the performative dislocation of value from the site of its inscription. Social conservatives, in turn, worked to reinscribe race in the body by revising the standards of racial identification just as the gold bugs revised the standards of monetary value to relocate the dollar's value in gold.

As sites for the articulation of monetary and racial discourses, passing novels are informed by both the cultural politics of race and the monetary politics of the gold standard. As the genre's name suggests, every passing novel chronicles the experience of at least one normatively black character who passes for white—that is, who is taken at face value despite his or her legal racial status. Contrary to contemporary critical assessments of the genre, however, the passing novel did more than just shift from critiquing fixed racialized subject positions at the turn of the century to celebrating the fluidity of racial identity during the Harlem Renaissance.[1] It also traces the transformation of what Gayatri Spivak calls strategic essentialism, the deconstructive strategy of using a reader's investment in essentialism—the belief in intrinsic value and its stability—to critique that investment. Most, if not all, passing novels employ strategic essentialism in some form or another. But an examination of the monetary metaphors that anchor these texts reveals how passing novel authors shifted their focus from critiquing essentialist definitions of racial difference to demonstrating the limits of strategic essentialism.

This chapter traces the coevolution of the passing novel and the gold standard from 1900 to 1933. In the process, it demonstrates how authors' use of strategic essentialism mirrors, and is in many cases a function of, the shifting logic of U.S. gold standard policy. Specifically, this chapter examines how pre-WWI passing novels serve strategic essentialist ends by conforming to the logic of the classical gold standard, and how the conflicting imperatives of postwar gold standard politics and Federal Reserve policies mirror the contradictory logic of Harlem Renaissance consolidation of and investment in the commodity of race.

## PLESSY, PASSING, AND PROGRESSIVISM: A PRELUDE

In Mark Twain's tragic novel *Pudd'nhead Wilson* (1894), a mulatto slave named Roxana secretly exchanges her infant son, Chambers, with her master's newborn heir, Tom. Indistinguishable half brothers who share the same father, Tom and Chambers unwittingly blur the color line as their unconscious passing continues into adulthood. Tom (who goes by "Chambers") grows up to become a cringing slave uncomfortable around whites even though he is legally white, and Chambers (who answers to "Tom") becomes the spoiled brat of Southern aristocracy in spite of his supposed "black blood." It seems at first that Twain's primary goal in *Pudd'nhead Wilson* is simply to deconstruct essentialist ideas about race—ideas that posited fundamental and intrinsic differences between ethnic groups, and tied these physical differences to less tangible traits like intelligence, temperament, and propensity for criminal behavior. But this assumption is complicated midway through the novel when descriptions of the half brothers' decentering of race give way to a backlash against the remaking of difference.

The turning point occurs when "Tom's" gambling debts become too great to manage, and he begins robbing houses to pay off his debtors.

After breaking into the home of Judge Driscoll, the man whom everyone thinks is his rich uncle, "Tom" botches the job and murders the old judge. David "Pudd'nhead" Wilson, a local lawyer hired to defend two Italian men blamed for the crime, eventually discovers not only that "Tom" murdered Driscoll, but that "Tom" is really Chambers: legally black, and legally the property of the deceased judge. Chambers's race, no longer portrayed as the emergent product of systemic processes of cultural inscription but relocated in his body, offers a post hoc explanation for his unlawful behavior, at least for the citizens of Dawson's Landing. By murdering Judge Driscoll, they conclude, Chambers proves himself to be the despicable other he "really" is. The evidence used by "Pudd'nhead" Wilson appears to reinforce the validity of this essentialist interpretation as Chambers's fingerprints, indexical signs of the body that render the body legible, simultaneously prove his guilt and assuage any anxieties the townspeople may have had over his passing. Order is restored when race is made real and readable again, and the color line is not only redrawn but underscored.

Twain, of course, didn't adhere to the racialist fantasy his characters find so comforting. Rather, his narrative demonstrates how legal and cultural frameworks that determine the meaning of difference, when informed by essentialist ideology, script responses to and simultaneously deny the "free play" of racial signifiers. Like the members of American society for which they stand, the citizens of Dawson's Landing conveniently forget or actively suppress the overwhelming evidence of race's socially constructed significance to embrace the happy ending of restored order that the legal inscription of racial essentialism provides. Chambers is sold downriver to settle his debts, and Tom is redeemed as heir to the Driscoll fortune. Of all the townspeople, the narrator alone seems to have lingering doubts about this return to normalcy, but as the novel's conclusion reveals, even he prefers denial to a troubled conscience. "The real heir suddenly found himself rich and free," he observes,

> but in a most embarrassing situation. He could neither read nor write, and his speech was the basest dialect of the negro quarter. His gait, his attitudes, his gestures, his bearing, his laugh—all were vulgar and uncouth; his manners were the manners of a slave. Money and fine clothes could not mend these defects or cover them up, they only made them the more glaring and the more pathetic. The poor fellow could not endure the terrors of the white man's parlour, and felt at home and at peace nowhere but in the kitchen. The family pew was a misery to him,

yet he could nevermore enter into the solacing refuge of the "nigger gallery"—that was closed to him for good and all. But we cannot follow his curious fate further—that would be a long story. (144)

Placing under erasure the questions that remain when race and the meaning of difference are (re)defined in essentialist terms, the narrator is freed from the burden of confronting either the social causes of Chambers's ill behavior or the consequences of Tom's translation. Such a confrontation would be a long story, indeed.

As Eric Sundquist has shown, *Pudd'nhead Wilson* prefigures racial essentialism's high-water mark, the *Plessy v. Ferguson* decision handed down by the United States Supreme Court in 1896.[2] This landmark case upheld the ruling of the Supreme Court of Louisiana which argued that Homer Plessy, who was one-eighth black in the eyes of the law, was rightfully jailed for sitting in a "whites only" railroad car in defiance of Louisiana's Separate Car Act of 1890. Affirming the constitutionality of "separate but equal" facilities and thereby legalizing post-Reconstruction de facto Jim Crow segregation, the *Plessy* decision epitomized the backlash against the remaking of racial difference exemplified by Homer Plessy's passing. In making their decision, eight of the nine Supreme Court justices ignored the arbitrariness of racial identification demonstrated by Plessy, whose skin was so light that he had to notify the train's conductor he was not legally white in order to stage his act of civil disobedience. Instead of reconsidering the validity of legal definitions of racial difference or the role legal discourse played in constituting the parameters of this difference, the court reified the essentialist myth of race by accepting the "one drop" doctrine, which dictated that a single drop of "black blood" made a person one hundred percent black (or one hundred percent nonwhite) in the eyes of the law. Justice Henry Brown's written opinion makes these essentialist assumptions clear in its proclamation that "legislation is powerless to eradicate racial instincts or to abolish distinctions based upon physical differences" (*Plessy v. Ferguson*, 163 U.S. 537 [1896]). Race was thus defined by the highest court in the nation, not in terms of face value, but as an intrinsic quality of the body.

As essentialist ideology was underwriting legal and social responses to the race question during the last decade of the nineteenth century, the money question was taking a similar, distinctly deflationary turn. Opponents of monetary and social Progressivism shared a common essentialist, anti-inflationary rhetoric during the 1890s. The reason for this similarity was that social and fiscal conservatives saw cultural relativism and the reformation of race in the same light as free silver agitation and the greenbackism that preceded it. To these critics, the intrinsic value of precious metals and the essential difference between blacks and whites were two sides of the same coin, and passing threatened them on two fronts, with inflated currency passing at face value on the one hand, and African Americans passing for white—or at least passing as citizens with all the rights of white men—on the other. Eighteen ninety-six turned out to be a watershed year for these critics, for not six months after the *Plessy* decision was handed down by the Supreme Court, gold bug William McKinley defeated free silver candidate William Jennings Bryan to become president of the United States.

Given the social, political, and economic climate of the 1890s it is no surprise that the passing novel came into vogue during the decade, or that authors of passing novels adopted the rhetoric of monetary reform in their texts. After all, the passing genre explores the consequences not of being something other than what one seems, but of circulating nonetheless. This explains why passing novels are rich in monetary metaphors, for passing is, in racial masquerade and political economy alike, a form of self-making in the marketplace and a means of renegotiating value. By crossing the color line, the passing character destabilizes racial boundaries and raises anew the questions that Plessy, the man, precipitated and *Plessy*, the decision, left unanswered. Highlighting (and exploiting) the slippage between face value and imagined intrinsic differences, like a silver dollar in circulation, the passing character relocates the authenticity of race in performance, at least while he or she is passing. The language and imagery of contemporary monetary debates, meanwhile, gave American authors a way to draw analogies between the race question and the money question and explore the larger question of value they have in common. This articulation is apparent in *Pudd'nhead Wilson* where Twain draws an explicit comparison between Chambers's racial passing and his gambling habit, implying that his passing for white is analogous to spending money he doesn't have. Conjoining the discourses of monetary and racial reform, Twain's novel portrays the cancellation of Chambers's debt and the redemption of Tom as coincident consequences of the restoration of racial order, or as consonant forms of deflation. The termination of racial passing in *Pudd'nhead Wilson* is thereby likened to the erasure of debt that inflated currency embodies.

The narrative strategies of authors like Twain who used money to comment metaphorically upon race took a new turn in 1900 when, under McKinley's leadership, the United States went on the gold standard. Ratified on March 14, 1900, the Gold Standard Act redefined the dollar's value in terms of gold alone. It abolished the bimetallic standard that had been on the books since 1792 (with a brief hiatus from 1873 to 1879, as the previous chapter explains), and thereby silenced the Populists' calls for the free coinage of silver at the post-1834 16:1 ratio. Squelching pro-silver dissenters who proposed inflationary monetary policies by dissolving the very standard that made them possible, the Gold Standard Act effectively did for the dollar what the *Plessy* decision did for race, revising the standards of value to delimit the dislocation of value from its imagined physical source to the signs upon its face.

African American authors writing after 1900 capitalized on the shimmering reflection between racial and monetary discourses in their texts, and the gold standard came to anchor the monetary metaphors of the passing novel just as it anchored the nation's currency. For pre-WWI novelists like Charles Chesnutt and James Weldon Johnson, challenging racial essentialism meant drawing analogies between post-*Plessy* racial politics and post–Gold Standard Act monetary politics, and undermining the myth of intrinsic value upon which they both relied. From a strictly anti-essentialist perspective, the gold standard was a form of monetary mystification, for while its adherents fetishized the intrinsic value of gold and pegged the nation's currency to it, the value of gold itself was always in flux. Because gold's value was subject to the same market forces as currency, as the value of gold went, so too went the price of money. The value of American money was therefore always already overdetermined by social relations, and the gold standard itself merely formalized collective social understandings of intrinsic value. By drawing analogies between this mystifying process and its racial analogue, authors like Chesnutt and Johnson sought to show that institutionalized racism was based upon the same essentialist pretenses as the value of money under the gold standard.

## PRE-WWI PASSING NOVELS AND THE CLASSICAL GOLD STANDARD

Set shortly after the close of the Civil War, Charles Chesnutt's *The House behind the Cedars* (1900) is a burlesque of both the tragic mulatto motif and the passing genre. In the novel, a very light-skinned African American woman named Rowena Walden decides to leave her hometown of Patesville and follow in the footsteps of her older brother John by passing for white in the nearby town of Clarence, South Carolina. In Clarence, Rowena, who goes by "Rena," falls in love with the white Southern aristocrat George Tryon, and they become engaged. But by a series of improbable coincidences Rena's secret is discovered by Tryon, who calls the wedding off. No longer able to pass for a white woman, Rena embraces her descent and begins a new life as a teacher at a school for black children in nearby Sampson County. While there she spends most of her time evading the unwanted advances of school superintendent Jeff Wain, an abusive man of mixed race whose delusions of grandeur mark both his affected speech and his bloated body. When Tryon, after a change of heart, begins visiting Rena's school and writing to her in hopes of rekindling their romance, Rena finds herself trapped between two men—and two destinies—she wants to avoid. After getting lost in a swamp during a rainstorm while trying to escape a confrontation with both men, Rena contracts a brain fever that eventually kills her, but only after Frank Fowler, a dark-skinned man with whom Rena grew up and who has loved Rena since childhood, rescues her and brings her home to Patesville.

Though its plot is conventional, especially in its resolution and accompanying restoration of racial order, the analogies the novel draws between the events of the narrative and the monetary metaphors that structure them are more complex. For out of the novel's portrayals of monetary and racial passing emerges a critique of essentialist social practice that calls into question the very standards that govern them both. While each turn of the plot, and therefore each step toward Rena's ruin, is precipitated by circulating inflated paper money, the association Chesnutt draws between racial masquerade and floating currency ultimately promotes an anti-essentialist reinterpretation of race, not an essentialist critique of funny money.

When *House* begins, the reader is introduced to John Warwick, who has just arrived in Patesville via steamboat from Clarence, South Carolina. The reader has not yet learned that John Warwick is really John Walden passing for white, but the novel's first monetary symbol, which coincides with John's return after a ten-year absence, provides a big hint that Warwick is not what he seems. Upon setting foot in the house where he grew up, John notices how "the screen standing before the fireplace was covered with Confederate bank-notes of various denominations and designs, in which the heads of Jefferson Davis and other Confederate leaders were conspicuous" (16). Apostrophizing the screen, John recites a line from *Hamlet*: "Imperious Caesar, dead, and turned to clay, / Might stop a hole to keep the wind away" (16). Confederate currency, of course, never had any precious metal backing whatsoever. It was always a fiat currency and thus, from an essentialist perspective, never had any real value. The Confederate notes set the scene in the Reconstruction South, but they also reflect the empty cipher that is Warwick's created persona. John confronts this screen as he confronts his past, for by returning to the eponymous house behind the cedars, John has returned to the home in which he grew up black, but had to leave in order to become white. The screen, then, acts as both a mirror into and an indictment of John's past.

The negative association Chesnutt draws here between John's passing and worthless money becomes part of a general anti-inflationary trend in the novel consistent with Reconstruction-era critiques of greenbackism and black ascendancy. In fact, the novel in general and its monetary metaphors in particular depend rather heavily upon the reader's familiarity with the money question of Reconstruction examined in the previous chapter. Chesnutt's narrator mockingly refers to "the government's promise to pay" that a greenback represents (254), and paper money is the catalyst for most of the plot's complications. For example, the reader learns that John and Rena's mother, Mis' Molly Walden, is poor because her father, who "had been at one time a man of some means," once "indorsed [sic] a note for a white man who, in a moment of financial hardship, clapped his colored neighbor on the back and called him brother" (156). Similarly, when Judge Straight, who knows of and sympathizes with John and Rena's passing, learns that Rena and Tryon are converging upon Patesville, he writes a note of warning to Mis' Molly and gives it to a black youngster named Billy to deliver. Judge Straight's mistake is that he pays the child to deliver the note *in advance* with another one of the government's promises to pay. "Make haste, now," he tells the boy. "'When you come back and tell me what she says, I'll give you ten cents. On second thoughts [sic], I shall be gone to lunch so here's your money,' he added, handing the lad the bit of soiled paper by which the United States government acknowledged its indebtedness to the bearer in the sum of ten cents" (121). Because the promise to pay passes as money, Billy doesn't deliver the note immediately; instead he "entered the grocery store and invested his unearned increment in gingerbread" beforehand (122). By the time the note is delivered it is too late, and Tryon has discovered Rena's secret.

The suspension of specie payments, the source of the greenback controversy Chesnutt satirizes here, finds its analogue in the monetary symbolism of Tryon's and Rena's affair. Early in the novel Tryon makes it plain that he believes in inherent racial characteristics. Accordingly, he expresses his belief in Rena's goodness—and his belief that this goodness is a function of her whiteness—by likening her to specie. Speaking to John prior to learning that he and his sister are passing, Tryon says, "All I care to know of Rowena's family is that she is your sister; and if you'll pardon me, old fellow, if I add that she hardly needs even you,—she carries the stamp of her descent upon her face and in her heart" (84).[3] Tryon reinforces the symbolic connection of Rena to specie again after he discovers her secret and curses, with a pun, that he was tricked by her "specious exterior" (251). Tryon's discovery of Rena's African ancestry, in turn, is likened to a suspension of specie payment, for in Tryon's eyes, Rena ceases to resemble the minted symbol of real (read: white) value, and begins to resemble a greenback: full of empty promise and passing in place of what once was real. Just in case the symbolic connection between Tryon's discovery of Rena's passing and the suspension of specie payments was too obscure, Chesnutt adds the following scene. John, knowing that Rena and Tryon have separately departed for Patesville, twirls a coin upon the floor and says, "Heads, he sees her; tails, he does not" (103). But as the coin is about to fall, John's son Albert "stretched forth his chubby fist and caught it ere it touched the floor" (103). If ever there was a pun on suspended specie, this is it.

With metaphors for inflated value dominating the novel up to the point of Rena's unmasking, it might seem as though Chesnutt was in league with the essentialists. But Chesnutt is really only baiting the reader, for the analogy he draws between monetary and racial passing is soon redirected toward anti-essentialist ends. This about-face relies heavily upon the novel's subplot, which revolves around the narrative's central monetary metaphor: an unpaid $500 note. After Rena has departed for Patesville to visit her sick mother, Tryon receives a letter from his mother asking if he could come to town to settle the family's claim against the estate of one Duncan McSwayne. She writes, "Your grandfather always believed the note was good, and meant to try to collect it, but the war interfered. He said to me, before he died, that if the note was ever collected, he would use the money to buy a wedding present for your wife" (99). On the one hand, the letter from Tryon's mother is little more than a plot device that puts Tryon on a collision course with his passing fiancée and thus also with the discovery of her hidden identity. But on the other hand, the fates of the unpaid note and of Tryon's future with Rena are, as the letter hints, inextricably linked.

They are also interconnected in the novel's symbolic economy, which becomes apparent after Tryon sees Rena on the street in Patesville and she faints to the ground overwhelmed by the significance of their ill-fated meeting. As Rena is brought into a nearby drugstore, revived, and sent home in a carriage, the narrator describes Tryon's thoughts. In his heart, remarks the narrator, "love and yearning had given place to anger and disgust" (142). But the paragraph describing Tryon's feelings and Rena's misfortune hasn't even ended before the matter of the $500 note is taken up again. "When Rena had been taken home," notes the narrator, Tryon "slipped away for a long walk, after which he called at Judge Straight's office and received the judge's report upon the matter presented. Judge Straight had found the claim, in his opinion, a good one; he had discovered property from which, in case the claim were allowed, the amount might be realized" (142–43). The juxtaposition of Tryon's discovery of Rena's passing and his meeting with Judge Straight about Duncan McSwayne's unpaid note is no mere coincidence, for as the novel progresses Tryon's attitude toward the debt the note embodies reflects his changing attitude about the racial status of his fiancée. For the moment, however, Tryon eschews attempting to collect on the note, and he leaves "the matter of the note unreservedly in the lawyer's hands" (143).

If at first Tryon was angered and disgusted to discover Rena's secret, and if Tryon's dread of racial passing is likened to postbellum ire over the suspension of specie payment (monetary passing), then Tryon's decision to defer collection of the unpaid note reflects some lingering doubts he has regarding his own essentialist beliefs about race and the value of racial difference. As payment of the note remains suspended, so also does Tryon try to suspend his belief that race is an intrinsic quality of the body, and accept Rena at face value. Tryon's internal struggles begin soon after Rena's "unveiling," at which time he begins having nightmares wherein his suppressed essentialist beliefs take shape. In one dream Rena appears before him "in all her fair young beauty . . . and then by some hellish magic she was slowly transformed into a hideous black hag. With agonized eyes he watched her beautiful tresses become mere wisps of coarse wool, wrapped round with dingy cotton strings; he saw her clear eyes grow bloodshot, her ivory teeth turn to unwholesome fangs" (146–47). But later, after much soul-searching, Tryon finds it harder and harder to reconcile the woman he knew and loved with the racialized other of his nightmares, and his feelings for her are gradually rekindled. So when a letter arrives at Tryon's home from Judge Straight reminding him of Duncan McSwayne's unpaid note, Tryon uses the note as an excuse to return to Patesville and see Rena. Rushing to the little town, Tryon "could no longer pretend obliviousness of the fact that some attraction stronger than the whole amount of Duncan McSwayne's note was urging him irresistibly toward his destination" (204).

The battle of Tryon's conscience with itself over the location of Rena's value symbolizes the tensions over the significance of race in turn-of-the-century American culture. This tension manifests itself most clearly when Tryon is en route to Patesville and he mutters to himself, "She ought to have been born white," before adding, "I would to God that I had never found her out!" (207). Tryon's exclamation summarizes his changing beliefs about race, shifting from essentialist outrage to a desire, not for a genuinely white body, but for the ignorance that would have allowed Rena to pass indefinitely. He eventually decides that it doesn't matter what Rena really is, racially speaking, for by marrying her "he would make her white; no one beyond the old town would ever know the difference" (208). But his desires to realize this constructivist plan are deferred when Tryon arrives in Patesville and sees Rena dancing with Wain. Exacerbated by jealousy, Tryon's essentializing tendencies return for a short while, but when he leaves the little town without collecting on Duncan McSwayne's note, the reader knows that he has not yet given up on a future with Rena—a future that depends upon the eternal suspension of the reality of Rena's race . . . or Tryon's belief in its reality, anyway. Tryon shows he is willing to let Rena pass forever by allowing the $500 note to do likewise.

Neither Tryon's nascent anti-essentialism nor the utopian vision it enables come to fruition, however, in part because Rena remains entrenched in the role prescribed for her by a racist society. Victims alike of a hegemonic racial order that estranges them from one another, Rena is sacrificed on the altar of essentialist difference while Tryon is denied union with the woman he loves. The return to racial order at the conclusion of *The House behind the Cedars* thus mirrors its analogue at the conclusion of *Pudd'nhead Wilson*, with both novels counting the cost of maintaining the racial state.

While Chesnutt's *House* uses monetary metaphors to critique essentialist standards in general, James Weldon Johnson's *The Autobiography of an Ex-Colored Man* (1912) links racial essentialism to the gold standard in particular. In the novel, which passed for autobiography when it was first published,[4] the unnamed narrator's earliest recollections of his white father and his black mother are characterized by the language and imagery of money, banking, and exchange. In his memory, the narrator syn-ecdochically condenses his father with the gold chain and the gold watch he wore, and he remembers that, in exchange for bringing him a pair of slippers when he came to visit, the man often gave him "a bright coin, which my mother taught me to promptly drop in a little tin bank" (3). If, as in *House*, whiteness and gold are praised for their intrinsic qualities, then Johnson's narrator literally banks on this connection, with each of his parents cultivating in him an essentialist view of black difference and white privilege. His mother later tells him that, thanks to his white father, he has "the best blood of the South" in him (12). But his father offers the boy a more symbolic reminder of his heritage: "I remember distinctly the last time this tall man came to the little house in Georgia," he writes—

> that evening before I went to bed he took me up in his arms and squeezed me very tightly; my mother stood behind his chair wiping tears from her eyes. I remember how I sat upon his knee and watched him laboriously drill a hole through a ten-dollar gold piece, and then tie the coin around my neck with a string. I have worn that gold piece around my neck the greater part of my life, and still possess it, but more than once I have wished that some other way had been found of attaching it to me besides putting a hole through it. (3)

Critics of Johnson's *Autobiography* miss the full significance of this gesture by overlooking the monetary history that informs it. For example, Houston Baker and Eric Sundquist each claim that the hole makes the coin worthless (436; *Hammers* 18), and Gayle Wald writes, "By putting a hole in the ten-dollar piece, the Ex-Colored Man's father takes it out of the realm of commerce and turns it into a keepsake, a 'sacred' object whose value, paradoxically, resides in its having been removed from commodity circulation" (145). These interpretations assume that gold coinage was, like present-day pocket change, token currency worth only the amount stamped upon it by the government, and that by defacing the coin the narrator's father negates its value. They ignore the trafficked interrelationship between face value and material worth upon which precious metal standards once depended, and thus misinterpret the significance of this particular monetary symbol. In light of the *Plessy* decision and its import after the turn of the century, the narrator's father's gesture is fraught with meaning, for in boring a hole through the coin he only negates the coin's *face value*. Under the gold standard, the coin would retain its commodity value, but the hole would end the slippage between face value and material worth because its precious metal value would still remain. The narrator's father therefore does to the coin what *Plessy* did to race, fixing its value in the body instead of the face.

The gold coin serves to remind the narrator of who—or rather what—he is, which is all right with him so long as he believes he is white, or that his father's "white blood" counts for something. This belief, and the essentialism that buttresses it, makes him "a perfect little aristocrat" in his early years (4). But his world comes crashing down when he discovers that his mother is not white but has been passing, and that he has therefore been passing too. The scene echoes W. E. B. Du Bois's own childhood entry into "double consciousness," the term Du Bois coined to describe the African American experience of trying to reconcile one's Americanness with one's African heritage, especially when the latter obviates the rights and privileges of the former. Johnson's narrator recollects:

> One day near the end of my second term at school the principal came into our room and, after talking to the teacher, for some reason said: "I wish all of the white scholars to stand for a moment." I rose with the others. The teacher looked at me and, calling my name, said: "You sit down for the present, and rise with the others." I did not quite understand her, and questioned: "Ma'm?" She repeated, with a softer tone in her voice: "You sit down now, and rise with the others." I sat down dazed. I saw and heard nothing. (11)

Once home from school he asks his mother, "Mother, mother, tell me, am I a nigger?" to which she replies, "No, my darling, you are not a nigger. . . . You are as good as anybody; if anyone calls you a nigger, don't notice them" (12). But when he asks, "Well, mother, am I white? Are you white?" she gives an incomplete answer: "No, I am not white," she says, "but you—your father is one of the greatest men in the country—the best blood of the South is in you—" (12). At this moment the narrator "did indeed pass into another world," and he discovers soon thereafter that every African American "is forced to take his outlook on all things, not from the viewpoint of a citizen, or a man, or even a human being, but from the viewpoint of a *colored* man," giving the African American "a sort of dual personality" (14).

The narrator's Du Boisian double consciousness turns to self-consciousness when he reads Harriet Beecher Stowe's *Uncle Tom's Cabin*, which, he claims, "opened my eyes as to who and what I was and what

Exploring the Limits of Strategic Essentialism   –   93

my country considered me" (29). The implied duality between "what I was" and "what my country considered me"—the very crux of double consciousness—finds its analogue in the gold piece the narrator wears and that Uncle Tom wore before him. As in the minstrel shows that *Uncle Tom's Cabin* redeploys, the coin signifies the slippage between face value (what the country considers it) and material value (what it is). By prescribing the relocation of value in the body, the hole—the mark of essentialism—underscores the very doubleness it seeks to negate. In short, Johnson's gold piece illustrates how essentialism lay at the root of double consciousness, which makes ethnicity and nationality antagonistic to one another. As the symbol not only of double consciousness but also of the essentialist ideology at its (absent) center, the narrator's golden pendant embodies the selfsame contradictions that the narrator embodies as he, like Uncle Tom, circulates in the symbolic economy of a book that contains him. Also like Uncle Tom, who is martyred in the name of Jacksonian hard money politics, the ex–colored man is figuratively crucified on the cross of racial essentialism while wearing the monetary symbol of the "Cross of Gold," William Jennings Bryan's metaphor for the gold standard. This, however, is where the similarity between Uncle Tom and Johnson's unnamed narrator ends. For if, as I argue in chapter 1, Uncle Tom's heroism is in part a function of his minstrel polyvalence (à la Jim Crow), then Johnson's narrator, by contrast, turns racial masquerade from a liberating practice into an expression of his own resurgent essentialism, and thereby becomes both the ex–colored man and the antihero of Johnson's novel.

The paradox of Johnson's narrator is that as he comes of age he becomes increasingly aware of and critical of essentialist practices and his own essentializing tendencies. But in the end he repudiates both his cultural relativism and his African heritage after seeing a black man lynched in the South. The narrator first begins to self-identify as African American when he hears his black classmate "Shiny" deliver Wendell Phillips's "Toussaint L'Ouverture" at their high school commencement ceremony. The speech, reports the narrator, made him feel proud to be "colored," and he "began to form wild dreams of bringing glory and honor to the Negro race" (32). His embrace of black culture becomes firmer following a chain of events that bring him to New York City, where he becomes an accomplished ragtime pianist. The narrator brings a border-crossing style with him to the piano, where he performs ragtime interpretations of the classical compositions he studied in his youth. As he learns that classical music can be "ragged" and ragtime can be made classic—that the boundaries that separate the two genres are fluid constructions—the narrator also discovers that the same fluidity characterizes racial categories because they are social constructions. While on the train that will take him into the Deep South to study black folk music, for example, he notes, "The main difficulty of the race question does not lie so much in the actual condition of the blacks as it does in the mental attitude of the whites; and a mental attitude, especially one not based on truth, can be changed more easily than actual conditions" (121). As for the essentialism that forms the basis of both the racist ideology he describes and the Jim Crow segregation it enables, the narrator surmises, "The difficulty of the problem is not so much due to the facts presented as to the hypothesis assumed for its solution" (121–22). He goes on to deconstruct the "generally accepted literary ideal of the American Negro"—the image of the shuffling, happy plantation slave—calling it the real "obstacle in the way of the thoughtful and progressive element of the race" (122).

The narrator's emergent constructivist outlook changes rapidly, however, after he arrives in the South and witnesses the lynching of a black man. Following the horrific scene in which the victim is burned alive, the narrator recalls, "A great wave of humiliation and shame swept over me. Shame that I belonged to a race that could be so dealt with; and shame for my country, that it, the great example of democracy to the world, should be the only civilized, if not the only state on earth where a human being would be burned alive" (137). With shame for both what he is and what his country considers him, the narrator decides "that to forsake one's race to better one's condition was no less worthy an action than to forsake one's country for the same purpose," and that he "would neither disclaim the black race nor claim the white race; but that I would change my name, raise a moustache, and let the world take me for what it would" (139).

The economic theme resumes when the narrator moves back to New York and chooses to capitalize on the essentialist beliefs of others by passing for white. Unlike Uncle Tom, who cashes in the symbol of his common circulation to become a savior to the antislavery cause, Johnson's unnamed narrator exchanges his desire to become "a great man, a great colored man" (32) for "a white man's success" (141). And as the narrator points out, a white man's success can be summed up in one word: "money" (141). Accordingly, he becomes a clerk in a wholesale house, and "began then to contract the money fever, which later took possession of me" (142). Eventually, he saves up a thousand dollars, call-

ing that day "an epoch in my life" (143). "And this was not because I had
never before had money," he muses—

> In my gambling days and while I was with my millionaire I handled
> sums running high up into the hundreds; but they had come to me
> like fairy godmother's gifts, and at a time when my conception of
> money was that it was made only to spend. Here, on the other hand,
> was a thousand dollars which I had earned by days of honest and
> patient work, a thousand dollars which I had carefully watched grow
> from the first dollar; and I experienced, in owning them, a pride and
> satisfaction which to me was an entirely new sensation. (143)

On the one hand, Johnson uses his narrator's financial success to
make a point about race and class, namely that by passing for white the
narrator is able to take advantage of the free market in a way that he
could not before. But on the other hand, the narrator's self-described
"honest and patient work" can only earn him top dollar if the white
businessmen for whom he works believe that he, too, is white. The
money he makes is therefore not just a measure of his labor, it is also
a touchstone for others' investment in his apparent whiteness and the
value it signifies. With this investment Johnson's use of the gold standard as a metaphor for racialist ideology comes full circle, for if the
coin the narrator wears is both the golden badge of essentialism and the
symbolic analogue of the narrator himself, then the investment of the
business establishment in the narrator's apparent whiteness is analogous
to the pegging of the dollar to gold.

Where Johnson's *Autobiography* makes its most original contribution,
however, is in its departure from its predecessors in the passing genre.
Unlike Chambers in *Pudd'nhead Wilson* and Rena in *The House behind
the Cedars*, Johnson's ex–colored man is never unmasked. As a result, the
transgressive power of his passing is substantially limited, for aside from
the reader and the white woman the narrator marries, nobody knows
that he is passing. Therefore, no one is forced to re-examine his or her
essentialist beliefs because the critique the narrator enacts depends upon
a difference they cannot perceive. To the reader, and to a lesser extent
the narrator's wife, the ex–colored man destabilizes the color line by
crossing it. But to everyone else he merely reinforces the color line by
conforming to the essentialist division it supposedly represents. Or, as
Gayle Wald puts it, "Because the very possibility and efficacy of passing
depend upon the concept of stable and diametrically opposed racial

identities of black and white, the Ex-Colored Man is continually fated to redraw the color line in the very process of crossing over it" (141). Though he often feels "like declaiming: 'I am a colored man. Do I not disprove the theory that one drop of Negro blood renders a man unfit?'" when his white peers make remarks "not altogether complimentary to people of color," he never does (144). The reason is that the color line enables his profit, just so long as he's on the white side of the line.

The ex–colored man's antiheroism manifests itself when he is seduced by the very essentialist values his performance mocks. This figurative seduction is perhaps best symbolized by the narrator's literal seduction by his future wife, who is a metonym for whiteness itself. "She was as white as a lily," recalls the narrator, "and she was dressed in white. Indeed, she seemed to me the most dazzlingly white thing I had ever seen" (144). This reawakening of the narrator's belief in the intrinsic value of whiteness leads to a resurgence of essentialist thought. He begins to doubt his ability to play the part of a white man, and, he recalls, "I began even to wonder if I really was like the [white] men I associated with; if there was not, after all, an indefinable something which marked a difference" (146). But his love for his future wife "melted away my cynicism and whitened my sullied soul and gave me back the wholesome dreams of my boyhood" (147). Of course, the boyhood he's referring to predates his fall from pre-colored grace and his entry into double consciousness—he is nostalgic for his own prelapsarian whiteness. He eventually shares the secret of his passing with her and only her. They are then married and have two children, but she dies delivering the second. With his white children beside him and the secret of his descent preserved, the ex–colored man truly begins to see himself not as ex-colored, but white. By the novel's end he is referring to himself as "an ordinarily successful white man who has made a little money" (154). Accordingly, the narrator puts his money where his mind is; so as he reinvests in whiteness, his money is invested in speculations that exploit minorities. He becomes, in effect, a slumlord, doubling his investment after taking equity in "a rickety old tenement-house" (143), before buying up additional flat-houses.

Though the ex–colored man enacts a deconstruction of the very idea of racial essences, his investment in the intrinsic value of racial difference (re)constitutes this difference along essentialist lines. The literal, financial investments he makes and from which he profits are the measure of this ideological investment and its returns, respectively. The resulting irony becomes clear in the concluding paragraphs of the novel when the narrator expresses his wish that he "were really white" (149), and posits, "I have never really been a Negro" (153). The adverb "really" in each observation provides a sardonic touch to both admissions, for the issue at the heart of the novel isn't whether race is real or not, but the degree to which people are invested in its stability.

This investment is the hinge upon which the novel's metacommentary turns, for Johnson's critique of essentialism depends in no small part upon the reader's belief in the inherent value of black culture, the ex–colored man's irrevocable membership in that culture, and the essential difference between it and white culture. In short, the reader must believe, as the ex–colored man does, in the inherent value of the birthright he "sells . . . for a mess of pottage" (154). This trade-off—a birthright for a mess of pottage—engraves the limits of strategic essentialism, for passing novels all rely to a greater or lesser extent upon the reader's investment in the passing character as an essentially *black* subject who, by crossing the color line, sells his or her birthright for something less authentic. The folly of the ex–colored man's investment in the inherent value of whiteness is thus a function of the reader's own investment in the inherent value of the narrator's blackness. The ex–colored man's seduction by race-writ-essentially holds a mirror to the reader's, and the results are equally mixed, for by accepting the very terms of the racial contract the author seeks to renegotiate, the reader, like the ex–colored man, simply exchanges one kind of essentialism for another. Walter Benn Michaels describes how attempts to replace racial identity with cultural identity often constitute "new ways of making the [same] mistake" by reinvesting such cultural constructs with racial meaning (*Our America* 134). And as Twain demonstrates in *Pudd'nhead Wilson*, to trade essentialisms is to swap one reductive ideology—one mistake— for another without confronting the hegemonic practices they enable. Of course, it is precisely this process of trading essentialisms and reinforcing racial meanings that James Weldon Johnson is using strategic essentialism to reveal. But this revelatory strategy is not without its limitations, as the example of postwar passing novelists demonstrates.

THE NEW ECONOMY AND THE LIMITS OF STRATEGIC ESSENTIALISM

By the mid-1920s it was clear that literary attempts to deconstruct racial binaries were doing little to precipitate the destruction of racism. The Great Migration of blacks to urban centers during and after the First

World War coupled with the tide of southern and eastern European immigration produced another, even stronger backlash against nonwhites in America; the "race science" of authors like Lothrop Stoddard and Madison Grant fueled the eugenics movement, which was perhaps the most obvious sign that essentialist ideology remained entrenched in the United States; and the Ku Klux Klan, which re-emerged in 1915, had over four million members by the mid-twenties (Robinson 116–18). But, paradoxical though it may seem in hindsight, especially given the conclusion of Johnson's novel, strategic essentialism wasn't just employed to combat this backlash, it formed the foundation of the New Negro movement in arts and letters. This elevation of a quasi-essentialist rhetorical strategy to the level of an aesthetic during the Harlem Renaissance is informed by the economic changes that characterized post-WWI America—popularly referred to as the start of a "new era" with a "new economy"—and heralded by a shift from money to market as the dominant metaphor in the passing novel of the 1920s. Like the dot-com bubble of the late-1990s, the new economy of the 1920s was characterized by explosive economic growth and intense stock market speculation. As the new economy approached a paroxysm of self-consumption that culminated in the 1929 stock market crash, some writers of the Harlem Renaissance began to question if the New Negro project of marketing of black authenticity was another such bubble waiting to burst. The passing novels of these authors therefore changed the genre's focus from delineating the limits of race to exploring the limits of *representations* of racial difference (that is, the (re)writing of race) as a vehicle for social change. In their books they drew analogies between the contradictory racial economics of New Negro literature, which used investments in racial essentialism to renegotiate the value of racial difference, and the competing logics of the new economy, which simultaneously adhered to and defied the gold standard and had come under popular scrutiny by 1928, the year the stock market began running out of control.

The new economy, along with the Federal Reserve System to which it is inextricably linked, was the product of three tectonic forces: the Panic of 1907, which led to the formation of the Federal Reserve System; the First World War, which gave the Fed powers it may not have been ready to exercise; and the Federal Reserve's implementation of the real bills doctrine after WWI, which symbolically turned commodities into gold. The Panic of 1907 was the product of an economic downturn that led to a stock market crash and the suspension of specie payments. The money shortage that ensued demonstrated the need for a more elastic currency in the United States. Popular demand for such seasonal elasticity led to the passage of the Aldrich-Vreeland Act of 1908, which allowed national banks to issue more notes on a broader range of securities and thereby increase the money supply when necessary. The Aldrich-Vreeland Act prefigured the Federal Reserve Act of 1913, which created a network of banks—a kind of decentralized central banking system—that could serve as lenders of last resort and provide the necessary elasticity to the nation's money with Federal Reserve Notes. As economist Richard Timberlake observes, Congress never intended the Federal Reserve System to be anything other than a fail-safe or "a self-regulating adjunct to a self-regulating gold standard" (255). But when the First World War broke out and the war's European belligerents went off the international gold standard to finance their war efforts, the Fed took an increasingly hands-on approach to managing America's money, the flow of gold between nations having become lopsided and erratic. The Fed's activism continued after the war when it took steps to help the countries of Europe get back onto the gold standard. To the chagrin of the Fed's laissez-faire critics, Federal Reserve policy was increasingly guided by an interventionist philosophy that sought to use legislation to *prevent*, not just relieve, the cycles of boom and bust that had so often plagued the U.S. economy. Economists Milton Friedman and Anna Schwartz point out that the Fed's operations often conflicted with what they call "the quasi-automatic discipline of the gold standard" (193). For instead of making monetary policies based upon the ebb and flow of gold, the Fed increasingly tied its operations to the flow of goods and services in the private sector (Timberlake 193). This shift is exemplified by the Fed's interpretation of the real bills doctrine, which allowed banks to provide credit or create money for borrowers whose goods were about to be sold on the market. The problem with the real bills doctrine, according to its critics, was that while gold could be monetized on fixed dollar terms, the monetization of goods amounted to banking on the future value of those goods. So while the Fed was treating the future return on these investments as "good as gold," critics of this practice were accusing the Fed of merely paying lip service to the gold standard. The result, observes political economist Allan Meltzer, was a fiscal policy in conflict with itself, and a Fed whose "aims . . . were incompatible" (262).[5]

Because the real bills doctrine increased the fluidity of credit in the name of gold standard fixity, postwar Federal Reserve policy adhered to the logic of strategic essentialism as closely as the New Negro movement in African American letters did during the same period. Triumphantly announced by Alain Locke in 1925, the New Negro movement combined community activism with a cultural program that, in addition to promoting strategic essentialism, commoditized race. Unlike pre-war passing novelists who worked to expose essentialist theories of race as empty ciphers, New Negro writers hoped to turn readers' investments in such theories into real change. In so doing, however, New Negro authors were banking upon the future value of race by investing in the future realization of an egalitarian, albeit racialized, society their work envisioned. The relationship of race to racial uplift in New Negro letters thus mirrored the relationship of commodities to gold under the real bills doctrine, for as the Federal Reserve was turning commodities into gold by monetizing their future value, New Negro authors were betting they could turn representations of black difference into a form of cultural capital from which all African Americans could profit. In short, they essentialized race—made it golden—in an effort to renegotiate the value of racial difference and profit from the change. If "The Story of Bras-Coupé" was like a greenback circulating within the symbolic economy of *The Grandissimes*, the pages of New Negro literature were like Federal Reserve Notes embodying investments in the future value of the commodity of race.

Early New Negro writers like Alain Locke and Walter White expressed their faith in this new literary economy and the profits it promised. But as the 1920s progressed, a growing number of African American authors began to suspect that investors in New Negro literary economics, like speculators in the new economy, were heading for a crash. By 1928, widespread fear that both of these markets could come tumbling down turned to anxiety over the inevitability of boom turning to bust. As Black Thursday approached on Wall Street, the brokers of New Negro cultural production began to panic when they realized that their speculative fictions could no longer be sustained.[6] Late Harlem Renaissance authors like Jessie Redmon Fauset and Nella Larsen therefore divested in the New Negro market and expressed their divestiture both in the language of postwar monetary policy and in conformity to the logic of the gold standard under the Federal Reserve. And, like White before them, Fauset and Larsen made the passing novel their circulating paper medium.

The antecedents of the New Negro movement can be found in a series of lectures Locke delivered in 1915 and 1916 entitled "Race Contacts and Inter-racial Relations: A Study of the Theory and Practice of Race." In these five lectures, Locke draws a fine distinction between biological race and cultural race, and demonstrates that although he agreed with anthropologist Franz Boas that biological race was a fallacy, he also thought that maintaining race as a cultural reality was necessary for enabling the ultimate acceptance and assimilation of African Americans into American society. Jeffrey C. Stewart describes this delicate balance when he writes, "Locke's pragmatic approach to the problem of race reminds us of [William] James's approach to the problem of war in 'The Moral Equivalent of War': Locke offered a cultural equivalent of race to his audience, both as a way for blacks to empower themselves and as a substitute for the more pernicious forms of race feeling and practice" (Locke, *Race Contacts* xxxiii). Locke's belief that the cultural equivalent of race could transform race relations found its expression in essays he wrote during the Harlem Renaissance, just as it informed the Harlem Renaissance itself. However, the balance Locke sought to maintain was undermined by his tendency to reinforce essentialist ideologies of race in these essays. For example, in "The Negro's Contribution to American Art and Literature" (1928) Locke observes that the Negro's "racial temperament" withstood his assimilation into Anglo-Saxon culture (234). Stewart comments on Locke's essentialist tendencies, and editorializes upon their incongruity with the cultural relativism of Locke's oeuvre, noting that as the 1920s progressed Locke increasingly "seemed to lend credence to the notion that blacks possessed an intrinsic nature" (xlvi). Stewart posits that Locke's "movement away from criticism of white paternalism and toward an essentialist view of racial character may have been influenced by his increasing dependence in the late 1920s on the financial support of Charlotte Mason, a white millionaire, who, in addition to being a fierce anti-Marxist, also believed that blacks and Indians were noble primitives who could reform Western civilization" (xlvi).

There's a better explanation for why Locke increasingly couched his New Negro constructivist arguments in essentialist language, however. On the one hand, Locke was practicing strategic essentialism to increase the value of Negro culture's currency in a rapidly expanding literary marketplace. But he was also yoking his strategic essentialism to the trope of analogizing the money question and the race question. Locke, who studied under Ralph Barton Perry and received his doctorate in value theory from Harvard in 1916, understood the contested nature of value. And Locke's tendency to deploy monetary metaphors when discussing the issue of racial discrimination shows that the author often riffed upon the tropic interaction between them.[7] This interaction extends to and informs Locke's New Negro enterprise, as the following discussion of Locke's anthology *The New Negro* (1925) illustrates.

Locke exemplifies the double gesture of the New Negro project in his foreword to *The New Negro* when he writes, "Whoever wishes to see the Negro in his essential traits, in the full perspective of his achievement and possibilities, must seek the enlightenment of that self-portraiture which the present developments of Negro culture are offering" (ix). This theme, that cultural texts reveal essential qualities, runs throughout Locke's introductory essay "The New Negro," which was originally published in the *Survey Graphic* Harlem issue of March 1925. In "The New Negro," Locke chronicles the Great Migration of blacks from the "medieval" South to the "modern" urban North and central Midwest (6). At the same time he describes another great migration in the arts from sentimental portrayals of African Americans to "scientific" ones. In the process, Locke describes a shift away from representation and toward reality; that is, away from the myth of "the Old Negro . . . a stock figure perpetuated as an historical fiction partly in innocent sentimentalism, partly in deliberate reactionism" (3) and toward "a realistic facing of facts" (5). "The Negro of to-day wishes to be known for what he is," he writes, "even in his faults and shortcomings, and scorns a craven and precarious survival at the price of seeming to be what he is not" (11). But as Locke himself writes, for an African American "to be known for what he is," he must remake himself in a symbolic marketplace where race is the currency; the "facing of facts" he craves must be produced, not by confronting essentialist representations of racial difference, but by taking them at face value.[8] The monetary metaphors Locke uses to describe the aims of New Negro cultural production, in turn, could also describe the process by which the Fed turned commodities into gold. "The intelligent Negro of to-day is resolved not to make discrimination an extenuation for his shortcomings in performance, individual or collective," he writes; "he is trying to hold himself *at par*, neither *inflated* by sentimental *allowances* nor *depreciated* by current social *discounts*" (8; emphasis added). Holding oneself at par, in this context, is to be known for what one is. But to be known for what he is, the black artist must first recreate himself in a New Negro literary marketplace. In short, he must use circulating paper to make himself golden by portraying as essential the difference he embodies.[9] Hence Locke's monetary metaphors: the New Negro transforms race into a circulating commodity by marketing black authenticity, and seeks a return on this investment that transcends the essentialism upon which this commoditized authenticity

depends. This, according to Locke, is how the New Negro will transcend the sentimentalism that makes his shadow "more real than his
personality" (4).

Just as the early to mid-twenties were characterized by faith in the
new economy, so too did authors like Walter White express their faith in
Locke's New Negro literary economy. Like James Weldon Johnson with
whom he worked in the NAACP, White believed that racial discrimination could not be ameliorated through direct action alone, but would
also require what David Levering Lewis calls "civil rights by copyright"
(xxviii).[10] The work of African American artists who sought to effect this
cultural revolution during the Harlem Renaissance took many expressive forms and represented several different theories of social reform,
but White was heavily invested in Locke's New Negro paradigm. Nowhere is this investment more evident than in White's passing novel,
*Flight* (1926).

Articulating White's faith in the transformative potential of Negro
culture, *Flight* tells the story of Mimi Daquin, a fair-skinned woman
of Creole descent who moves from city to city in search of her identity.
After moving from New Orleans to Atlanta, from Atlanta to Philadelphia, and from Philadelphia to Harlem, Mimi finds that she cannot
make a living as a colored woman no matter where she goes. So she
leaves Harlem to pass for white, and secures an apartment in the lower
nineties. Meanwhile, Mimi's dark-skinned son Petit Jean, who was born
of a love affair with Atlanta black bourgeoisie-member Carl Hunter, sits
in an orphanage getting older. Mimi never reclaims the boy, although at
the novel's end it is implied that she is coming to collect him after more
than twelve years' separation. During the intervening years, Mimi has a
successful career as a seamstress and dressmaker, and marries a wealthy
(and bigoted) white stockbroker named Jimmie Forrester. But financial success isn't worth the trade-off of living amongst miserable and
racist white people, and Mimi becomes more despondent than ever.
Mimi's ennui is at its acme when she meets a Chinese scholar named
Wu Hseh-Chuan, who puts Mimi's discontent into words for her. For
the most part, Wu Hseh-Chuan's observations amount to a Marxist
critique of modern capitalism. What sticks with Mimi, however, is the
scholar's observation, "Only your Negroes have successfully resisted
mechanization—they yet can laugh and they yet can enjoy the benefits
of the machine [White's metaphor for industrial capitalism] without
being crushed by it" (282). During the last of a number of clandestine
trips she takes to Harlem, Mimi confirms Wu Hseh-Chuan's thesis with

her own primitivist revelation. Observing the lack of black desire, Mimi exults, "Here was leisureliness, none of the hectic dashing after material things which brought little happiness when gained" (294). This revelation leads to the novel's conclusion, which depicts Mimi walking down the steps of the home she shared with Jimmie, leaving her husband without revealing the secrets of her past, and walking resolutely toward "*Petit* Jean—my own people—and happiness!" (300).

In order to turn Negro culture into cultural currency, White has to imagine race outside of the relations of production, or in essentialist rather than constructionist terms. This is why, as the novel progresses, Mimi increasingly conceives of race as an amalgam of inherent characteristics. It is also why golden metaphors accompany Mimi's essentialist investments. For instance, while working as a dressmaker Mimi "would run through her fingers a fragile bit of silk or chiffon . . . as a miser would his gold" (225). Having likened the materials of her trade to gold, the narrator then extends the metaphor by likening the differences that give them value to ethnic differences. "Most of all she loved the passionate reds, the vivid blues, the more pronounced shades," notes the narrator. "In a world of indefinite gropings [*sic*] they were to her positive, real things instead of the vaporous and lighter shades" (225). Clearly, racial difference, materiality, and value are all enmeshed in White's rhetoric.

Mimi also rejects the constructionist arguments of the political Left. When her passing-induced ennui leads her to attend progressive lectures at the Rand School and at Cooper Union, the economic theories and descriptions of class conflict espoused there fall flat for her. The fact that she likens this failure to alchemists' futile attempts to turn lead into gold is all the more symbolic given the logic of the gold standard to which earlier passing novels adhered and her own golden metaphors for the value of racial difference. "Most of the theories advanced there seemed to her visionary and impractical," observes the narrator—"the burning intensity of most of the students and hearers frightened and repelled her. Like alchemists of old searching, probing, seeking diligently for the mysterious and elusive secret by which baser metals could be changed into gold, so many of these seemed intent on finding some panacea which could be applied to all problems, economic, social, political, and in a flash solve them all" (221). The implicit argument being made here is that race, like gold, has intrinsic value, and Marxist arguments that describe the value of racial difference as an emergent ideological product of material conditions are but failed attempts to use leaden theories of social construction to account for golden racial essences. This alchemic metaphor is only one example of White's symbolic relocation of race in the body. Over the course of the novel, Mimi grows to see black resistance to industrialization and the acceleration of industrial capitalism as an inherent quality of Negro culture. After hearing a group of black convicts singing while working on the chain gang, for example, Mimi "marveled at their toughness of fibre which seemed to be a racial characteristic, which made them able to live in the midst of a highly mechanized civilization, enjoy its undoubted advantages, and yet keep free that individual and racial distinctiveness which did not permit the surrender of individuality to the machine" (94).

The strategy of Mimi's, and by extension White's, deployment of essentialist rhetoric is consistent with the logic of Locke's New Negro manifesto, and revealed through the novel's self-reflexive gestures. In *Flight*, White imagines black liberation as a consequence of embracing Negro essentialism, and he connects this embrace to the circulating paper of the literary marketplace via depictions of Mimi's reading practices. Throughout the novel, Mimi uses literary fiction to re-evaluate her place in the world. And as Mimi uses literature to self-reflect, Mimi's relationship to literary fiction becomes self-reflexive when she looks back upon the turning points in her life and concludes that "they were to her almost as though she had read of them in a novel" (236). White seeks, through his own novel, to replicate Mimi's New Negro awakening, and he demonstrates in the process the degree to which New Negro strategic essentialism adheres to the real bills doctrine. Just as future commodities must be materialized in order to keep the Fed's circulating paper from becoming inflationary, so too must the reader make race real for a return on White's investments in New Negro futures to be realized. White's aim, then, is to help the reader "become golden" by embracing his or her essential negritude, and to keep the circulating paper of his novel from becoming inflated in the process. This gesture toward a shared golden future appears on the final page of the novel when, just before the reader closes the book containing Mimi's story, the narrator reports that "another book in her [Mimi's] life was being closed" (300). And after this chapter in her life comes to a conclusion, Mimi becomes more golden, "the rays of the morning sun dancing lightly upon the more brilliant gold of her hair" (300).

White may have been a champion of Locke's New Negro paradigm, but for many members of Harlem's literati, exuberance for Lockeian strategic essentialism and the marketing of Negro culture waned at the same time anxieties over the inevitable stock market bust were reaching their peak. Though their role in the stock market collapse has been disputed by contemporary scholars such as Barry Eichengreen, the Fed's policies during the 1920s were popularly seen as contributors to both the runaway stock market boom of the mid- to late twenties and the bust that ensued.[11] For example, H. Parker Willis, the first secretary of the Federal Reserve Board, published an article in May of 1929 called "The Failure of the Federal Reserve," which faults the Fed for encouraging "the constantly rising tide of speculative transactions at higher and higher prices" in the stock market (547). Passing novel authors drew analogies between the self-contradictory logic of the Fed's simultaneous adherence to the real bills doctrine and the gold standard on the one hand and the oxymoronic logic of strategic essentialism on the other. Both, they warned, were leading to a crash. As much as Locke's New Negro project conforms to the logic of the real bills era in U.S. monetary policy, so also does the rhetoric of Locke's critics resemble that of the Fed's critics, as Jessie Redmon Fauset's novel *Plum Bun* (1928) demonstrates.

As the nursery rhyme around which its narrative is structured would suggest, *Plum Bun* takes the market, not money, as its central metaphor. The novel tells the story of Angela Murray, a light-skinned African American woman who moves from her native Philadelphia to New York and passes for white. Her attempts to spare herself from the confines of color in a racist society alienate Angela from her sister, Virginia, who inherited her father's darker skin, and whom Angela must publicly disown to maintain the illusion that she is white. The comforts she desires lead Angela to seek a wealthy white husband, but after she is spurned by young millionaire Roger Fielding, Angela begins a slow return to her sister and to her heritage.

*Plum Bun* offers a performative critique of the passing novel that cuts two ways. The first half of the novel follows the formula of early passing novels like *The House behind the Cedars* to the letter, right down to the gold standard metaphors that anchored these texts. The latter half of the novel, however, in adhering to the logic of New Negro strategic essentialism, critiques this logic by demonstrating its shortcomings.

The novel's incorporation of the monetary metaphors of early passing novels is evident from the opening chapter, which describes how Angela's mother, with whom Angela would spend her Saturdays passing, instilled in Angela a belief that "the possibilities for joy and freedom" were "inherent in mere whiteness" (14). Her father, in turn, took his wife and daughter's "little excursions . . . at their face value" (16).

Angela meditates on the representational nature of passing and power, and in the process articulates her faith in the inherent value of whiteness when she notes that "she possessed the badge, and unless there was someone to tell she could possess the power for which it stood" (73–74). Angela decides that, in order to have the power and comfort she desires, "it would be better to marry . . . a white man" after she moves to New York (88). A love affair ensues between Angela and the bigoted aristocrat Roger Fielding, and the novel's plot begins to parallel that of Chesnutt's *House behind the Cedars*. Accordingly, Fauset's novel deploys a host of monetary metaphors. Angela admits that passing makes her a sort of "confidence" woman (109). More importantly, Angela comes to define her value in relation to Roger, who is likened to gold so often that the analogy grows redundant. The reader is told of Roger's "golden recklessness" (142) and "his golden keys which could open the doors to beauty and ease" (142); he can speak "words of gold" (160); Angela broods upon "the broad, golden highway of Roger's existence" (197); he represents "a golden way out of her material difficulties" (199); and he promises "golden memories" (233). Not surprisingly, Roger was trained as "a mining engineer" (226), another connection to the precious metal with which he is associated.

Given Angela's initial characterization of "white blood" as inherently valuable and her own passing as a type of representation of whiteness without inherent value, Angela's love affair with Roger assumes a monetary symbolism consistent with the logic of the pre-war classical gold standard. She passes—that is, she circulates—and his whiteness (and the wealth for which whiteness was a precondition) lends value to her passing. She describes Roger as "a blond, glorious god" (129), and in this white god she trusts.

But if the first half of the novel adheres to the logic of the classical gold standard, the second half embodies the contradictions of Lockeian strategic essentialism by conforming to the paradoxical logic of postwar Federal Reserve policy. After Roger spurns Angela, her value is no longer determined in relation to him and his perceived inherent value. In the process, Angela goes from being a character in a book who wishes she could be a character in a book (183), to self-reflexively commenting on Fauset's narrative by aestheticizing essentialist difference in her own work. If Angela is a fictional character who comments ironically upon the role she plays in a novel about race, then her own representations of difference in essentialist terms hold a mirror up to the book that contains her. In short, Angela's paintings and the investment of others in the social order her art depicts act as mirrors in the text through which Fauset examines—and invites the reader to examine—her own role in the (re)production of difference.

Aside from the portraits Angela paints on commission and the work she does as an illustrator for a fashion magazine, Angela's artistic production is condensed into two works. The first, an allegorical sketch of Life, offers a reflexive wink to the reader, for as Fauset represents life in her novel, her protagonist does so at a more literal level in her art. The second, called *Fourteenth Street Types*, is a painting Angela conceives upon first arriving in New York, and which, upon completion, wins her an award to study abroad in France. Taking its cue from Angela's other work, this painting also holds a mirror up to the text that contains it. And, like *Plum Bun*, *Fourteenth Street Types* essentializes difference with mixed results. As their description as types suggests, Angela's studies are caricatures of the despondent people she sees around Fourteenth Street, and it is clear from Angela's plans for her masterpiece that she continues to think in essentialist ways. While formulating her painting, for instance, Angela often recalls images "of the countenance of a purse-proud but lonely man, of the silken insanity of a society girl, of the smiling despair of a harlot. Even in her own mind she hesitated before the use of that terrible word, but association was teaching her to call a spade a spade" (111).

At the same time that Angela is constructing her types and calling "a spade a spade," Fauset is describing Angela's own consolidation of Lockeian essentialism. Like Mimi in *Flight*, Angela goes from one kind of essentialism to another when her affair with Roger ends and her affair with Anthony Cross begins. After breaking up with Roger, Angela decides that the aptly-named Anthony Cross, who crossed the color line himself years ago, is perfect for her, and "she would make herself inexpressibly dearer and nearer to him when he came to know that her sympathy and her tenderness were real, fixed and lasting, because they were based and rooted in the same blood" (294). This blood argument extends to other characters in the novel to whom Angela feels a renewed obligation even as she continues passing.

Angela's gradual embrace of New Negro essentialism reaches its peak at the same time that Angela's art achieves recognition. The coincidence is no accident, for if *Fourteenth Street Types* comments upon the text that contains it, then the fallout this painting produces constitutes a critique of Lockeian strategic essentialism. After *Fourteenth Street Types* wins a prize that allows Angela to travel to France to study art,

Angela gives herself away defending another classmate, Miss Powell, who won the same trip but was refused passage based upon the color of her skin. Ironically, when the donor of the prize discovers that Angela is not white, he no longer sees *Fourteenth Street Types* as art, but as "ethnology" (359). The divestment in Angela's art continues when she is fired from her illustrating job, ostensibly for deceiving her coworkers.

Unlike Mimi in White's *Flight*, Angela's embrace of black essentialism does not lead to the promotion of Negro culture. In fact, when she goes to France on her sister's money she spends her time studying Anglo, not Negro, art. And, as the changing reactions to Angela's essentialist art illustrate, identity politics trump content in the eyes of white arbiters of culture for whom an artist's racial identification overdetermines the message she seeks to convey. Fauset thereby uses *Fourteenth Street Types* to anticipate reactions to her own work outside of Harlem's literati. Her novel ends with Anthony's arrival at Angela's flat in France, and the reader is left to presume that they live happily ever after. But the romance of Fauset's conclusion is undercut by the caricature of Angela's art, which reveals the sanguine optimism of the novel's ending to be as stereotypical as any one of Angela's types. *Plum Bun* therefore conforms to the same formula as *Fourteenth Street Types*, only it takes race as its subject instead of class. Fauset also anticipates the reader's divestment in the New Negro formula that Walter White's *Flight* exemplifies so perfectly. Her novel becomes ethnology, not art, in order to critique Lockeian strategic essentialism as overinflated, and to suggest that the concept of civil rights by copyright is a romantic fantasy.

Whereas *Plum Bun* demonstrates the limitations of Lockeian strategic essentialism, Nella Larsen's *Passing* (1929) likens the outcome of New Negro narrative speculation to a financial panic. The novel follows Irene Redfield as she struggles with the threat that Clare Kendry's passing represents. An old acquaintance of Irene's, Clare reappears in New York after a twelve-year absence with a wealthy white husband named John Bellew and a burning desire to reconnect with African Americans in Harlem. Irene quickly finds herself trapped between Clare's competing desires for white security and black society, and she begins to suspect her husband, Brian, of having an affair with Clare. Irene's fear and clouded judgment gradually erupt into the narration, which becomes similarly disoriented. This is why, when John Bellew bursts in upon a party Clare is attending to confirm that his wife is not the white woman he thought she was, it remains unclear to the reader how Clare falls from the sixth-floor window to her death below. But it is implied that Irene, fearing that John Bellew would divorce Clare and that Clare would then pursue Brian, unconsciously precipitated Clare's demise.

Unlike the literary figure she embodies, Clare refuses to be "neither black nor white," to borrow Langston Hughes's formulation, but insists upon being *both* black and white, much to Irene's chagrin. Irene masquerades as white from time to time for the sake of convenience, as she admits to her friend Felise late in the novel, but her occasional crossing of the color line is something different from Clare's straddling of it. To pass, in this context, is not to masquerade on certain occasions but to marry white and live the white life—to cross over instead of get by. The irony is that Irene, as a black woman, feels more threatened by Clare's passing than anyone else. Even John Bellew seems shocked at the novel's conclusion, less by Clare's death than by Irene's apparent hand in it. In short, it is hard to determine who has more invested in Clare's racial status, John or Irene.

Larsen draws several parallels between John Bellew and Irene Redfield to highlight the similarities between their essentialist beliefs. John, who is described as "some sort of international banking agent" (56), is an investor in more ways than one. Among the things he has invested in most heavily is the inherent value of racial difference. Elaborating on how he came upon the nickname "Nig" for Clare, he remarks to Irene, "When we were first married, she was as white as—as—well as white as a lily. But I declare she's gettin' darker and darker. I tell her if she don't look out, she'll wake up one of these days and find she's turned into a nigger" (67). He justifies his glib comment by saying to Clare, "I know you're no nigger, so it's all right. You can get as black as you please as far as I'm concerned, since I know you're no nigger. I draw the line at that. No niggers in my family. Never have been and never will be" (68). If this weren't enough to solidify his faith in racial essences, John goes on to rehearse a litany of racist stereotypes about black people, calling them "black scrimy devils" and so forth (70).

Irene, however, is no less invested in the inherent value of racial difference than John is. In a revealing financial metaphor, Irene wonders "how one accounted for oneself" when he or she was passing (37). And while she asserts that "white people were so stupid" when it came to telling who was white and who was passing (18–19), Irene claims that she can identify a person's race regardless of his or her skin color. It's "just something," she remarks, "a thing that couldn't be registered" (141). Irene is also contemptuous of the porting of "race," both in the passing of Clare and the appropriation of black performance by white entertainers. She notes that many white people come to Harlem "to get material to turn into shekels" (125), a veiled reference to Jewish entertainers who performed in blackface. And she refers to Clare's white life as a form of acting (89). In Irene's mind, Clare is *really* black, just as to John she is *really* white despite the color of her skin.

The implicit comparison Larsen makes between John's racism and Irene's investment in racial difference takes on added significance when the reader learns that Irene works with the Negro Welfare League. Her essentialism, combined with her work for racial uplift, makes her resemble New Negro advocates like Walter White. But the similarity Larsen highlights between Irene's essentialism and John's bigotry casts doubt upon the effectiveness of Irene's work as a reformer and thus also upon the entire New Negro project she symbolizes.

Clare, meanwhile, is described with golden metaphors. She has a head of "gold hair" (45), a "golden" personality, and a pair of "golden feet" (134), and she looks "golden, like a sunlit day" to Irene (137). Clare is also characterized as "cold, and hard" by Irene (5), a description that lends monetary significance to Clare's goldenness by invoking the image of cold, hard cash. As this characterization reveals, the question of value clings to Clare throughout the novel. On more than one occasion Clare quotes her father's maxim, "Everything must be paid for" (62, 129), and Irene notes that "Clare hadn't precisely reckoned the cost" of her actions, and therefore had "no right to expect others to help make up the reckoning" (88).

With Clare's racial status up in the air, John and Irene's investments in Clare's essential whiteness or blackness are not unlike speculations on gold futures. Irene in particular weighs the value—the cost—of Clare's passing against the security she stands to lose if found out by her husband. But instead of leading to a New Negro renaissance, these speculations lead instead to an extended panic punctuated by a crash. Thus at the novel's climactic moment when Clare is confronted by both John and Irene, Clare's descent from the top-floor window anticipates both *the* iconic image of the stock market crash—a body falling from a tall building—and the effects the crash had upon an inflated futures market. In one fell swoop, Larsen closes the book on the passing genre's New Negro incarnation with a cautionary tale about reformers' investments in black essentialism, however strategically (or ironically) it may be deployed. Like Irene, Larsen is unwilling to stake security upon such gambles. But unlike Irene—and thus unlike Walter White—Larsen argues for the value of the liminal position Clare occupied but could not maintain.

Larsen's novel announces the limits of Lockeian New Negroism, which many scholars, Nathan Huggins most infamously, treat as a failure and a foregone conclusion.[12] These critics proclaim, as Kenneth Robert Janken does, that while the New Negro movement "could uplift African Americans' spirit and had the potential to erase some whites' prejudice, [it] simply could not do the heavy lifting of eradicating the nation's pervasive and race-based economic and social inequality" (90). The veracity of Janken's comments notwithstanding, the movement couldn't catalyze a social upheaval not because its ambitions were over-inflated, but because it was in many respects ahead of its time. There was nothing inherently limiting about New Negro strategic essentialism; it just relied upon symbolic economies that had yet to gain ascendance in America. As a rhetorical strategy, strategic essentialism is predicated upon acceptance of the principles of cultural relativism, and Boas's ideas were just getting a toehold when Locke was writing in the teens and twenties. Locke may have helped promote cultural relativism, but he arrived too early on the scene to see it come to its fruition.

The New Negro movement's demise cannot be separated from changes in American money that characterized the era and to which Locke and his successors tied their critique, for as Marc Shell argues, epistemic changes in thought tend to accompany tectonic shifts in monetary policy in general and changes in the form of money in particular. The form a society's money takes helps set the standard for the kinds of thoughts it is possible to think in that society. In other words, monetary policy and epistemology are inextricably linked. The changes in the form of American money this chapter describes eventually paved the way for a poststructural model of thought when money's value became, like Lockeian formulations of race, a cultural reality separate and distinct from its former essentialist self.

Ironically, the crash of 1929 eventually led to the creation of a constructivist, managed currency system as part of the New Deal, which was itself a precondition for the poststructural zeitgeist that Locke's rhetorical strategies anticipated but from which they could not yet benefit. The history of strategic essentialism therefore parallels the genealogy of the term "racialism," which, as Rohit Barot and John Bird have illustrated, emerges and circulates during the first quarter of the twentieth century only to disappear and re-emerge in the 1960s as part of the poststructural turn.[13] Epistemic breaks are seldom the synchronic processes that the word "break" would suggest, and thus while the idea of racialization may have emerged at the turn of the century, it didn't become "true" for decades—people, collectively speaking, weren't yet ready for it or for the discursive, culturally constructed model of race it represented. "Racialization," like strategic essentialism, therefore disappeared from the cultural scene to re-emerge at a more opportune moment in the future. The monetary changes that comprised the New Deal were not without their own challenges, however, as the following chapter on Ralph Ellison's *Invisible Man* (1952) illustrates. But because Ellison was able to tie his critiques to the changes in money's form that followed the crash of 1929, he was able to connect his ideas about race to a model of value that was already in the ascendancy and was itself precipitated by monetary policy changes that Ellison allegorizes.

# 4

## BLACK IS . . . AN' BLACK AIN'T

### *"Invisible Man" and the Fiat of Race*

*Let Ras run that race, he was a race man; I had graduated.*
RALPH ELLISON, ORIGINAL TYPESCRIPT OF *Invisible Man*

*Money, get back.*
*I'm all right Jack keep your hands off of my stack.*
*Money, it's a hit.*
*Don't give me that do goody good bullshit.*
PINK FLOYD, "MONEY"

In the mid-1990s it was discovered that, when cued up properly, the music and lyrics of Pink Floyd's 1974 album *Dark Side of the Moon* appear to follow the visual action of MGM's 1939 film *The Wizard of Oz*. According to the authors of "Dark Side of the Rainbow," a Web site dedicated to this popular cultural phenomenon, replacing the movie musical's soundtrack with Pink Floyd's acid-rock classic produces a series of synesthetic resonations wherein the audio and video fall into lockstep. One such convergence occurs as Dorothy traverses the boundary that separates the black-and-white world of her transplanted home and the Technicolor land of Oz, a transition heralded by the album's hit song, "Money." Starting with a "cha-ching" and the sound of cascading coins, which accompanies Dorothy's first steps into Munchkin Land, the song marks the unconscious return of a monetary allegory that anchored L. Frank Baum's original novel, *The Wonderful Wizard of Oz* (1900), but was written out of the 1939 film starring Judy Garland.

This allegory was first examined in 1964 by Henry Littlefield, a high school history teacher who reinterpreted Baum's novel as a "Parable on Populism," and was later re-examined by scholars like Hugh Rockoff, John G. Geer, and Thomas R. Rochon. As described in chapters 2 and 3, the Populist movement in general and the presidential election of 1896 in particular turned upon the money question to such a degree that the choice of monetary standard—bimetallism or gold monometallism—dictated one's choice for president. According to Littlefield, Rockoff, Geer, and Rochon, *The Wonderful Wizard of Oz* is a retrospective commentary on 1890s Populism in which the movement's adherents, rhetoric, and political fallout are all represented allegorically.[1] Central to the novel's Populist subtext is the monetary imagery that animates it in much the same way that the Populist movement itself was animated by the money question. In this Populist interpretation of the novel, Dorothy's trek down the yellow brick (read: gold) road in her silver—not ruby—slippers serves as a metaphor for the progress of bimetallism, the monetary standard the Populists supported.[2] And as Ranjit Dighe has shown, Dorothy's experiences in the Emerald City allegorize the folly of pure fiat greenbackism, that is, the issue of paper money not backed by precious metals, which a majority of Populists denounced in favor of a more conservative but still inflationary hard money policy grounded by what Rockoff calls "a genuine bimetallic standard" (753). The objective correlative of Populism's portrayal of unfettered greenbackism, the Emerald City in the Land of Oz isn't really emerald at all, just as greenbacks aren't really money; in the context of Baum's narrative economy and the political economic agenda it articulates, both are illusions foisted on the public, one by the U.S. government and the other by the humbug Oz, who requires everyone within the city's walls to don spectacles with green lenses. The green glasses—ideological state apparatuses, literally—produce an illusion of value analogous to that of fiat paper money, which converts faith in its value into value itself.[3]

Ralph Ellison's *Invisible Man* (1952), which begins with a synesthetic album-listening experience resembling the Pink Floyd/*Wizard of Oz* audio-visual "mash-up" of the 1990s, riffs heavily upon Baum's novel as it approaches its conclusion. As anyone familiar with Baum's story knows, Dorothy's journey down the yellow brick road to the Emerald City begins with a symbolic change of shoes when she trades her own worn pair for the silver slippers formerly owned by the Wicked Witch of the East. The unnamed narrator of Ellison's novel—the invisible man—is similarly re-shod before taking the steps that will lead him to his rendezvous with destiny. Immediately prior to the event that propels the narrative toward its climax, the shooting death of Tod Clifton, the narrator purchases a brand new pair of two-toned shoes in a store on Fifth Avenue. He himself alludes to the apparent incongruity of this act when he recalls, "Then I decided, of all things, to shop for a pair of new shoes" (429). Ellison's allusions to Baum's book become more substantial once the narrator leaves the scene of Clifton's demise and returns to Harlem. On the run from Ras the Exhorter and his henchmen, the narrator enters a drugstore and purchases a pair of sunglasses with green lenses to wear as part of a disguise. These glasses not only resemble the green spectacles that make Oz's Emerald City emerald, they also serve a similar function within Ellison's narrative, for through their tinted lenses Harlem and its inhabitants assume a new value. The similarities to Dorothy and her journey to the Emerald City continue when Ellison's narrator—now commonly mistaken for Rinehart, a member of the Harlem underworld—goes to meet the Brotherhood higher-up, Hambro, and discovers him to be a charlatan just like the so-called wizard of Oz. Echoing Dorothy's lamentation that Oz was in fact "the Great and Terrible Humbug" (110), the invisible man concludes, "It was all a swindle, an obscene swindle!" (507).[4]

These yet-unmapped and untapped allusions to Baum's novel are consistent with Ellison's poaching of the American literary tradition, which he frequently if not obsessively signifies upon in *Invisible Man*. Heteroglossic and intertextual to an extreme, *Invisible Man* has inspired a generation of literary critics who have spent the last fifty-plus years productively mapping the myriad of allusions the novel makes. Alan Nadel and Valerie Bonita Gray have written book-length studies devoted entirely to this subject.[5] Kun Jong Lee comments on the breadth of this critical phenomenon, writing, "Scholars have noted or demonstrated Ellison's allusions to almost every major writer in the European, American, or African American literary traditions" (421). And Rudolf F. Dietze exclaims, "The more thoroughly familiar one becomes with the work of Ralph Waldo Ellison the fewer are the chances of finding a major literary work published before 1950 that does not have some bearing on *Invisible Man*" (25). Mark Busby's list of authors whose influence can be found in the novel appears to confirm Dietze's hyperbolic claim; the list includes Benjamin Franklin, James Fenimore Cooper, Ralph Waldo Emerson, Edgar Allan Poe, Frederick Douglass, Herman Melville, Mark Twain, Booker T. Washington, W. E. B. Du Bois, James Weldon Johnson, T. S. Eliot, Ernest Hemingway, William Faulkner, Zora Neale Hurston, and Richard Wright, and these are just the *American* authors on Busby's list.[6]

Although literary critics like Busby, Lee, Gray, Dietze, and Nadel have been productively mapping the allusive landscape of *Invisible Man* ever since its publication in 1952, Ellison's references to Baum's *The*

*Wonderful Wizard of Oz* have somehow gone either unnoticed or unaddressed. This could be due to the apparent superficiality of the resemblance between the two novels. After all, what's in a new pair of shoes, some green spectacles, and a city-bound journey marked by disillusionment? But if Ellison riffed on *The Wonderful Wizard of Oz* to incorporate its monetary symbolism into his own narrative, then to pass over Ellison's allusions to Baum's novel is to overlook their contribution to a broader monetary allegory of Ellison's own creation—an allegory whose monetary logic is anchored by the novel's more prominent and widely-recognized literary allusions. This chapter reconstructs the monetary logic of *Invisible Man*, which the allusions to Baum's *Wizard* radically reshape, and demonstrates how Ellison, like the authors who preceded him, turned to money in order to comment on race and literature's role in the renegotiation of the value of racial difference.

As his critical essays demonstrate, Ralph Ellison was preoccupied not only with the American literary tradition, but with its torque on race and articulation of racialist ideology. Of especial concern to Ellison was the role American literature played in the dehumanization of African Americans. As he argues in "Twentieth-Century Fiction and the Black Mask of Humanity" (1953),[7] the black man, "both as man and as a symbol of man," was "pushed into the underground of the American conscious" so thoroughly that whites could not see a human being when they looked at him—only a black mask (90). By turning the counterfeit stereotypes of black America into "images of reality," he proclaims, American authors elevated the cultural currency of the minstrel clown and kept it in constant circulation (84). The antidote, Ellison believed, would be to realize an American literature that not only rendered intelligible the processes by which racist stereotypes acquired their currency but also affirmed rather than denied the humanity and individuality of African American men and women.

To these ends, Ellison's *Invisible Man* reorganizes the American literary tradition around three authors whose texts renegotiate the value of racial difference: Harriet Beecher Stowe, Herman Melville, and Richard Wright. At the same time, Ellison positions his novel alongside the work of these authors to examine the shifting role of literature in the epistemology of race. As I have demonstrated throughout this book, money marks the spot where American literary interventions into the race question turn back upon themselves, and each of these authors used money, and in particular the language and logic of monetary reform, to comment on both the currency of race and his or her own participation in its circulation. Concomitant with this narrative strategy, Stowe's *Uncle Tom's Cabin*, Melville's *The Confidence-Man* (1857), and Wright's "The Man Who Lived Underground" (1944) each turn upon a single monetary symbol that condenses the critique it articulates into a fungible sign. Ellison, in turn, deploys these narratives in *Invisible Man* by putting the monetary symbols that anchor them back into circulation. These texts, by way of the monetary symbols upon which they turn, form the foundation of the narrative economy of *Invisible Man*—an economy that Ellison establishes ultimately to call into question both the value of his own contribution to the American literary tradition and literature's changing role in the renegotiation of racial difference. The allusions to Baum's *The Wonderful Wizard of Oz* cannot be fully appreciated outside of this monetary context, for they function collectively as a mirror in Ellison's text through which he self-reflexively examines his own participation in the social construction of race while articulating his own ambivalence about literature's efficacy as a vehicle for social justice.

Interwoven within this allusive narrative framework (and inseparable from it) is Ellison's own monetary allegory, which relies upon an established analogical connection between race and the gold standard in American literature—a connection whose history is mapped by the first three chapters of this book. Like Dorothy in Baum's novel, the narrator of *Invisible Man* stands in for the dollar at a time when the standards that give it value are in flux. In fact, the turning points of the narrative correspond with key events in the (d)evolution of the monetary standard during the 1930s. They even occur during the same months. But *Invisible Man* is more than an allegory for the end of the gold standard; it is simultaneously a metaphor for writing race in American literature.

*Invisible Man* is inherently self-reflexive, to the point that it rehearses its own creation and dissemination in the novel's prologue and epilogue. And while *Invisible Man* is a narrative about narratives, its protagonist is a narrator who self-consciously inscribes himself in the act of chronicling his journey "from ranter to writer" (Ellison, "Change the Joke" 111). In Ellison's hands, this self-conscious self-making becomes a metaphor for writing race, the value of which is weighed against the value of money after the gold standard. Ellison draws this analogy between money and race throughout the novel, and he punctuates it with allusions to Baum's *Wonderful Wizard of Oz*. Using Baum's narrative to hold up a mirror to his own text, Ellison draws a parallel analogy between Baumian ambivalence about fiat money and his own wariness about the relocation of race's authenticity in performance, that is, the fiat of race. The result is a proto-postmodern examination of an epistemological turn that began with the devolution of American money toward simulacra and would eventually encompass race's demotion from essence to metaphor to sign. Tracing the arc of this turn, Ellison anticipates the changing role of literature—itself a form of circulating paper—in the revaluation of racial difference.

Ellison's critique, like the plot of the novel itself, breaks neatly into two sections that examine the cultural currency of race and the narrative economy that sustains it, respectively. In the first half of the novel, Ellison examines how the value of racial difference is maintained and the black mask that occludes the humanity of African Americans is reproduced. This occlusion is described by the narrator in the prologue when he observes how others "see only my surroundings, themselves, or figments of their imagination—indeed, everything and anything except me" (3). This blindness is a cultural phenomenon, he notes, "a matter of the construction of their *inner* eyes, those eyes with which they look through their physical eyes upon reality" (3). To show how the cultural currency of race, which blinds the "inner eyes" of others, is reproduced, Ellison draws analogies among four circulatory mediums: blood, money, narrative, and power. In the process, Ellison demonstrates how the value of racial difference, maintained by narratives like Jim Trueblood's, conforms to the cyclical logic of the gold standard to promote the very blindness the narrator laments in the prologue. As chapter 3 of this project describes in detail, the myth of the gold standard was anchored by the illusion of intrinsic value. In truth, gold merely *represented* intrinsic value, and the gold standard obscured the fact that gold's commodity value was overdetermined by market forces. In other words, gold embodied the illusion that its value was based on something other than its circulation and the social relations upon which such circulation depends. Like the dollar under the gold standard, the narrator embodies an illusory faith in the intrinsic value of race, which is in reality socially constructed. As gold embodied the illusion of intrinsic value within the myth of the gold standard, the narrator, like gold standard currency, represents faith in the illusion that behind the circulating images of race lay something of essential value.

If Ellison equates the value of racial difference with the value of money under the gold standard in the first half of *Invisible Man*, in the second half he explores the challenges of renouncing the proverbial gold standard of racial essentialism and embracing race as a social construction while continuing to live in the racial state. Riffing explicitly upon changes made to U.S. monetary policy in the wake of the stock market crash of 1929, Ellison likens the cultural project of decoupling race from the physical differences it signifies to the removal of gold from circulation and the accompanying elevation of all forms of paper money to legal tender status by the government during 1933 and 1934, the temporal setting of the novel's second half. These changes, which heralded the end of the gold standard in the United States, put gold and paper money on divergent paths: gold flowed into the Treasury's vaults by executive order of the president while fiat paper money circulated in its place. Drawing an analogy between race and post–gold standard paper currency, Ellison shows that while the essentialist pretenses that anchored both the theory of race and the domestic gold standard may have been abandoned, the value of race, like the value of fiat paper money, is maintained by the economy in which it circulates.

The analogy Ellison draws between the values of money and race takes allegorical form in the novel when, following his own personal crash and ensuing depression, the narrator exchanges his golden faith in racial essentialism for a new paper-based identity from the Brotherhood along with three hundred dollars in crisp, new Federal Reserve Notes to which this new identity is symbolically linked. Like the post–gold standard dollar for which he then stands, the narrator gets pulled in two different directions. His paper persona, created by executive order of Brotherhood president Jack, circulates to maintain the organization's veneer of color-blind post-racial harmony, while he is driven underground, first figuratively and then literally, like gold into Fort Knox.

The narrator naïvely thinks that by joining the Brotherhood he is representing the black community in the political sense, but, as he gradually comes to realize, he is chosen as spokesman because he represents racial difference itself. Used by the Brotherhood in much the same way that the Fed used gold removed from circulation during the New Deal, his blackness becomes a "natural resource" (303) that Jack and the committee use to "back" their message that race doesn't matter. His circulating image and its egalitarian connotations are not convertible to his personal experience, however, as the narrator eventually discovers. To play upon the *Wizard of Oz*–inspired lyrical pun around which the plot turns, as the Brotherhood uses the narrator to pay lip service to "the Rainbow of America's Future" (385), the narrator learns to "get *over*" *the rainbow* by realizing the limits of the self-serving representational logic of the organization that exploits him.

Ellison makes his most incisive move when his examination of the economics of race reveals the degree to which these economics overdetermine the value of his own novel. Ellison's multilayered allegory ultimately functions as a performative critique of writing race and the difference it makes, for while the narrator remains underground, the paper upon which his story is printed continues to circulate aboveground in the form of *Invisible Man*. Equating the pages of the novel that contains the narrator with the pieces of paper that name him and set him running, Ellison shifts his focus from the cultural currency of race to the literary economy that keeps it circulating. Enlarging the scope of his examination to include the American literary tradition itself, Ellison's novel turns the mirror onto itself to examine its place within the literary tradition, a tradition that the second half of the narrative reconstructs. The result is aporetic, for *Invisible Man* cannot escape the influence of the narratives it contains; it cannot plunge outside of literary history because the racial economics of the narratives it contains overdetermine its meaning. Ellison's observations about the end of one kind of gold standard dovetail with Baum's cautionary tale about the illusory value of fiat money when Ellison reveals himself to be another "buggy jiving" (581) humbug offering paper promises of future action that he cannot deliver.

### BEFORE: TURNING BLOOD INTO MONEY

In the first half of *Invisible Man*, Ellison signifies upon a centuries-old metaphor comparing a nation's money to a person's blood. Ellison's namesake, Ralph Waldo Emerson, was just one of many prominent Americans to reinforce this association when he wrote, "money is another kind of blood. *Pecunia alter sanguis*: or, the estate of man is only a larger kind of body, and admits of regimen analogous to his bodily circulations" ("Wealth"). Contemporary historian Michael O'Malley examines how this ubiquitous analogy, in conjunction with hard money rhetoric, was used to prop up essentialist definitions of race and thereby support discriminatory social and political policies that relied upon race as a stable system of classification. "Thomas Hobbes understood money as the blood in Leviathan's body," writes O'Malley, "and the metaphor served proslavery Southerner John C. Calhoun equally well nearly two hundred years later" (372). Taking the intrinsic value of precious metals as a given, persons like Calhoun who had a vested interest in maintaining racial difference would argue that race and money were two sides of the same coin. That is, if money was in accord with natural law only when it could be converted to the precious metals that gave it value, then race was similarly meaningful only when it could be located in the blood. Any attempt to view race outside of the body was, like fiat money, considered a violation of natural law. Observing that precious metal monetary standards and essentialist definitions of race rely upon consonant theories of intrinsic value, O'Malley asks, "What is race but a theory of purity in blood?" (372).

In the first half of *Invisible Man*, Ellison turns the hard money standard/purity of blood analogy O'Malley describes on its head by demonstrating how essentialist conceptions of racial difference and the gold standard both *obscure the absence* of intrinsic value, and thereby maintain the illusion of intrinsic value itself. Race *is* like the gold standard, Ellison illustrates, not because each is an expression of natural law, but because both are discourse-dependent social constructions that insinuate the intrinsic value upon which they appear to depend. So, unlike Burnside, the vet who is accused of "trying to change some blood into money" for financial gain by one of the other vets (81), Ellison turns blood into money in order to render intelligible the formalizing of race, and to identify the source(s) of its value.

Despite his statements to the contrary and claims of greater self-awareness, the narrator exhibits a blind faith in the authenticity of race (or the purity of blood) in the first half of the novel. This faith is most clearly demonstrated by the narrator's interactions with Mr. Norton, especially during their experience at the aptly named Golden Day. Mr. Norton, a caricature of whiteness with his white hair, white skin, and white suit, is the very embodiment of white difference to the narrator. The narrator's faith in the essential nature of this difference becomes evident (although not self-evident) when he is shoved up against the unconscious trustee beneath the stairwell of the Golden Day. There are many reasons for the narrator to be in awe of or even to fear Mr. Norton—his wealth, his influence, and so forth—but when he finds himself not two inches from the man's face he begins screaming unconsciously because he "had never been so close to a white person before" (86). Mr. Norton's power and prestige, markers of his social being, fall by the wayside and he becomes "a mass of whiteness" and "a formless white death" in the narrator's eyes (86); he is distilled down to the essence he represents to the narrator. Recognizing the source of the narrator's fear, the mad vet/physician pulls him away and reassures him, "He's only a man. Remember that. He's only a man!" (86). But when the narrator proves himself deaf to the truth he is being told, the vet follows his correct diagnosis of Mr. Norton's illness with an accurate appraisal of the narrator's unconscious essentialism. Drawing an analogy between the narrator's faith in the intrinsic value of racial difference and the circulation of the blood in which the narrator locates it, the vet tells the revived Mr. Norton, "He believes in you *as he believes in the beat of his heart*. He believes in that great false wisdom taught slaves and pragmatists alike, that white is right" (95; emphasis added).[8]

If, as the vet articulates, faith in the purity of blood is another name for the reification of race, then Ellison's monetary metaphors reveal how the intrinsic value of racial difference, or rather the illusion that race has intrinsic value, is analogous to the value of gold under the gold standard. Riffing upon the long-established analogy between monetary and racial essentialisms, Ellison portrays the narrator's relationship to Mr. Norton as an allegory for the relationship of the dollar to gold. If gold represents intrinsic value under the gold standard and the dollar embodies faith in this value, then Mr. Norton and the racial difference he represents stand in for the former while the narrator, who embodies faith in this difference, plays the part of the latter. These roles and the larger allegorical framework of which they are a part are rendered subtly but explicitly throughout the opening chapters. For example, the narrator twice likens Mr. Norton to St. Nicholas, a figure so closely associated with gold that his name is a metonym for the precious metal itself.[9] The narrator characterizes Mr. Norton using golden nicknames and locates his own value in the investments of his golden trustee, and the events that demonstrate his blind faith in the essential nature of race take place in the Golden Day, a metaphor for the gold standard era. But the monetary significance of the narrator's relationship to Mr. Norton and the golden faith in race it represents is perhaps best illustrated when the vet, in the act of exposing the lie upon which essentialism is erected, uses marketplace metaphors to describe Mr. Norton as a representative of an intrinsic value he doesn't actually possess. "The clocks are all set back and the forces of destruction are rampant down below," he warns Mr. Norton—"They [the other vets] might suddenly realize that you are what you are, and then your life wouldn't be worth a piece of bankrupt stock. You would be canceled, perforated, voided, become the recognized magnet attracting loose screws. Then what would you do? Such men are beyond money, and with Supercargo down, out like a felled ox, they know nothing of value" (93).[10]

The vet's speech articulates the constructionist view that Mr. Norton's value is dependent upon the trust others put in the difference he represents, not the other way around. The same is true for the narrator's trust, upon which Mr. Norton's fate depends (45). In light of the vet's comments, the monetary logic of this relationship and the fate about which Mr. Norton speaks becomes clear: the dollar may be defined by its gold content just as race can be determined by the contents of the blood, but the price of gold—its value—*follows* the value of the dollar, just as Mr. Norton's fate is determined by the narrator's actions. Essentialism, it follows, is the gold standard of race, obscuring the fact that the value of racial difference, like the value of the dollar, is maintained through a much more elaborate process of circulation and exchange.

The vet confirms for the reader what the narrator fails to recognize for himself: that the value of racial difference has no essential basis. Ellison provides another blood metaphor to reinforce this point by locating Mr. Norton's illness in his blood. Although the vet's diagnosis is delivered in the narrator's absence and thus out of the reader's proverbial earshot, the reader can see that Mr. Norton exhibits all the symptoms of anemia: rapid heartbeat,[11] unusually pale skin, confusion, and fainting. One of the prostitutes at the Golden Day offers the reader a hint as to the source of his illness when she says that Mr. Norton "needs a drink. Put some iron in his blood" (92). If, as the essentialist view of race dictates, the authenticity of race is located in the blood, then the narrator's trust in this authenticity is further ridiculed when the source— Mr. Norton's blood—is shown to be lacking. "Anemia" literally means "want of blood."

If intrinsic value itself is a social construction, as the vet's exposure of Mr. Norton announces, and the value of racial difference is in fact an emergent property of an ongoing process of exchange, then how is the gold standard of race maintained? Through performance—specifically, through performance that reifies hegemonic ideologies of race by dovetailing into (and therefore reinforcing) established ways of seeing. Hence the idea that race has cultural *currency*, the value of which is maintained through (re)circulation. Ellison uses monetary currency to symbolize the cultural currency of race, showing in the process how the same circulatory logic determines the value of each. To cement the analogy he draws between gold standard political economy and the economics of race, Ellison includes the Battle Royal and Trueblood episodes, in which black performances of self-marginalization are exchanged for white investments in the maintenance of racial difference. The monetary symbols upon which each of these episodes turns illustrate how racial performativity conforms to the logic of the gold standard by perpetuating the illusion that race has intrinsic value. By including such performances, Ellison prefigures Foucault's argument that power circulates within a disciplinary society. Bledsoe, who is engaged in an elaborate performance of his own, describes such power circulation and his own complicit role as a disciplined subject when he tells the narrator, "This is a power set-up, son, and I'm at the controls. You think about that. When you buck against me, you're bucking against power, rich white folk's power, the nation's power—which means government power!" (142). Bledsoe facilitates the circulation of power by facilitating the ideology of white supremacy, particularly by wearing the mask of servitude. However, as Bledsoe himself knows, maintaining an illusion through constant repetition is how "it becomes the truth" (143). Ellison is keen to point out that performances like Bledsoe's have no value outside of the sociocultural context that makes them profitable and/or necessary for survival. Hence he deploys the Battle Royal and Trueblood episodes, which show racial performances in the discursive contexts that make them meaningful. The monetary symbols that anchor each of these episodes in turn highlight how the cultural currency of race, as a trope of difference, is a function of its circulation within a symbolic economy.

In the battle royal, black men are pitted against one another for the entertainment of a white audience, after which the narrator and his co-combatants compete to gather what appear to be five-dollar gold coins from an electrified rug.[12] "Get the money," yells the emcee. "That's good hard American cash!" (28). But instead of hard money, the coins turn out to be "brass pocket tokens advertising a certain make of automobile" (32). Aside from anticipating the narrator's futile attempts to grasp the illusion of intrinsic value that Mr. Norton represents and extending the monetary symbolism by having the narrator once again measure his self-worth in gold like the dollar under the gold standard, this pursuit of gold without intrinsic value finds its analogue in the narrator's postfight speech, which incorporates quotes from Booker T. Washington's "Atlanta Compromise" oration of 1895. A marginalizing performance just like the speech that inspired it, the narrator's address is rewarded with "a scholarship to the state college for Negroes" (32). In his dream that night, the scholarship becomes "an engraved document containing a short message in letters of gold" (33). The golden message, "To Whom It May Concern . . . Keep This Nigger-Boy Running" (33), is the golden reward for his performance—a reward that perpetuates inequality by keeping white power circulating and thereby maintaining the racial hierarchy. In short, the scholarship keeps the system running by keeping the narrator running.

The Trueblood episode introduces narrative as another vehicle for racial performativity, and cannot be fully appreciated apart from the themes of blood and money, the circulation of power, and the logic of the gold standard that binds them all together. As Houston Baker has observed, the Trueblood episode draws an explicit analogy between storytelling and the economics of minstrelsy as Jim Trueblood exchanges his performance of the minstrel mask for Mr. Norton's investment in it. Mr. Norton wants the narrator to write to him so he "can observe in terms of living personalities to what extent my money, my time and my hopes have been fruitfully invested" (45). His investment in Trueblood's story is the other side of this same coin, for Trueblood, like the narrator, performs his own marginalization and, perhaps more importantly, raises such marginalization to an aesthetic through repeat performances. Before telling his story to Mr. Norton, Trueblood reveals that many of the local white folks have rewarded him, not so much for impregnating his daughter, but for telling the story of how it happened—a story that, as the narrator surmises, encourages rather than challenges the fantasy among white men "that all Negroes do such things" (58). Trueblood tells Mr. Norton that after he found out the school "was tryin' to get rid of us 'cause they said we was a disgrace," he

> went down to see Mr. Buchanan, the boss man, and I tole him 'bout it and he give me a note to the sheriff and tole me to take it to him. I did that, jus' like he tole me. I went to the jailhouse and give Sheriff Barbour the note and he ask me to tell him what happen, and I tole him and he called in some more men and they made me tell it again. They wanted to hear about the gal lots of times and they gimme somethin' to eat and drink and some tobacco. Surprised me, 'cause I was scared and spectin' somethin' different. Why, I guess there ain't a colored man in the county who ever got to take so much of the white folkses' time as I did. So finally they tell me not to worry, that they was going to send word up to the school that I was to stay right where I am. (52–53)

In exchange for his encore performances, which affirm rather than challenge white supremacist ideology, Trueblood is given "more work now than I ever did have before" (53). But Mr. Norton's investment in the story and by extension the difference it upholds, the hundred-dollar bill, shows why he is, in the vet's words, "a trustee of consciousness" (89). The hundred-dollar bill is the objective correlative of Mr. Norton's investment in racial difference—a difference that stories like Trueblood's, however artful they may be, help to maintain. As a piece of gold standard paper currency, Norton's hundred-dollar bill, like Trueblood's narrative, helps maintain the illusion that something of intrinsic worth lends it value. By portraying the free exchange of one for the other, Ellison equates them, and the bill becomes a metonym for race itself. Moreover, by echoing the narrator's allegorical role as the dollar under the gold standard, Ellison also likens the narrator's unconscious following of "the white line" (46) to the reward Trueblood receives for his conscious performative reinforcement of it. Hence the pun on Jim Trueblood's name, for Ellison uses his narrative to argue that the *true blood* of race is performance. And, like the hegemony of white power it helps to maintain, Trueblood's performance circulates, in part because a few of the "big white folks . . . from the big school way cross the State . . . wrote it all down in a book" (53).

Trueblood is rewarded for his tale while the narrator is punished because, despite his wholehearted (and blind) faith in the illusion that "white is right," the narrator brings Mr. Norton into contact with individuals who give the lie to this illusion. Trueblood burlesques his own marginalization while the vet's proclamations expose Trueblood's performance for what it is: a performance—one in which Mr. Norton has already invested heavily, just as he has invested in the narrator and the school. The narrator's inability to maintain appearances vexes Bledsoe, who raves, "You don't even know the difference between the way things are and the way they're supposed to be" (142). Bledsoe's admonition describes the gap between race and "race," between an illusory essence and its sign, only he speaks with an irony too sophisticated for the narrator to grasp. For instead of asserting that race relations ought to be more democratic than they are, Bledsoe is chastising the narrator for not knowing the difference between maintaining the illusion of race (the way things are "supposed to be" when catering to powerful whites like Mr. Norton), and the realities of "race" ("the way things are" in fact socially constructed). Like Trueblood, Bledsoe knows how to exploit this discrepancy; he's fully aware of the economics of "race" that elude the narrator. The question remains, however, whether Bledsoe does more harm than good by "act[ing] the nigger" to achieve his power, especially if it means "hav[ing] every Negro in the country hanging on tree limbs by morning" in order to keep it (143).

Having established that the value of racial difference is socially constructed through an ongoing process of exchange in a sociocultural marketplace, Ellison next turns to drawing analogies between the symbolic economy that gives race its currency and *the* American economy. If, like Mr. Norton's hundred-dollar bill, U.S. currency acts as a metonym for race in the first half of the novel, then the appearance of black men "chained to money" (165) on Wall Street not only reinforces a symbolic link between race and money, it suggests that a broader symbolic economy sustains it. Just as the economy, synecdochically represented here by Wall Street, maintains the value of money by incessantly recalculating the value of difference that keeps it circulating, larger cultural forces maintain the cultural currency of race. As his focus upon Trueblood's Faulknerian yarn and depiction of its exchange for Mr. Norton's hundred-dollar bill illustrate, Ellison sees the literary marketplace in general, and the American literary tradition in particular, as the cultural equivalent of the U.S. economy, right down to the gold standard whose logic they share.

So what happens when America goes off the gold standard of race? That is, what social, cultural, and political changes occur when large segments of the population reject the fallacy of biological race but continue to live in a segregated society? Ellison addresses these questions in the second half of *Invisible Man* and examines how the established symbolic economy of race and its complex relationship to the lived realities of black life in America thwart the efforts of critics and artists, and in particular American literary authors, bent upon reforming American society. The keys to understanding and organizing this complexity, along with Ellison's efforts to transcend the very quandary he identifies, are the real-life changes made in U.S. monetary policy during the Depression upon which Ellison riffs in the second half of the novel. Incorporating the language and logic of New Deal monetary policy, Ellison draws analogies between FDR's monetary reforms and the reformation of race from essence to social construction. In the process, Ellison stakes a claim about race, civil rights, and black aesthetics that prefigures the poststructural turn and anticipates his novel's role as the negative reflection of the Black Arts Movement.

AFTER: THE NEW DEAL

The monetary symbolism of *Invisible Man*, which was subtle but pervasive throughout the first half of the novel, becomes much more overt in the second half as generalizations about race and its conformity to the logic of the gold standard give way to specific allusions to Depression-era monetary policy. The New Deal, which brought about the end of the gold standard in the United States, encompassed a series of laws and executive orders enacted by President Roosevelt from March 1933 to January 1934. Aimed at remedying the Depression that followed the stock market crash of 1929, the New Deal began on March 9, 1933, with the passage of the Emergency Banking Act. This piece of legislation put the president in charge of the Federal Reserve banks, declared an emergency banking holiday, and authorized the issuance of nearly two billion dollars in Federal Reserve banknotes that were printed and distributed to banks prior to reopening on March 13, 1933. The international gold standard was officially suspended the next day when Roosevelt signed an executive order prohibiting the export of gold. Then on April 5, 1933, domestic gold was recalled by an executive order requiring "all persons [to] deliver on or before May 1 to a Federal Reserve bank or a branch or agency thereof, or to any member bank all gold coin, gold bullion and gold certificates owned by them or coming into their ownership on or before April 28" (Crawford 35). Beginning in May 1933, all forms of currency, including the new Federal Reserve Notes, were declared legal tender by the Thomas Inflation Amendment, and on June 5, 1933, the gold clause was abrogated, meaning that contracts that specified payment in gold could then be paid with any legal tender currency, including Federal Reserve Notes. All of these acts and orders were consolidated on January 30, 1934, when FDR signed the Gold Reserve Act into law. Under this act, the president was granted the authority to manage the nation's money, an authority which included but was not limited to the power to change the gold content of the dollar. Roosevelt used these new executive powers to fix the gold value of the dollar at the approximate level it currently stood in world markets on January 31, 1934.[13] The Gold Reserve Act also nationalized the gold that the Federal Reserve banks collected following the executive order of April 5, 1933, and transferred ownership of this gold to the U.S. Treasury. Finally, the Gold Reserve Act provided that gold should no longer be coined, that gold coin should no longer be paid out by the United States, and that any and all gold coin still in circulation should be withdrawn, melted into bullion, and kept in the Treasury vaults (Crawford 1–83).

The New Deal created a new monetary standard that, unlike the gold standard it replaced, had no pretensions about the socially constructed nature of monetary value. In fact, the New Deal made a virtue of this arbitrariness. Whereas the gold standard maintained the illusion that the value it upheld was intrinsic and that the standard itself was entirely self-regulating, the new standard didn't pretend to be anything but a managed currency system. Gold remained the metallic base of this new system, but because the president could revise the dollar's gold content at any time and because U.S. currency could no longer be exchanged for gold, the dollar remained only loosely tied to the precious metal. The dollar was thus transformed from a signifier of essential value to the sign of its absence, while the power to effect such a transformation was consolidated into the hands of the president, who became the primary arbiter of the dollar's value.

The turning points in the plot of *Invisible Man* take place during the same period as the monetary policies of the New Deal, from the spring of 1933 to the winter of 1934. The math gets a little tricky at times, but Ellison drops hint after hint to help the reader locate the temporal setting of the novel's main episodes. In the prologue, the narrator says that his grandparents, who were slaves, were told they were free "about eighty-five years ago" (15). The Emancipation Proclamation declared Southern slaves free in 1863, but there was no way for the Union to enforce this order until the Thirteenth Amendment abolishing slavery was ratified after the surrender in 1865. The narrator's grandparents, being Southern slaves, were therefore probably not freed until 1865. The narrator's recollection of his grandfather's admission that he had "been a spy in the enemy's country *ever since I give up my gun back in the Reconstruction*" reinforces this (16; emphasis added). Eighty-five years after 1865 places the time-present of the prologue and epilogue in the year 1950. The battle royal therefore takes place in 1930, "some twenty years" earlier than the prologue and epilogue (15).[14] Then, "near the end of [the narrator's] junior year" of college—three years after the battle royal—he is kicked out of school (37). The mad vets of the Golden Day episode, then, stand in for the Bonus Army—World War I veterans who wanted their Service Certificates paid earlier than their 1945 redemption date to ease their financial hardships during the Depression. The fact that the narrator's expulsion occurs during the spring of 1933 when the New Deal was just getting underway is no mere coincidence. The narrator even puns on the name of FDR's programs when, having taken up residence at Men's House in Harlem, he spreads the letters Bledsoe wrote for him "upon the dresser like a hand of high trump cards" (163). But the narrator's new deal doesn't fully get underway until the events of the narrator's "first northern winter" (260)—the same winter the Gold Reserve Act was signed into law in January 1934. As the nation was at the lowest point of the Depression, the narrator is at the nadir of what his landlord, Mary Rambo, calls "hard times" (258). But after his impromptu speech at the Harlem eviction and his initial conversation with Brotherhood president Jack over cheesecake and coffee, the narrator remarks, "I had begun to lose my depression" (295). The monetary policies of the New Deal, of course, marked the beginning of the end of the Depression, and these policies find their allegorical counterparts in the novel when the narrator joins the Brotherhood. As the dollar went off the gold standard and was given a new paper identity in the form of crisp, new Federal Reserve Notes, the narrator, who stands in for the dollar, exchanges his old identity for "a name written on a slip of paper" by Brotherhood president Jack (309). If the monetary symbolism of the narrator's new paper identification and its association with post–gold standard currency weren't obvious enough, the reader is informed that the narrator keeps his new paper name in his wallet alongside the three hundred dollars in "crisp and fresh" banknotes he acquired from the same source (327, 316).[15]

The narrator's new identity accompanies his new role as spokesman for the Brotherhood, a role that paradoxically requires him to embody the very difference that the Brotherhood supposedly devalues. In other words, the Brotherhood needs the narrator's black body, and specifically the difference it represents, to lend credence to their message that racial difference is overinflated and insignificant. As the president of the Brotherhood, Jack continually pays lip service to the Brotherhood's claims of color-blindness, chastising the narrator for talking "in terms of race" (292), and lashing out at Emma when she asks, "Don't you think he should be a little blacker?" (303). But Emma's question gives the lie to the Brotherhood's egalitarian rhetoric, the persuasiveness of which relies upon the narrator's ability to represent the very difference the Brotherhood claims to be irrelevant. And so, like the dollar after the abolition of the gold standard—and in particular like the new Federal Reserve Notes with which he is newly associated—the narrator goes from signifier of race's essential value to the sign of its absence. Where he embodied faith in the intrinsic value of racial difference in the first half of the novel, the narrator stands in for "race," the sign of an always already metaphorical and culturally constructed trope of difference, in the second half. So also begins the narrator's journey underground. For just as recalled gold went into the vaults of the Treasury (and eventually into Fort Knox) as fiat paper circulated in its place, the narrator undergoes his transformation at an apartment building named for the underworld, the Chthonian, when he denounces race for "race." Accordingly, he replaces his gold standard–esque essentialist assertion, "I am what I am" (266) with its constructionist equivalent, "I am what they think I am" (379).

But as the episode immediately following this scene at the Chthonian illustrates, the narrator's new role as both representative of his race and "race" itself lead him to reinforce rather than destabilize the very racialist associations the Brotherhood purports to ameliorate. This episode, in which the narrator breaks the iron bank full of coins he found at Mary Rambo's, extends Ellison's monetary metaphor by illustrating how the narrator's performances as Brotherhood spokesperson conform to the logic of the post–gold standard era. As the dollar remains tied to gold for which it cannot be exchanged, the narrator continues to signify a difference that has no real referent when he assumes the role of "race." And just as U.S. currency performs the functions of gold while marking its absence after the gold standard, "race" marks the absence of race while performing its functions as a trope of difference. The bank, which takes the form of a gross minstrel caricature with the caption "Feed Me," cements an association between gold standard era hard money and investments in racial performance that Ellison forged in the first half of the novel—an association that, unlike the bank itself, the narrator cannot break in the second half. Try as he might, his efforts to discard the broken image and the coins invested in it are thwarted by a host of other people, and the narrator ends up placing them in his beloved briefcase, which accompanies him to the novel's end and thus also into his underground vault. His inability to discard the racist image and the investments made in it prefigure his inability to recondition the cultivated expectations of others in his role as Brotherhood spokesman. As he keeps the contents of the bank in circulation by keeping them with him throughout his journey, so also does he unwittingly reify a trope of black difference through his role as "race."[16]

Race, like U.S. currency after the gold standard, may be culturally constructed, but as the narrator gradually discovers it has real-life consequences, especially when its circulation obscures inequities that race helps (re)produce. Race may be a construct, but racism remains a reality. The controversy surrounding the death of Tod Clifton provides the most salient example of the simulacral and self-regenerating nature of race and concomitant consequences of racism. As the narrator gradually comes to understand, Clifton wasn't killed for his ideas or his role in the Brotherhood, but "because he was black" (469). Jack responds to this revelation by accusing the narrator of "riding 'race' again," while

Brother Tobitt[17] complains, "Black and white, white and black. . . . Must we listen to this racist nonsense?" (469). Denouncing the narrator for playing the proverbial race card, the Brotherhood's committee members hide behind their portrayal of race as an ideological construct void of intrinsic value, all the while ignoring (and hence exacerbating) the institutionalized racism that precipitated Clifton's demise.

In his attempt to destroy the Brotherhood, or precipitate the Brotherhood's destruction of itself, the narrator first follows his grandfather's advice (and Trueblood's example) by performing the minstrel mask. Choosing to affirm the Brotherhood's misconceptions by providing an "optimistic chorus of yassuh, yassuh, yassuh!" to its members (509), the narrator foreshadows his own discovery of the limitations of this tactic by likening their reception of it to the racist, thick-lipped bank choking on coins: "So I'd accept it [invisibility]," he recalls, "I'd explore it, rine and heart. I'd plunge into it with both feet and they'd gag. Oh, but wouldn't they gag. . . . I'd overcome them with yeses, undermine them with grins, I'd agree them to death and destruction. Yes, and I'd let them swoller me until they vomited or burst wide open. Let them gag on what they refused to see. Let them choke on it" (508). But just as "feeding" the bank amounts to investing in the image it represents, the narrator's strategy only lends currency to the stereotype he performs. Affirming the relocation of authenticity in performance, he surmises, "By pretending to agree I *had* indeed agreed" (553). The only alternative solution the narrator can propose is to write about his experiences. This, he remarks elliptically, is the "only . . . way to destroy them" (564).

But given the narrator's demonstration that racial performance reifies tropes of difference by maintaining their cultural currency, along with the New Deal monetary logic to which this demonstration inheres, the solution he proposes and executes, namely to write the narrative the reader holds in his or her hands, is rendered problematic right from the start. For while the narrator's body sits in an underground vault like gold in Fort Knox, his paper narrative circulates aboveground in his place, just like his Brotherhood identity did earlier. Drawing a three-way analogy between post–gold standard paper money, the slip of paper that names the narrator, and the paper pages of the narrative that contains him, Ellison implicates his own literary endeavor—his own writing of race and restaging of racial conflict—when he uses the narrator's story to reflect upon his own. This self-reflection is demonstrated in the epilogue, where Ellison's narrator proposes a shift from writing race to assuming the "socially responsible role" of an activist (581), but he never emerges from his hole to effect this change; his activism is perpetually deferred. Likewise, Ellison's novel, coextensive with the bounds of the narrator's story, may offer the "possibility of action" (579), but the action is suspended indefinitely. Rather than signal the failure of the novel, however, Ellison's self-reflexive gestures and the limitations they reveal enable him to demarcate the limits of (re)writing race as a means of attaining social justice. Which is where the allusions to Baum's *Wonderful Wizard of Oz* reenter the picture.

As a narrative that (re)writes race, *Invisible Man* circulates as fiat and conforms to the logic of the post–gold standard era. Baum's book, by contrast, examined the possibility (and articulated the popular/Populist fear) that such a fiat era would come to pass. By employing Baum's tale as a mirror through which he reflects upon his own text, Ellison signals his ambivalence about the solution he and his narrator together propose. These allusions to Baum render problematic writing's role in the negotiation of the value of racial difference, the history of which Ellison reconstructs and ultimately punctuates with *Invisible Man*.

Ellison's allusions to Baum's tale begin during the Chthonian episode when the narrator joins the Brotherhood and acquires his new paper identity. To steer his readers toward Baum's original novel, Ellison begins these allusions with references to language and imagery exclusive to the wildly popular 1939 MGM movie musical, which, as Francis MacDonnell has demonstrated, can be read as "an allegory of Franklin Roosevelt's New Deal" (71). Riding in the car with Jack and three other members of the Brotherhood past Central Park on his way to the Chthonian, the narrator echoes the movie's chant of "Lions and tigers and bears, oh my!" when he remarks, "Somewhere close by in the night, there was a zoo with its dangerous animals. The lions and tigers in heated cages, the bears asleep" (299). The oversized knocker on Emma's apartment door echoes its cinematic counterpart at the Emerald City gates, and the narrator's feeling that "a curtain had been parted and I was being allowed to glimpse how the country operated" (306) not only echoes the film's climactic moment ("Pay no attention to that man behind the curtain!"), but foreshadows his own discovery that Hambro, and by extension the Brotherhood itself, is a humbug.

Once the narrator assumes his new identity, however, all of Ellison's references to *The Wizard of Oz* are exclusive to the turn-of-the-century novel. The key symbol Ellison borrows from Baum is the pair of green spectacles, the "Rineharts," which enable the narrator to walk through Harlem incognito and see what he had failed to see before, namely that

W. W. Denslow illustration of Dorothy and her companions wearing the green spectacles, from an early edition of Baum's novel entitled *The New Wizard of Oz*, 107.

"the world in which we lived was without boundaries. A vast seething, hot world of fluidity" (498). Pausing to reflect upon the role the green glasses played in this revelation, the narrator laughs and admits he "had been trying simply to turn them [the glasses] into a disguise but they had become a political instrument instead" (499).

But the role the green spectacles play in Baum's original novel and their role in Baum's monetary allegory significantly undercut the political promise of the invisible man's vision. In Baum's *Wizard*, the green spectacles maintain the illusion that the Emerald City is emerald, and they are required wearing for anyone who wants to enter the city. As the guardian of the gates explains to Dorothy, "If you did not wear spectacles the brightness and glory of the Emerald City would blind you. Even those who live in the City must wear spectacles night and day. They are all locked on, for Oz ordered it when the City was first built, and I have the only key that will unlock them" (81). However, as Oz admits when he is exposed as a humbug, the Emerald City is no greener than any other city: "My people have worn green glasses on their eyes so long that most of them think it really is an Emerald City," he admits (109). Like the value of fiat money, which the emerald illusion produced by the spectacles metaphorically echoes, the apparent value of the Emerald City is maintained by social contract; the city is emerald because everyone agrees to wear the spectacles that make it appear so, just as greenbacks circulate at face value because everyone agrees to accept them as legal tender. Within the context of Baum's monetary allegory, however, the vision of the people and the value of fiat paper money this vision emulates are both flawed and fragile, just like the illusion of power that Oz maintains through his trickery.

Besides a palpable metaphor for the fiat of race and the blindness it reproduces, Ellison found in Baum's monetary allegory a metaphor for the role racialist ideology plays in maintaining white hegemony. When Dorothy leaves the Emerald City for the first time to find the Wicked Witch of the West, she discovers that without the green glasses everything she brought with her from the Emerald City isn't green. "Dorothy still wore the pretty silk dress she had put on in the palace," Baum writes, "but now, to her surprise, she found it was no longer green, but pure white. The ribbon around Toto's neck had also lost its green color and was as white as Dorothy's dress" (90). When coupled with these examples from Baum's novel, Ranjit Dighe's observation that "Baum drew much of the inspiration for the Emerald City from the grandiose 'White City' that was specially created for the 1893 Columbian Exposition" (82n) suggests that the Emerald City is in fact white, coated with its own special brand of "Optic White." If the vision one sees through the green spectacles, the value of fiat currency this vision symbolizes, and the writing of race this value resembles are shimmering reflections of one another, then Ellison begs the question: are his narrator's revelations about the destabilizing potential and value of Rinehart as tainted (or tinted) as Dorothy's view of the Emerald City through the green spectacles? Similarly, is the narrator's investment in paper's promise—in (re)writing race—as fraught as Oz's utopia, reifying a trope of difference that, like the green spectacles, makes the White City look less white? Consider the following.

The narrator's vision through the green glasses is characterized by uncertainty and/or ambivalence; its sheer difference from the vision (or lack of vision) he has always known leads him to question the nature of reality ("What is real anyway?" he asks), and to make a series of epiphanies like, "Perhaps the truth was always a lie" (498). If, as Ellison suggests, looking through the green glasses is a metaphor for experiencing race as it is (re)constructed by American fiction, then the narrator experiences firsthand the symbiotic relationship between writing race and the racialized realities that such writing naturalizes when he wears the Rineharts. Rinehart, the undisputed star of this metafictional vision, is the black protagonist/everyman of such narratives, and by standing in for him, the narrator self-reflexively comments upon his own role as a black everyman in Ellison's novel.[18]

This commentary is informed by Ellison's own critical essays on the history and politics of the American novel, which explore the selfsame gap between reality and possibility that the narrator of *Invisible Man* examines through the green glasses. For example, in "Society, Morality and the Novel" (1957), Ellison writes, "We repay the novelist in terms of our admiration to the extent that he intensifies our sense of the real— or, conversely, *to the extent that he justifies our desire to evade certain aspects of reality which we find unpleasant beyond the point of confrontation*" (697; italics in original). This quote dovetails nicely with Ellison's assertion in "Twentieth-Century Fiction and the Black Mask of Humanity" that "if the word has the potency to revive and make us free, it has also the power to blind, imprison and destroy. The essence of the word is its ambivalence, and in fiction it is never so effective and revealing as when both potentials are operating simultaneously" (81). In Ellison's economy, a novelist is most successful when he or she both intensifies our sense of the real and uses fiction to reveal to readers their desire to avoid certain aspects of reality—especially when this avoidance is enabled by fiction. Hence Ellison's strategy of using fiction to both reveal its limitations and turn readers' realizations of these limitations into potential catalysts for social action.

This tension between revival and freedom on one hand and blindness, imprisonment, and destruction on the other (that is, between reality and avoidance, rind and heart) characterizes the entire Rinehart episode. On the one hand, the narrator's vision, like the American fictional text whose reinscription of race it symbolizes, provides the narrator with a self-awareness that he lacked up to this point. But on the other hand, the only roles black men appear to play in this emerald metanarrative are those of pimps, hustlers, and preachers—an apparent contradiction of the narrator's own realization that identity is fluid. Instead, identity is reinscribed as racialized subjects are reproduced by cultural texts. The narrator's vision through his Rineharts, like the view of race through the lens of American fiction, may help one imagine changes, but it can also work to prevent their realization. Ellison drives this point home by revealing how the full implication of the narrator's actions—the reality of his situation—cannot be confronted until he draws out his "Rineharts . . . only to see the crushed lenses fall to the street" (557). What he must confront with his own eyes, not through the lens(es) of literary fiction, is Ras the Exhorter turned Ras the Destroyer. It's just such a confrontation that the green spectacles had, up to this point, enabled the invisible man to avoid, just as the green spectacles enable visitors to the Emerald City to avoid seeing the city's real color—Oz says it will blind them, but it is the glasses themselves that are blinding. The irony of this is not lost on Ellison, who uses the green spectacles to reveal how writing race—and reading it—conceals as much as it reveals. In the process, Ellison marks the limits of his own contribution to the social construction of race. For while it may create "the possibility of action," as Ellison argues through his narrator (579), the word must be made real through a process that modern fiction can only catalyze.

Ellison doesn't just touch on this relationship between words and deeds and fiction's role as catalyst for social action, he also examines the trajectory of its evolution across a century. To these ends, Ellison not only uses the language and logic of monetary reform to self-reflexively mark the limits of his own text, but he also incorporates the monetary symbolism of his predecessors to reconstruct the history of American literary interventions into the race question—interventions that, like his own, turned upon contemporary references to the money question. Further reinforcing the symbolic connection between American fiction and U.S. currency he draws in his own text, Ellison treats the monetary symbols of Stowe, Melville, and Wright—symbols upon which each of these authors' attempts to renegotiate the value of racial difference turns—as shorthand for the narratives that contain them, namely *Uncle Tom's Cabin*, *The Confidence-Man*, and "The Man Who Lived Underground." Re-creating the American literary tradition of writing race, organizing this tradition around the evolution of the money question, and punctuating it with his own narrative, Ellison reflects upon the history of the money/race connection to declare a limit to, and effectively close the book on, this narrative strategy.

Ellison begins his retrospective with the same text with which I begin this book, *Uncle Tom's Cabin*. His references to Stowe's novel and its monetary symbolism occur during the eviction episode, the consequences of which will launch the narrator into the world of the Brotherhood. Surveying the elderly couple's meager belongings that lie on the sidewalk, the narrator notices a coin "pierced with a nail hole so as to be worn about the ankle on a string for luck" next to a greeting card "with a picture of what looked like a white man in black-face seated in the door of a cabin strumming a banjo beneath a bar of music and the lyric 'Going back to my old cabin home'" (272). Here, Ellison returns to *Uncle Tom's Cabin* and the money/minstrelsy connection that Stowe deployed in it, the significance of which is explored more fully in chapter 1. As the novel progresses chronologically, so also does Ellison's retracing of the money/

race/literature connection. In the process, Ellison reveals how literature's political agency (and thus also its use of monetary metaphors) was altered by an epistemological turn that emphasized the discursive nature of both truth and value—a turn that his literary predecessors helped to redirect, in no small part through their use of money. Stowe's romantic racialism thus gives way to Melville's deconstruction of truth—and in particular the truth of race—as Ellison ceases to signify on *Uncle Tom's Cabin* and starts to make allusions to *The Confidence-Man*.

Ellison incorporates Melville's text into his own by deploying the racist caricature/coin bank, which refers explicitly to Black Guinea, a "grotesque negro cripple" (and possible confidence man) who appeals to the charity of a crowd of white passengers and catches the coins they toss in his mouth, swallowing his pride "while still retaining each copper this side the oesophagus [*sic*]" (13, 14). Ellison was forthright about Melville's influence on this particular symbol. As Ellison wrote to his friend and literary cohort Albert Murray in a letter dated August 9, 1954, "I guess I told you that the bank image in *Invisible* was suggested by the figure of Black Guinea. That son of a bitch with his mouth full of pennies!" ("To Albert Murray" 79). Susan Ryan observes that neither Black Guinea's sympathizers nor Melville's readers can be sure if Black Guinea is really black, and they therefore remain uncertain whether or not he deserves the charity for which he humiliates himself. This is due, in large part, to the efforts of another beggar who tells the crowd of sympathizers that Black Guinea is "some white operator, betwisted and painted up for a decoy. He and his friends are all humbugs" (18). By tying the question of racial authenticity to what Ryan calls "the epistemology of doing good" (686), Black Guinea challenges the epistemological assumptions that overdetermine the value of racial difference—a difference in which the passengers have invested, and whose value is condensed in the coins Black Guinea consumes. By deploying Black Guinea in symbolic form and forging a connection between the bank that represents him and the narrator who resembles him, Ellison prompts his readers to examine the questions of race and authenticity that surround Black Guinea and his narrator alike. The result is a similar uncertainty, that is, more ambivalence.

If riffing on *The Confidence-Man* enabled Ellison to question the nature of truth and with it the fluid value of racial difference, then incorporating Richard Wright's "The Man Who Lived Underground" provided Ellison with both a metonym for the relocation of race in performance and a method for rewriting Wright who, in Ellison's eyes, restaged black victimization in a way that foreclosed readers' attempts to imagine alternatives to it. "The Man Who Lived Underground," which Ellison's prologue and epilogue uncannily resemble, therefore forms the underground foundation of *Invisible Man*. Just as *The Grandissimes* became a vehicle for Cable's revision of "Bibi" in the form of the Bras-Coupé episode, *Invisible Man* becomes the vehicle for Ellison's revision of Wright's naturalism.[19]

"The Man Who Lived Underground" begins in medias res as protagonist Fred Daniels flees from the police after signing a confession for a murder he didn't commit. Daniels then takes to the sewers to escape the policemen who beat him, just as Ellison's narrator takes refuge in his "hole" to escape from men he thinks are club-brandishing police officers. While underground, Daniels steals money from a safe along with a typewriter and a radio from the businesses that surround him. He wallpapers his hole with the money and writes on the typewriter while listening to the radio, having tapped into the wiring beneath the streets like Ellison's unnamed narrator does in the prologue and epilogue of *Invisible Man*. To Daniels, the money he uses for décor is not unlike Robinson Crusoe's money; it has no value in the underground. The hundred-dollar bills he uses to paper his underground lair are "just like any other paper" to him (54). Daniels's efforts to write on the typewriter are equally symbolic, and they anticipate Ellison's revision of the narrative. While in the office from which he steals both the typewriter and the money Daniels pauses twice to type his name. But once he returns underground he tries to repeat the procedure only to discover that he's forgotten his name! Instead he types two versions of a six-word narrative: "It was a long hot day" (61). Like Ellison would after him, Wright draws an implicit analogy between the bills, his protagonist, and his narrative. And just as Ellison would do after him, Wright connects the value of his protagonist to post–gold standard fiat money, which Wright goes to great lengths to fetishize:

> He [Daniels] took a wad of green bills and weighed it in his palm, then broke the seal and held one of the bills up to the light and studied it closely. *The United States of America will pay to the bearer on demand one hundred dollars*, he read in slow speech; then: *This note is legal tender for all debts, public and private*. . . . He broke into a musing laugh, feeling that he was reading of the doings of people who lived on some far-off planet. He turned the bill over and saw on the other side of it a delicately beautiful building gleaming with paint and set amidst green grass. (60)[20]

For Wright, the hundred-dollar bills collectively serve as a metaphor for Daniels's socially constructed worth and his undervaluation by society. They also echo Daniels's typewritten narrative—his representational paper shadow—that has no value in the underground. Ellison took Wright's monetary symbolism and transformed it from a meditation on the social contracts that uphold the values of money and racial difference to a metaphor for writing race. In the process, Ellison identifies Wright with the very shortcomings that "The Man Who Lived Underground" dramatizes, for as Daniels wallpapers his hole with the money Wright associates with his protagonist's narrative, Ellison's unnamed narrator puts his proverbial "notes from underground" into circulation in the form of *Invisible Man*. And while Daniels returns to the hole only to be shot to death and to remain, like his typescript, submerged forever, Ellison's invisible man entertains the hope of emerging from his subaltern space—an emergence that depends entirely upon the reader's ability to imagine a way out for him.

As this brief literary and monetary history incorporated into the pages of *Invisible Man* reveals, Ellison drew a sharp distinction between twentieth-century narratives represented by Wright's tale and their nineteenth-century predecessors when it came to writing race. To Ellison, twentieth-century American authors like Wright were failing to fulfill the promise that the great novelists of the nineteenth century had realized before them. As he argues in "Society, Morality and the Novel," the American novel, "which in the hands of our greatest writers had been a superb moral instrument" in the nineteenth century, "became morally diffident, and much of its energy was turned upon itself in the form of technical experimentation" in the twentieth (708). Ellison's National Book Award acceptance speech underscores his locating of this fissure at the turn of the century: "If I were asked in all seriousness just what I considered to be the chief significance of *Invisible Man* as a fiction," he began, "I would reply: Its experimental attitude and its attempt to return to the mood of personal moral responsibility for democracy which typified the best of our nineteenth-century fiction."

All of the narratives Ellison incorporated into his novel took paper form, but where these narratives could be exchanged for some real change in the nineteenth century, they were relegated to the status of legal tender paper money in the twentieth. The reason, as Ellison's reconstruction of the American literary tradition illustrates, has everything to do with the economics of race and the recalculation of literary value. As Henry Louis Gates, Jr., argued, writing race performs a double gesture in the act of renegotiating the value of racial difference, and each of the narratives Ellison incorporated into *Invisible Man* decenters race while reifying this trope of difference. But as his adoption of Richard Wright's story indicates, Ellison was pessimistic about the role of writing (that is, the value of circulating paper) in ameliorating the causes of racism in the twentieth century.[21] The reason for Ellison's pessimism has less to do with writing itself than it does with epistemology, for the real change that nineteenth-century fiction was able to effect was predicated on faith in the reality of race and the real value of money to which it was likened. So while Harriet Beecher Stowe could write the book that started the great war between the states, Ellison could only contribute to what he called "that fictional *vision* of an ideal democracy in which the actual combines with the ideal" (*Invisible* xx). Ellison therefore found himself caught in the middle as his desire to achieve nineteenth-century ends was forestalled by the twentieth-century historical and cultural milieu in which he operated. Referring to Baum allowed Ellison to symbolically return to 1900 and strike a balance between the moral responsibility of nineteenth-century fiction and the formal self-reflexivity of twentieth-century literature.

With this assertion, the logic of Baum's *Wizard* once again shimmers to the surface of Ellison's novel, for if the unnamed narrator of *Invisible Man* plays the part of Dorothy in Ellison's symbolic return to the Land of Oz, then Ellison is the wizard behind the veil who, despite the humbuggery of his methods, achieves results nonetheless (right down to his inability to get his main character back home again). In fact, the wizard's success in providing a heart for the Tin Woodman, courage for the Cowardly Lion, and a brain for the Scarecrow is dependent upon his exposure as a good man but a bad wizard. Only instead of being exposed as a humbug by a ragtag group of meddling interlopers, Ellison himself casts the veil aside to reveal how the machinery of culture works and the virtual reality of race is maintained. The result is not a denunciation of writing as an agent of social and political change, but a demonstration of its limitations. Remember, the Emerald City is not where journeys end, but where they begin anew, and Ellison used his novel to demarcate a point of departure and a change of direction. But though his narrative marks this limit, taking the next step—the step out of the underground that eludes his narrator and Wright's, too—is more problematic.

If *Invisible Man* constitutes Ellison's (bank)notes from the underground, then it is only fitting that the novel's epilogue would contains a paraphrase of the pluralist motto, *e pluribus unum*, which appears on every piece of U.S. currency. "Our fate is to become one, and yet many," notes the narrator (577). But Ellison's allusions to Baum's *Wizard* and the fears of a fiat future Baum articulated undercut this pluralist promise with proto-poststructuralist ambivalence.[22] This is because Ellison knew that his democratic message, like the Brotherhood's that relies upon the difference his narrator represents, depended on a vehicle that rewrites race. The green spectacles, then, compromise the epilogue's gestures toward an egalitarian, post-racialist future in which the promise of democracy could be fully realized. This is not a contradiction of Ellison's self-proclaimed democratic individualism, but a performative demonstration of Ellison's belief that, as long as the concept of racial difference is considered common sense, one is condemned never to eradicate, but forever to renegotiate, its value. Hence the difficulty of taking that first step out of the Chthonian labyrinth in which the narrator, like Ellison, both finds himself and rewrites himself.

## EPILOGUE: ELLISON AND THE BLACK ARTS MOVEMENT

Ellisonian ambivalence and the cultural currency of race would take center stage in the Black Arts Movement (BAM) of the 1960s and 1970s, which rejected Ellison's liberal individualism for black nationalism—a position which had the corollary effect of altering Ellison's own political capital in the eyes of literary critics.[23] The plot of *Invisible Man* and its narrator's struggles with Ras and his followers therefore prefigure Ellison's own struggles with Amiri Baraka (formerly LeRoi Jones) and other black nationalists in the decades after the novel was published. *Invisible Man* gives voice to Ellison's belief that, in art as in life, race was a limiting force standing in the way of cultural and political democracy. In the process, Ellison's novel articulates the double bind of the black artist who sought to transcend the limitations of race without denying the reality of black experience. The BAM, by contrast, took another approach, illuminated by an unlikely film that completes the *Wizard of Oz/Invisible Man* cycle: *The Wiz* (1978).

As if following the lead of Ellison, who turned L. Frank Baum's monetary allegory into a meditation on race and identity, William F. Brown and Charlie Smalls adapted *The Wonderful Wizard of Oz* into a Broadway musical in which all the characters are black. Brown and Smalls's urbanized take on Baum's novel was then turned into a screenplay by Joel Schumacher that became the campy classic of disco cinema known as *The Wiz*. Directed by Sidney Lumet (who always wanted to make a film version of *Invisible Man*)[24] and starring Diana Ross as Dorothy, Michael Jackson as the Scarecrow, Nipsey Russell as the Tin Man, and Ted Ross as the Lion, *The Wiz* retains the theme of self-discovery that characterized Baum's novel, but with an all African American cast. The film also restores the monetary metaphors of Baum's classic story: Dorothy's slippers are once again silver, the gate to the Emerald City has become a bank vault, and the wizard's palace is none other than the twin towers of the World Trade Center. And as the iconic imagery of American money makes its return, so also is the wizard cycle completed when the film riffs upon a scene from *Invisible Man*.

No sooner have Dorothy and her three companions assembled for the first time than they "ease on down" the yellow brick road to the subway. A mysterious figure in black approaches; from his two hands dangle dancing paper dolls just like the two-faced Sambo dolls that Tod Clifton made dance when he wasn't "on the lambo" (*Invisible* 433). In a move of which Ellison would approve, the dolls begin to grow and grow, until what seemed like harmless marionettes become menacing figures, just as they do in the narrator's emerging consciousness. Rather than spit in their faces, though, Dorothy and her cohorts turn from the dancing dolls and escape the underground to complete their mission and realize their self-worth . . . unlike the narrator of *Invisible Man*.

Although a G-rated movie adapted from a children's novel, *The Wiz* echoes many of the broad themes of the BAM, in particular its preoccupations with black nationalism. The film itself is not a BAM text, being derived from a white author's work and disconnected almost entirely from the politics of Black Power. Yet its focus on performativity, its anti-materialist critique, its black nationalist themes, and its occasional Pan-African rhetoric constitute a commentary on the BAM as seen through the prism of a mainstream black theatrical production. This broader perspective upon the BAM and its influences becomes clear when the film comments explicitly upon the antagonism between BAM imperatives and Ellisonian priorities, and prizes the former at the expense of the latter.

In the movie, as in the play, everyone is black—a total cultural separation has occurred and New York is thus transformed into the antithesis of Baum's White City. Freed from the forces of white hegemony, the principals of *The Wiz* prove they can make it on their own. Ellison, of course, would have rejected this simplistic ending just as his narrator rejected the separationist overtures of Ras the Exhorter. But then, the BAM was in no small part a rejection of Ellisonian ambivalence. To the movement's adherents, the arts were supposed to clarify and underscore the self-worth of African Americans and provide what Larry Neal called the "Vision of a Liberated Future," not reprise the factors that complicate and frustrate efforts to turn words into deeds. These principles are clearly represented, albeit in sanitized form, in *The Wiz*. For example, Dorothy tells the Scarecrow that he's not unintelligent, but that he's "the product of some negative thinking"—a G-rated way of saying he has internalized the colonized mindset and concomitant self-hate that Frantz Fanon, Malcolm X, and others identified in the 1950s and 1960s. As for the film's gestures toward Pan-Africanism and black nationalism, the Lion—a.k.a. Fleetwood Coupe de Ville—reminisces about being a king in an African paradise, and he longs to regain the courage he had there via his own symbolic back-to-Africa movement.

It should come as no surprise, given these preoccupations, that despite the film's faithfulness to the spirit of Baum's novel, the green glasses do not appear in *The Wiz* in any form. Omitting them enabled the filmmakers to eliminate the self-reflexive device and the ambivalence it produces in the hopes of sending a clear, unambiguous message to youngsters, especially black youngsters, about their self-worth. However, as Ellison asked in his criticism of the Black Arts Movement, how accurate can this estimation of self-worth be if it is predicated on the separation of culture along racial lines—a segregation that would not, and, in Ellison's view, should not, ever take place? Given this tension and the film's explicit rejection of Ellisonian ambivalence, the black figure with the marionettes just might represent Ellison himself, upon whom the principal characters must turn their backs and run in order to escape the underground. Obscured almost to the point of invisibility, his appearance (or disappearance) at the center of the film underscores the degree to which Ellison's narrative is the absent center of *The Wiz*, and Ellison himself speaks on the lower frequencies of the Black Arts Movement.

# CONCLUSION

*The liquidity of Jes Grew has resulted in a hyperinflated situation, all you hear is more, more, increase growth . . . Suppose we shut down a few temples . . . I mean banks, take money out of circulation, how would people be able to support the appendages of Jes Grew, the cabarets the jook joints and the speaks.*

ISHMAEL REED, *Mumbo Jumbo*

*They think
it's flesh
and blood here*

*When it's coin,
and legal tender
silver certificates*

*instead of organic
parts*

AMIRI BARAKA, "PRIMITIVE WORLD:
AN ANTI-NUCLEAR JAZZ MUSICAL"

The conclusion of *Invisible Man* anticipates both the arrival of the cultural turn and its failure to ameliorate the social ills that race reproduces. The reason for this failure, as Ellison himself foresaw, is that the cultural turn, like race, is another construction of contested value. Moreover, it's a construction whose value is in no small part pegged to the value of racial difference, and persistent conflicts over the latter forestall the anti-essentialist objectives of the former. Suffice it to say that racism and racial essentialism are still alive and well despite the cultural turn, giving the lie to contemporary claims of a post-racial present.

The persistence of race in contemporary America recalls Michael Omi and Howard Winant's observations about how social constructions evolve: they either coexist in institutional and imaginative forms or they don't exist at all. The upshot of this observation is that for change to take place, there must be reciprocation not only between/among the frameworks through which the body is read, but also between these discursive frameworks and the social practices they sanction. However, while changing the way race is represented may be necessary for changing the institutional form that race assumes, it is not sufficient to effect this change in and of itself. To invoke Ellison once more, you have to change the joke to slip the yoke, but slipping the yoke takes more than merely changing the joke.

By promoting commerce between literary, monetary, and racial discourses, the authors examined in this book could only change the joke. This isn't a shortcoming, per se. Rather, the work of these authors makes legible the limitation of fiction's agency, and illustrates how fundamental race has been to the formation and evolution of the social, political, and cultural frameworks that promote and perpetuate the materialization of racial difference. It seems almost too commonsensical to mention, but race remains deeply engrained in the nation's legal, practical, and expressive fabric—its social and cultural memory banks. The writers whose work I examine in this book may have raised readers' awareness of the processes by which racial difference is materialized by way of analogy to a more visible and, for many white Americans whose racial status only appears unvexed, more tangible form of materialized difference. But this approach could only go so far.

Ishmael Reed explores the limitations defined by these authors in his novel *Mumbo Jumbo* (1972), which chronicles the outbreak of a "psychic epidemic" called Jes Grew (5). Its name drawn from Harriet Beecher Stowe's characterization of Topsy, Jes Grew's effects may, as one official explains, know "no class no race no consciousness," but its source is obviously black (5). Jes Grew is opposed by a group of Atonists called the Wallflower Order, whose plans to combat the outbreak include grooming "a Talking Android who will work within the Negro, who seems to be its classical host; to drive it out, categorize it analyze it expel it slay it, blot Jes Grew" (17). What ultimately contains the spread of Jes Grew and the influence of black culture it represents isn't an Atonist conspiracy, however, but a systemic resistance to what Jes Grew represents. In other words, Jes Grew is not defeated so much as neutralized by the hegemony it challenges. The fever doesn't break because of any one group's culture jamming or even as a direct result of the burning of the Book of Thoth, the text that Jes Grew seeks. Rather, the status quo remains intact by absorbing the impact of the "anti-plague" on many fronts. Jes Grew may be a movement in need of a text to keep it from being "mistaken for entertainment" (211), but the text, while necessary, isn't sufficient for overcoming the Atonists or the hegemony they represent. Of course, Reed doesn't suggest that one should stop trying to "change the joke" through cultural production, or that such commentaries have not been effective catalysts for change. Indeed, he concludes his novel with an explanation of why a new text is needed—a text that a new generation will write.

The new generation of writers and artists Reed called to action continues to use money to comment on race. However, this particular form of changing the joke has taken an ironic, self-reflexive turn in contemporary American culture. To fully understand and appreciate the cultural work these writers are doing, one needs to know the cultural history this book traces and the persistent analogy between race and money it engages—an analogy that took on new significance when money achieved its poststructural perfection in electronic data while American race relations remained medieval.

Many contemporary artists continue to use money in their texts as a means to reclaim something, be it a critique that money once made possible or a historical narrative that remains obscured. The monetary theme that characterizes the work of so many hip-hop fashion designers, for instance, is more than just bling; it is a tongue-in-cheek comment on slavery's transformation of persons into money and, by extension, an expression of self-possession by the wearer—a self-possession that slavery once denied. Double-edged commentaries like this remain salient in part because reminders of slavery's transformation of persons into movable property remain visible in contemporary popular cultural texts, which, not coincidentally, continue to incorporate monetary symbols. The operatic version of *Amistad* presented at the 2008 Spoleto Festival USA, for example, takes place on a stage in the form of a ten-dollar gold piece from 1839. This coin functions as a literal "contact zone" where actors playing black slaves and white slave-masters meet. Artist John W. Jones takes this literalized connection between money and slavery a step further in his paintings, which recontextualize, reanimate, and rehumanize the images of slaves featured on many antebellum Southern

Still image from Spoleto Festival USA 2008 production of *Amistad*. Photograph by William Struhs © 2008, used by permission of William Struhs.

currencies. Money doesn't exactly mark the spot where black and white meet in John W. Jones's art; instead, his paintings reveal how American money has itself functioned as a contact zone for representations of whiteness and blackness. But, as the staging of *Amistad* described above demonstrates, money continues to mark the spot in the literary and popular cultural text where racialized bodies converge. Only now, this contact zone signifies the ironic persistence of race in a society in which postmodernism is the coin of the pop culture realm. The irony is compounded by the fact that the simulacral nature of money is largely taken for granted while the hyperreality of race is not. Two contemporary artists have raised this irony to an aesthetic: painter Michael Ray Charles and cinematographer Spike Lee.

Michael Ray Charles and Spike Lee both take the cultural politics of race as their subject. Charles's paintings invoke and/or include racist caricatures from advertisements and the minstrel stage in order to critique contemporary racial politics. These images are controversial and confrontational, to say the least. For instance, Charles painted a blackface version of the National Basketball Association's (NBA) logo in which a grotesque minstrel stereotype dribbles a basketball and runs à la Jerry West toward the viewer while sporting white gloves on his hands and a price tag around his neck. The caption that accompanies this figure reads, "The NBA is TANTASTIC." Spike Lee's films are equally frank in their approach to the issues of race, representation, and the materialization of difference. Frequently apocalyptic, movies like *Do the Right Thing* (1989) and *Jungle Fever* (1991) explicitly render the racial codes that structure American society while exploring their consequences.

The work of these two artists converges in Spike Lee's film *Bamboozled* (2000), which features two of Michael Ray Charles's paintings as mirrors in the text. The tropic network of racial, monetary, and literary signification is dense at these points of irruption. To untangle the web these two artists weave, I must first examine one of the film's subtexts as articulated by Michael Ray Charles in a portrait of the artist taken by photographer Patrick Demarchelier. This portrait appears alongside reproductions of Charles's paintings in the exhibition catalogue of his show "Michael Ray Charles, 1989–1997: An American Artist's Work," which was staged at Blaffer Gallery, the Art Museum of the University of Houston in 1997. In the photograph Charles addresses the camera, intently returning its gaze over the rims of his glasses, his chin resting on the butt of his left hand. Everything about the image appears to be consistent with the conventions of promotional photography, except that tucked into the corner of Charles's mouth is a shiny penny.

At first glance, Charles appears merely to be playing the part of Black Guinea for the camera—a gesture that is rich with symbolism in and of itself. But this gesture takes on additional meaning when one discovers that Charles affixed a Lincoln cent to each and every painting in the show as well as to each copy of the exhibition catalogue itself. By playing the part of Black Guinea in order to represent himself as an artist and to reflect on his own role as one who traffics in vexing/vexed racial imagery, Charles accomplishes two things: he echoes the instability that his art foregrounds, and raises anew the issues of race and authenticity that Melville raised in *The Confidence-Man*. Black Guinea, the reader will recall, may or may not be a white man in blackface. The authenticity of his racial status is determined by the investments of others—investments represented by the pennies they toss into Black Guinea's mouth. By attaching pennies to the stereotypical images in which American culture has historically invested, Charles can simultaneously depict the performances in which many have invested over the years and render these investments legible by way of the currency to which they are literally affixed. At the same time, Charles's portrait encourages the viewer to second-guess the motives of the artist, who, like Black Guinea, may or may not be a confidence man. Is he, as some critics have claimed, merely recycling and thereby reinforcing racial stereotypes, exploiting the investments of others in order to feed his own image as an artist, or does he satirize and thereby raise awareness of the processes by which racial stereotypes acquire their currency? The resulting uncertainty, I would argue, is the goal, not merely a byproduct, of Charles's art.

A similar instability lies at the heart of Spike Lee's *Bamboozled*, which is more or less a blackface version of *The Producers*. The film's protagonist, Pierre Delacroix (né Peerless Dothan), decides he's had enough of the racist practices of his employer, the Continental Network System, and more than enough of the obnoxious claiming of his white boss, Thomas Dunwitty, so he hatches a plan to get himself fired and thus released from his contract. Thinking he might simultaneously expose the racism of the network executives and insure his termination in one fell stroke, Delacroix pitches a show called *Mantan: The New Millennium Minstrel Show* to Dunwitty who, in turn, sells it to the higher-ups at CNS. *Mantan* is nothing more than a nineteenth-century minstrel show performed on a soundstage, and much like *Springtime for Hitler* in Mel Brooks's *The Producers*, the show is a hit despite Delacroix's efforts to make the show as offensive as possible. The drama of the film, however, lies in Delacroix's evolving need to justify his accidental success to himself and rationalize his complicity in the spectacle he helped to create.

Delacroix's complicity is expressed via the racially charged images with which he begins to surround himself. Not long after tasting the success that had been denied to him for so long, Delacroix begins collecting racist memorabilia from the nineteenth and early twentieth centuries. His collection begins with a gift from his assistant, confidante, and former lover, Sloan Hopkins, in the form of what she calls a "jolly nigger bank." It is the very bank that the protagonist of *Invisible Man* could dash to pieces but never discard. Like Dunwitty, Delacroix fails to see how the token with which he's been presented critiques his role as a willing purveyor of racist imagery, at least at first. This becomes clear in the scene upon which the entire movie turns as Delacroix, alone in his office, begins feeding quarters into the bank one by one. As he does so, the viewer is presented with a series of stills of the objects that surround Delacroix—the lawn jockeys, ceramic mammies, etc. he's acquired—to the sound of quarters being fed into the bank. Each image is accompanied by the sound of a single coin falling into the bank. The final image the viewer sees is a painting by Michael Ray Charles called *Bamboozled* that depicts the head of another minstrel stereotype at the bull's-eye of a dartboard, a slot cut in the top of its scalp like a piggy bank. Running along the top and bottom of this painting is the line, "Bamboozled—The Amazing Game of Deceit N Conquer." After the viewer is presented with this image, Delacroix once again appears in real time sitting back in his desk chair, a quarter sitting in the bank's iron hand waiting to be propelled into its mouth. Suddenly, the bank springs to life and lifts its outstretched hand to its mouth to consume the coin. It then repeats the gesture over and over unassisted before becoming dormant once more. Echoing the painting that shares the film's name, Lee uses this scene to suggest that racist stereotypes, upon becoming hegemonic, become self-sustaining. They become hyperreal. Delacroix may have been investing in the image just for fun, just as he pitched *Mantan* with tongue firmly planted in cheek, but the result in both cases turns out to be more than he bargained for. Each stereotype takes on a life of its own, constituting an authenticity it appears only to represent.

This postmodern twist on Ellison's invocation of Black Guinea cannot be fully decoded without considering the seemingly incongruous inclusion of Michael Ray Charles's painting amongst the racist memorabilia—coin bank included—in Delacroix's office, or fully appreciated without more closely examining the questions surrounding racial satire raised by Charles. Despite what the viewer's early impressions might suggest, *Bamboozled* is not a satire but an exploration of satire's limitations. This is why the movie begins with Delacroix explicitly addressing the camera and reciting the dictionary definition of satire, making it clear from the onset that he knows precisely what satire is, at least in the academic sense. Yet he draws no practical distinction between Charles's paintings and the sources they critique, both of which compete for the viewer's attention in the visual vocabulary of the film (Sloan, too, has one of Charles's paintings hanging in her home). One can only assume that Spike Lee, who is the actual owner of Delacroix's museum of racist images and the proud owner of several Michael Ray Charles paintings, *is* able to draw this distinction. But his protagonist is either unwilling or unable to do likewise. This failure to discriminate is inseparable from Delacroix's complicity in the success of the *New Millennium Minstrel Show*, which he explicitly pitches as a satire despite all evidence to the contrary—evidence corroborated by the fact that he has already announced to the viewer that he knows exactly what satire is and what it is supposed to do. Perhaps Delacroix seeks to assuage his feelings of guilt over the vehicle of his long-deferred professional success by erasing or at least ignoring the distinction between the image and its critique, between satire and the satirized. Or perhaps, having experienced firsthand the disconnection between authorial intent and audience reception, he no longer finds it necessary to draw this distinction because others will draw it for him in accordance with their own sensibilities, however uninformed they may be. Like the viewer of Michael Ray Charles's paintings, then, the viewer of *Bamboozled* is left to ponder, but not resolve, this paradox.

As is the case with the Book of Thoth in *Mumbo Jumbo*, the agency of these texts is overdetermined by the larger problem of institutionalized racism they critique. Spike Lee drives this point home in the film by illustrating how Charles's painting won't extricate Delacroix from his conflicted position no matter how he interprets the image. If anyone's conscience were to be pricked by the painting that shares the film's name, it would be Delacroix's. But the viewer cannot know what Delacroix feels about this image or why he conflates it with the stereotypes it explodes. All he or she can know is that regardless of how Delacroix interprets this image, he must continue to function within a racialized social system that only recognizes him when he affirms certain stereotypes and/or promotes the continued distortion of cultural lenses through which African Americans are viewed. The ambivalent logic of Charles's *Bamboozled*, then, extends to Delacroix's role in *Bamboozled*. Delacroix plays the Sambo role to get ahead, and he is rewarded with recognition by the television industry. But while the irony of this role and its resemblance to that of the coin bank may or may not be lost on Delacroix, it is clearly lost on the industry higher-ups who shower him with accolades. The consequences of this disconnection soon become clear. By the end of the film Delacroix has become the Sambo he thought he was only pretending to be in order to get ahead, and he appears in blackface for the remainder of the movie to signify his debasement.

The issues of agency and its limitations here are numerous. Delacroix may never have intended *Mantan* to be a satire, and yet it is frequently interpreted as such by bit players in the film. Similarly, he may have intended his own Sambo role to be ironic, yet it is taken prima facie for reality because it confirms the very distorted image that *Mantan* helps to maintain. In short, Delacroix may have tried to play the confidence man, but he became Black Guinea nonetheless, discovering in the process what Charles's paintings satirized all along: that the Sambo role, like most racial stereotypes, is more real to others than he is. This hyperreal confusion, more than anything else, accounts for the collapsing of satire and satirized in *Bamboozled*.

Charles's paintings engrave the social relations that turn cultural performances into (hyper)realities, but as Delacroix's transformation from confidence man to Black Guinea illustrates, the very conditions these images satirize can turn such representations from satirical to perversely realistic, and thereby foreclose their subversive potential. The agency of *Bamboozled*, Lee implies self-reflexively, is similarly circumscribed by the cultivated expectations and vested interests of its viewers. They may get the Ellisonian joke at the heart of the film and the invisibility it makes visible, but the yoke will still be hard to slip no matter how the joke is interpreted. But while Lee may have no control over how his film and its use of charged racial images will be interpreted, he, like Charles, foregrounds this instability with monetary metaphors that make this lack of agency legible.

In both Michael Ray Charles's paintings and Spike Lee's film, money is a sign of frustrated agency rather than a path to continued reform. The analogies both artists draw between race and money are not, as they were in the past, employed to take advantage of a rhetoric or logic of reform that they could share. Instead, they function as reminders of the need for a systemic approach to social reform—one that addresses both the institutional and the ideological forms of racial formation that Omi and Winant describe. They also function as reminders that the rhetoric of monetary reform reached the end of its usefulness for artists and critics like Charles and Lee. The coins affixed to Charles's paintings and the coins invested/ingested into the image the bank represents in *Bamboozled* do not function as sites for the articulation of discourses of monetary and racial reform. Instead, they mark the persistence of institutionalized racism and the absence of authorial agency in an era when monetary reform is a thing of the past. Once U.S. currency became or was embraced as the data it always already was its value could no longer be changed simply by changing its form. As a result, the persistent analogy whose history this book traces broke down. Artists like Michael Ray Charles and Spike Lee use the fracturing of this analogy, as well as the cultural memory of its former effectiveness, to reflect upon their own roles as cultural commentators in a postmodern society.

# NOTES

1. Omi and Winant are joined by other critics who agree that race defies simple definition as either a purely ideological construct or a fixed biological reality, an illusion or an essence. For example, Brett St. Louis burlesques critics who seek to resolve the radical irreconcilability between realist and constructivist positions on race when he writes, "Attempts at definitive racial understanding have arrived at the following conclusions: race does/does not exist and we should/should not use the concept" (29–30). Rohit Barot and John Bird echo St. Louis's intentional ambiguity when they write, "As [Michael] Banton, [Robert] Miles and many others have argued, the concept of 'race' should now be abandoned by sociologists as signifying nothing; this despite other claims— Winant, most noticeable—that the dustbin is not empty" (601).

2. Howard Winant offers an abbreviated version of this formula in "Whiteness at Century's End" when he writes, "Racial formation is the articulation of culture and structure, signification and social organization." In the October 2008 special issue of *PMLA*, "Comparative Racialization," Omi and Winant reprise their definition of "racial projects," and renew their call for cultural commentators to "systematically address structural racism and the inextricable connections between it and the politics of identity" ("Once More" 1565).

3. The double-bind that Gates describes has led a cadre of contemporary scholars, Paul Gilroy foremost among them, to propose that race be eliminated altogether as a category of difference. Gilroy, who laments the tendency of cultural critics to endlessly repeat "the pious ritual in which we always agree that 'race' is invented but are then required to defer to its embeddedness in the world and to accept that the demand for justice requires us nevertheless innocently to enter the political arenas it helps to mark out," argues that the invalidation of racial determinism and the increasing visibility of the means of racial (re)production make this the time to take some bold steps toward fulfilling a post-race cosmopolitanism (52). Howard Winant mocks such declarations when he writes, "Race is here to stay, baby. Go home and tell your momma" (*New Politics* xix).

4. See Goldberg 1–7.

5. According to Mikhail Bakhtin, novels are inherently heteroglossic, containing many ideological "voices" that stand in interaction and are, in turn, articulated by the reader who populates them with meanings that are themselves contingent and socially determined.

6. Echoing W. E. B. Du Bois and Ralph Ellison, Smith equates visibility with value in the passage from which this quote was extracted. She writes, "In accord with the changing interests and other values of a community, various potential meanings of a work will become more or less visible (or 'realizable'), and the visibility—and hence value—of the work for that community will change accordingly" (10). Lindon Barrett, in turn, examines the contingencies of racial signification in his book *Blackness and Value*, in which he argues "that in U.S. cultural logic the abstract entities 'value' and 'race' keenly reflect one another, even to a point at which they might be considered isomorphic" (1).

7. See chapter 1 of *The Latino Body: Crisis Identities in American Literary and Cultural Memory*, in which Lima illustrates "how the Mexican body ultimately became conflated with 'blackness' in the public sphere," and "how 'whiteness' became the organizing principle for the construction of American citizenship and identity for Mexicans in the nineteenth century" (16). See also chapter 8 of Martha Menchaca's *Recovering History, Constructing Race: The Indian, Black, and White Roots of Mexican Americans*, in which she writes of how white Mexicans were awarded full citizenship in the aftermath of the violated Treaty of Guadalupe Hidalgo, "while *mestizos*, Christianized Indians, and *afromestizos* came under different racial laws" (217).

8. Gross describes the mutually constitutive relationship between the legalization of racial mythologies and the lived social practices they sanctioned when she writes, "Legal rules passed by high courts and legislatures had to be translated into practical action on the ground. Witnesses, lawyers, and litigants learned to tell stories that resonated with juries or with government officials. At the intersection of law and local culture, we can see the day-to-day creation of race" (12).

9. The term "New Economic criticism" was coined by Martha Woodmansee and Mark Osteen to distinguish between the economic criticism of the late 1970s and early 1980s and contemporary scholarship that interrogates the intersections of literary, cultural, and economic discourses. See Woodmansee and Osteen 3–50.

10. Appropriately enough, Poe's "The Gold-Bug" was first published in the *Dollar Magazine*.

11. Calhoun's rhetoric is an example of what Joseph Fichtelberg calls the "systemic metaphors of circulation" that characterized the early American republic (4).

12. Hoeller writes, "Hurston's story racializes the debate about the color (and substance) of legal currency as it tracks the destructive repercussions of

the gold standard's arrival in an African American community. At first sight, Hurston seems to suggest that silver money is black, good money and that gold is the evil money of white corporate America. She links silver money to a playful, working-class, gift-giving community and gold money to the deceptively seductive lures of the city and its corporate structure. But her story does not quite yield to such a schematic interpretation because silver money can only be earned within a racialized, industrial economy and the gold money that appears in the story is not really gold but gilded silver coin" (762–63).

13. In *Our America*, Michaels reproduces the dualism of race and the discourses surrounding it when he writes, "Anti-essentialist defenses of race amount to nothing more than new ways of making the mistake. As absurd as the one-drop rule of Jim Crow is, the no-drop rule of anti-essentialism is even more absurd. Omi and Winant cite two 'temptations' that they believe must be resisted in thinking about race: the first is the temptation 'to think of race as an *essence*, as something fixed, concrete and objective'; the second is 'to see it as a mere illusion.' Their point, of course, is that in seeing race as a social construction we can avoid both the temptations. But if to see race as a social construction is inevitably (even if unwillingly and unknowingly) to essentialize it, then race really is either an essence or an illusion. The two 'temptations' are the only choices we have" (134).

14. Melville's minstrel signifying is examined by Eric Lott, who writes that *Moby-Dick* contains several "minstrel-show feints and jabs: Melville has Pip close the 'Doubloon' chapter with a snippet of 'Old King Crow' (1843), one of the most popular minstrel songs in the 1840s, and Fleece comes forth with a sermon straight out of the minstrel show" (163).

15. See *Oxford English Dictionary* entry for "tin."

16. There are a multitude of publications in popular media that address the money question from any given angle. What follows is but a tiny cross-sectional sample of such publications. Working-class assessments of Andrew Jackson's war against the Second Bank of the United States and his administration's hard money policies can be found in "Conclusion of Mr. Benton's Speech" and "A Sound Currency" from the February 8, 1834, and March 8, 1834, issues of *Workingman's Advocate*. The contours of the money question during Reconstruction are clearly visible in articles published in *Harper's Weekly* and Horace Greeley's *New York Tribune*. See, for example, "The Silver Dollar" and "Specie Payments" in the June 23, 1877, and December 18, 1869, issues of *Harper's Weekly*, and "Effects of Unlimited Silver" and "The Silver Heresy" in the January 1, 1878, and January 3, 1878, editions of the *Tribune*. The monetary inflections of the presidential election of 1896, which led to the passage of the Gold Standard Act of 1900, are particularly clear in two publications: the *North American Review* and the *Overland Monthly*, each of which gave ample opportunities for Republicans and Populists/Democrats to make their cases. See Adams, Miller, and Craig; Bryan; Irish; Lane; Levy; and Valentine. Finally, for analysis of the managed

currency system that accompanied the New Deal, see the *Life* editorial essay "Where There's Life, There's Hope" in the January 1934 issue, as well as articles by Crowther and Garrett in the *Saturday Evening Post*.

17. The Greenback Party was formed in 1874. The circumstances surrounding its formation are examined in detail in the third chapter of this project. Although it was no longer a contender on the national political scene after 1884, the Greenback Party lingered well into the twentieth century.

18. Richards echoes Charles Beard, whose book *An Economic Interpretation of the Constitution of the United States* (1913) portrays the drafting of the U.S. Constitution as a reaction against agrarian soft money interests. Beard observes that, because "substantially all of the merchants, money lenders, security holders, manufacturers, shippers, capitalists, and financiers and their professional associates" supported the Constitution and "substantially all or the major portion of the opposition came from the non-slaveholding farmers and the debtors," it stands to reason that the Constitution protected the economic interests of the former group at the expense of the latter (17).

## 1. JACKSONIAN ABOLITIONISM

1. After quoting Stowe's own assertion that "the worst abuse of the system of slavery is its outrage upon the family," Ashworth puts this outrage in socioeconomic terms, writing, "It was the sin of the slave system that it engulfed the family within the market economy" (180, 185).

2. Joseph Fichtelberg describes this Jeffersonian nostalgia as a Democratic expression of the period's monetary anxieties. Describing the reaction of Jacksonian Democrats after the Panic of 1837—a panic caused in no small part by Jackson's own monetary policies—he writes, "As different elements of classical republicanism gradually gave way. . . . Democrats clung to the yeoman ideal of Jefferson and John Taylor of Caroline, even as market uncertainties threatened the average man's ability to order his affairs" (124–25).

3. Throughout this chapter I use phrases like "the Age of Jackson" and "Jacksonian America." I am following the practices of historians like Arthur M. Schlesinger, Jr., and Robert V. Remini who describe the "Age of Jackson" as a period characterized by Andrew Jackson's political and ideological influence that transcends the years of his presidency and extends more or less up to the Civil War. Remini describes the Age of Jackson as the period beginning with Jackson's election in 1828 and ending with the start of the Mexican War in 1846. But Remini also notes that the Mexican War was just the beginning of "a long tragic drift into secession and civil war, developing almost inexorably out of the Mexican conflict" (*Age* ix). Schlesinger is more forthright in stating his belief that Jackson's influence and political protégés held sway up to and even beyond the American Civil War. Schlesinger describes Andrew Johnson, who became president after Lincoln's assassination, as "a Jacksonian from Jackson's own state" (497).

4. The association Jacksonians drew between gold specie and the health of the nation is reflected in the rhetorical practice of calling gold coins "Benton gold lozenges" after the Jacksonian hard money advocate Thomas Hart Benton (Wilentz 114). Benjamin Mifflin called quarter eagles "Dr. Benton's yellow lozenges; a panacea for all diseases in the chest" (qtd. in O'Leary 94).

5. Pierson describes Republican gender ideology as an inseparable part of Stowe's abolitionist and free labor appeals. "Women's roles in *Uncle Tom's Cabin* are not antagonistic to wage-labor capitalism," he writes; "rather, Stowe depicts wage labor as not only a viable option for women but also as a significant weapon with which to counteract the devastating effects of Arthur Shelby's unthinking patriarchy and his disastrous slaveholding" (77).

6. The social changes to which Pierson refers here are shifting gender ideologies and threats to white supremacy.

7. Stowe's choice to attempt this rhetorical tightrope walk in *Uncle Tom's Cabin* could account for what Samuel Otter has called "the characteristic peculiarity" of Stowe's thinking about race (18). Stowe's racialism, I suggest, was less characteristically peculiar than it was politically expedient.

8. Gresham's Law dictates that "bad" money drives "good" money out of circulation, so if the price of gold was low and the price of silver was high, gold would circulate as money while silver would be hoarded as bullion. This is exactly what happened after the Coinage Act of 1834.

9. The very existence of the gold dollar coin is a testament to the abundance of gold in America after 1848. The gold dollar was the smallest coin ever minted in the United States. It was but three-quarters of the size of a Roosevelt dime. Given its minuscule size, it would have been much easier for Uncle Tom to conceal a gold dollar on his person than a silver dollar almost four centimeters in diameter. Furthermore, because it consisted of only 1.7 grams of gold, this dollar would have been much easier for George Shelby to bore a hole through than the era's silver dollar, which weighed in at 26.73 grams.

10. Eric Lott describes the three parts of the minstrel show of the period, writing, "In the late 1840s and early 1850s, as the first part began to be devoted to more sentimental music (sometimes performed without blackface), [Dan] Emmett's and other companies added a stirring middle or 'olio' section containing a variety of acts (among them a stump speech), the third part then often comprising a skit situated in the south" (140). Jason Richards compares the antics of Harry Harris to those of T. D. Rice's onstage likeness-in-miniature, four-year-old Joseph Jefferson III: "In those days," he writes, "Rice would emerge behind a mask of burnt cork, sporting red-and-white stripes for pants and a long blue coat that boasted a star-spangled collar. On one occasion he improvised an act that became a national legend. In a gunny sack slung over his shoulder, he carried on stage four-year-old Joseph Jefferson III, likewise arrayed in the colors of Old Glory. During his song-and-dance sequence, Rice rolled his mini mimic from the sack, and Joe performed an imitation Jim Crow"

(206). Noting the resemblance between Joseph Jefferson and Harry Harris, Richards notes, "Stowe must have known this story" (206).

11. For example, the narrator of John Smith's 1840 tune "Jumbo Jum" states, "Not a great way from Nashville, as snug as a mouse, / Dare lives a great man in a very nice house, / Every body ought to cherish him, you know who I mean, / It's massa General Jackson of the battle of Orlean." Sam Dennison signals this homage as formulaic when he calls it an example of "the usual political salute to Jackson" (78).

12. The version of "Jim Crow" published by E. Riley, 29 Chatham St. in New York around 1932 addresses the nullification debate with the lines: "De great Nullification, / And fuss in de South, Is now before Congress, / To be tried by word ob mouth. . . . / Wid Jackson at de head, / Dey soon de ting may settle / For ole Hickory is a man, / Dat's tarnal full ob mettle" (qtd. in Lhamon, *Jump* 100–101).

13. This history of Jackson's war against the Second Bank of the United States is drawn primarily from Robert V. Remini's book *Andrew Jackson and the Bank War: A Study in the Growth of Presidential Power*.

14. The reference to Nicholas Biddle is implied rather than explicitly stated in the line, "I teld dem dare be Ole Nick, / Wat wants de bank renew; / He gib me so much mony, / O lor, dey want it too." The tune continues its commentary on the Bank War with the lines, "O den I go to Washinton / Wid bank memorial; / But find dey tork sick nonsense, / I spend my time wid Sal." Another minstrel song called "Jim Brown" published in the *Jim Along Josey Roarer* songster published at 52 Chatham Street, New York, and 11 N. Sixth Street, Philadelphia, extends this critique of Biddle with the lines, "I play upon de fife—I play upon de fiddle. / I'm opposed to de bank, an don't like Biddle."

15. The identity of the author of this minstrel tune is uncertain. Sam Dennison notes that the song "was sung by George W. Dixon and Bob Farrell, both of whom claimed authorship of the song. Another blackface performer of the period, George Nichols, claimed credit for the piece, although Farrell is usually conceded the dubious honor" (58–59). And Barbara Lewis writes, "According to T. Allston Brown, George Washington Dixon sang his prize extravaganza 'Zip Coon' on the stage of the Arch Street Theatre on June 19, 1834. The S. Foster Damon songbook agrees that 'Zip Coon' was first performed and published in 1834, but in that reference (with George Odell indicated as a source), it is Bob Farrell who is credited with introducing the song" (267).

16. Jackson's veto message to Congress is contained in the second volume of *A Compilation of the Messages and Papers of the Presidents, 1789–1897*, which was edited by James D. Richardson. See pp. 576–91.

17. Arthur M. Schlesinger, Jr., explains that hard money policy advocates "reiterated constantly that they had no intention, as their opponents charged, of doing away with the banking system and establishing an exclusively metallic currency. As Calhoun stated the issue with characteristic precision, 'The

question is, not between credit and no credit, as some would have us believe, but in what form credit can best perform the functions of a sound and safe currency'" (525).

18. David R. Roediger examines the evolution of this analogy between wage-labor capitalism and chattel slavery in *The Wages of Whiteness: Race and the Making of the American Working Class*. Roediger observes how "instances of comparison between wage labor and chattel slavery between 1830 and 1860 were . . . both insistent and embarrassed. They could not have been otherwise" (66). As for the ubiquity of this comparison in "the labor and radical Democratic press of the 1840s," Roediger writes, "*white slavery* was the most common phrasing of metaphors regarding white workers' oppression with *slavery of wages* second and *wage slavery* a very distant third" (72). Roediger adds that while this analogy had its origins with Jacksonian Democrats, by 1860 many labor radicals "had come to support the Republican party, where they were joined by a large number of abolitionists" (80). Concomitant with this shift was an embrace of free labor ideology by wage-earning Northerners, which put them at odds with proslavery Southerners.

19. Walter Benn Michaels explains how monetary metaphors, labor, and the desire for self-possession converge in his book *The Gold Standard and the Logic of Naturalism* (1987). Michaels's observations can be applied to an examination of minstrelsy's monetary preoccupations, and help us better understand the constitutive differences upon which money and minstrelsy both depend, and which Stowe's novel worked out. Michaels describes literary production as the means by which an author produces—and reproduces—herself. The desire to write, he notes, is the desire to possess oneself. His exemplar is Charlotte Perkins Gilman's "The Yellow Wallpaper" (1892), in which "being oneself depends on owning oneself, and owning oneself depends on producing oneself" (13). Producing, writes Michaels, "is thus a kind of buying—it gives you title to yourself—and a kind of selling too—your labor in making yourself is sold for the self you have made" (13). Marks on paper, then, represent an author's desire for self-possession—the desire to produce and consume the self. The body of Gilman's unnamed narrator, like the body of her text (her diary) and the body of the text that contains it ("The Yellow Wallpaper"), is always already the site of market exchange. Each is, in Michaels's economy, "a subject in the market" (28). Drawing an analogy to paper money—more marks on paper—Michaels observes a similar kind of representational self-possession. Comparing Carrie Meeber's desire "to be equal to [the] feeling [of pathos] written upon her countenance" in Theodore Dreiser's *Sister Carrie* (1900) to paper money under the gold standard, Michaels writes, "The desire to live up to the look on your face (to become what is written on your face) is the desire to be equal to oneself (to transform that writing into marks). It is, in the logic of the gold standard, the desire to make yourself equal to your face value, to become gold" (22). This difference between face value and the self, however, is essential and constitutive.

As Michaels puts it, "to achieve that equality is to efface both writing as writing and money as money; it is to become not Carrie but Hurstwood, a corpse in a New York flophouse. This is why the discrepancy is constitutive—when the self becomes equal to its body, as Dreiser sees it, it dies" (22).

20. This skit, which appears on pp. 11–15 of George Christy's *Essence of Old Kentucky* (1852), is part of what W. T. Lhamon, Jr., would call the same "lore cycle" as "De New York Nigger," which Lhamon examines closely in *Raising Cain* (see especially pp. 46–55). In "De New York Nigger," abolitionist and founder of the American Tract Society Arthur Tappan runs off with the narrator's mixed-race lover: "He walk a little furder an tink he die a laffin, / To see his Dinah walkin' wid Massa Arfy Tappan. / Ole Bobolition Glory, he live an die in story, / De black man's friend, wid de black man's hourii" (qtd. in Lhamon, *Raising* 48).

21. "New Jim Brown, 'Bout de Sputed Territory" appears in the *Jim Along Josey Roarer: An Entire New Collection of Negro Songs* published by Turner and Fisher, 52 Chatham Street, New York, and 11 N. Sixth Street, Philadelphia. The song comments upon the "Aroostook War," which grew out of a border dispute between the United States, Great Britain, and the colonial government of New Brunswick. Until 1842, Great Britain and the United States each claimed ownership of both sides of the upper St. John River valley. This dispute appears to remain unresolved at the time this song was written, hence the narrator's description of what Maine *will* gain when the border is redrawn. For a detailed explanation of this border dispute, including descriptions of principal actors like New Brunswick Lieutenant Governor Sir John Harvey—the "John Harvy" referred to in the song—see Gagnon.

22. As Eric Foner has noted, Salmon P. Chase was not just the architect of the greenbacks; he was almost single-handedly responsible for transforming the American antislavery movement from a moral crusade to a political movement. Foner writes, "Chase developed an interpretation of American history which convinced thousands of northerners that anti-slavery was the intended policy of the founders of the nation, and was fully compatible with the Constitution. He helped develop the idea that southern slaveholders, organized politically as a Slave Power, were conspiring to dominate the national government, reverse the policy of the founding fathers, and make slavery the ruling interest of the republic" (73). This connection between Chase's monetary policies and his antislavery politics would not have been lost on Griffin and Christy's audiences.

23. In a 1975 *American Quarterly* article entitled "Blackface Minstrelsy and Jacksonian Ideology," Alexander Saxton attributes this song to Dan Emmett. However, Emmett appears to have penned his own take on legal tender fiat currency in the form of "Greenbacks! New Song for the Times," which contains the lyrics: "How are you Green-backs ten or twenty! / Four forty on the turnpike gate; / How are you Father Abra'm? / From one to five, I have got plenty!" Both songs were performed by Bryant's Minstrels. Hans Nathan clari-

fies the relationship of the two versions to each other in "Two Inflation Songs of the Civil War."

24. See Zwarg's essay, "Fathering and Blackface in *Uncle Tom's Cabin*."

25. Esther Cleophes Quinn reminisced about Rice's attire: "His display of jewels was most ridiculous. In the folds of his cravat would nestle a cluster pin, containing eight or ten costly gems, each unlike, and sufficient in size and luster to do service alone. His sunshiny waistcoat would show for buttons double rows of gold guineas, but sometimes this extraordinary style would be supplemented by an even more unique set of fastenings in the way of a representation of coins of all nations, one each of the highest denomination of the different countries being used." This description of Rice was found on a newspaper clipping dated August 25, 1895, that was glued in the back of an edition of John Briggs's *The History of Jim Crow* contained in the Boston Public Library's Allen A. Brown collection (**T.87.6). The original source remains unknown.

26. Curiously, there are two characters named Sambo in *Uncle Tom's Cabin*. The first appears at the slave warehouse where Tom is sold to Legree, and mocks Adolph's appearance. The second is waiting for Legree at his plantation when he arrives. The former is described as being full of "trick and grimace," but the same could be said for the latter.

27. In *Raising Cain*, Lhamon writes, "Eliza is interesting enough as an abolitionist's stereotype—mulatta Madonna crosses Ohio River with child to freedom. But what made her legendary was Stowe's addition of minstrel leaps and contorted twists" (97). He goes on to observe how "Eliza's bloody crossing became the cover image for the book, the scene featured on posters for the subsequent Tom plays when it went back onto the minstrel stage, and the central image of the Tom movies" (97).

28. See Fredrickson 110–18.

29. I refer here to Stowe's observations about the readability of *Uncle Tom's Cabin*, which, as she describes in *A Key to Uncle Tom's Cabin*, explain why her first novel did not accurately represent slavery. "A work which should represent it strictly as it is," she writes, "would be a work which could not be read. And all works which ever mean to give pleasure must draw a veil somewhere, or they cannot succeed" (5).

30. This curious mixture of racialism and religion was part and parcel of Stowe's historical and cultural milieu. Take, for example, Charles Kingsley's *Alton Locke* (1850), in which the author observes, "The black is more like an ape than the white man—he is—the fact is there; and no notions of an abstract right will put that down: nothing but another fact—a mightier, more universal fact—Jesus of Nazareth died for the negro as well as for the white. Looked at apart from Him, each race, each individual of mankind, stands separate and alone, owing no more brotherhood to each other than wolf to wolf, or pike to pike—himself a mightier beast of prey—even as he has proven himself in every age" (qtd. in Banton, *Idea* 67). Michael Banton's paraphrase of this quote,

"Men and races are unequal in nature but equal in Christ" (67), summarizes Stowe's romantic racialism as much as it does Kingsley's argument.

31. The experiences of George Kunkel chronicled here are drawn from an interview with Kunkel published in the May 27, 1883, issue of the *Commercial Gazette* entitled "The Original Uncle Tom Tells How the Play Was First Produced."

32. The mansion depicted on the back of the 2001 Kentucky State commemorative quarter is Federal Hill. According to the Web site maintained by the United States Mint, Stephen Foster wrote the song "My Old Kentucky Home, Good-Night!" while visiting Federal Hill in 1852 ("Celebrate"). This myth of the song's origin whitewashes not only Foster's minstrel past, but also the song itself. My pun on this "big house" as the counterpoint of the slave cabin is entirely intentional.

## 2. REAL CHANGE

1. See, for example, William C. Brownell's review in the *Nation*, which criticizes the story of Bras-Coupé and the murder of Clemence for unduly taxing the reader's emotions "in behalf of a cause already won."

2. See the anonymous review of the novel in the December 1880 *Atlantic Monthly*, which describes Frowenfeld as "the chorus; for though his action occasionally affects the story, his chief function is to ask the questions and bring out the prior conditions, and especially, as we have hinted, to be the external conscience." Scholars seldom fail to cite this review when writing about *The Grandissimes* or disagree with the reviewer.

3. See, for example, Schölin Tipping's "The Sinking Plantation-House: Cable's Narrative Method in *The Grandissimes*," which posits that "the Frowenfelds demonstrate the liking for pattern and order which is a part of their religious belief in a universe where all is arranged for the best" (66).

4. See, for example, the "Topics of the Time" column in the November 1878 issue (volume 17, issue 1, pp. 146–49), which dismisses the Greenback Party, or the same column in the October 1879 issue (volume 18, issue 6, pp. 935–39), which speaks offhandedly of such topics as specie payments, the silver question, and the soft money question.

5. The exact dollar figure is disputed. William G. Sumner's *A History of American Currency* puts the sum of greenbacks in circulation at the end of the Civil War at $428,160,569 (211); Henry V. Poor's *The Money Question* lists the circulating greenback debt as $433,160,569 (102).

6. Economics professor Ranjit S. Dighe lucidly summarizes the origins of the Civil War debt and the choice between devaluation and deflation in *The Historian's "Wizard of Oz": Reading L. Frank Baum's Classic as a Political and Monetary Allegory*.

7. See Unger 138–39, which examines the Social Science Association, an or-

ganization whose members constituted a who's who of middle-class dissention, and who represented the hard money interest. Members included Daniel Coit Gilman, president of Yale and later first president of Johns Hopkins University, George William Curtis of *Harper's Weekly*, and William Cullen Bryant.

8. Pages 59–60 of Walter T. K. Nugent's *The Money Question During Reconstruction* flesh out greenbackism's differential definition against gold monometallism.

9. Nugent writes, "The greenbackers and the gold monometallists split completely on policy, but they both believed and used the rhetoric of civilization, law, prevailing monetary principles, and producerism. They ranked the rhetoric differently, however. . . . Both groups claimed Adam Smith, Jean-Baptiste Say, and various of the Utilitarians, as ideological ancestors" (*Money and American Society* 38).

10. See Halévy, who writes, "What is known as Utilitarianism, or Philosophical Radicalism, can be defined as nothing but an attempt to apply the principles of Newton to the affairs of politics and of morals" (6).

11. A Greenback Party history published in 1952 continues the tradition of quoting Mill, noting, "An inconvertible paper made a legal tender is universally admitted to be money" (*Greenback Party* 18), even though in his *Principles of Political Economy* (1848) Mill denied that increasing the money supply would stimulate economic growth—a central tenet of producerism (Unger 39).

12. Prior to 1876, most Americans had no idea that silver had been demonetized at all (Weinstein 9–10).

13. See John Stuart Mill's *Utilitarianism* (1861), which claims: "The creed which accepts as the foundation of morals 'utility' or the 'greatest happiness principle' holds that actions are right in proportion as they tend to promote happiness; wrong as they tend to produce the reverse of happiness. By happiness is intended pleasure and the absence of pain; by unhappiness, pain and the privation of pleasure" (7).

14. See Cable's letter to his mother, Rebecca Boardman Cable, dated January 10, 1866, in which he describes "the beauties of the *science* of Trade" (Rubin 33).

15. Cable's references to social science can be found in at least two sources. While en route to Toronto by train in November 1889 Cable "talked social science" with an Englishman during a layover in Buffalo (Bikle 207–8). And in his essay "My Politics" Cable wrote: "Even as a novelist I felt bound to study social science from as many points of view as I could" (23).

16. Cable actually hedges on the year of the Nancanou-Fusilier duel that leaves Aurora, née Aurora De Grapion, a widow. When she first visits the Grandissimes' counting room, Aurora observes that eighteen years have passed "since any representative of the De Grapion line had met a Grandissime face to face" (121). Agricola puts the duel twenty years before the time-present (328). Doing the math, however, shows that the duel took place seventeen years ear-

lier. The ambiguity of the year is intentional, since it allowed for the interpellation of the reader in the years subsequent to 1878, namely the years that the novel was serialized and thereafter.

17. Samuel Dana Horton, secretary of the American delegation to the Monetary Conference of 1878 and author of such works as *Silver and Gold and Their Relation to the Problem of Resumption* (1876) and *The Silver Pound and England's Monetary Policy since the Restoration* (1887), proclaimed Newton to be the father of modern bimetallism.

18. Louis D. Rubin, Jr., observes that "Bibi" underwent little revision prior to being included in *The Grandissimes* "apparently with little change" (81). Arlin Turner hedges even less than Rubin in his assessment, noting only that "Bibi" "became the episode of Bras-Coupé" (*George W. Cable* 54).

19. Section 4 of the Fourteenth Amendment validates the public debt of the United States while declaring void any debts incurred "in aid of insurrection or rebellion against the United States," including "any claim for the loss or emancipation of any slave." That the Fourteenth Amendment extends civil rights and equal protection under the law for African Americans while addressing public debt is a coincidence too rich to avoid comment.

20. When Honoré retells "The Story of Bras-Coupé" to Frowenfeld, the apothecary asks, "And you suffered this thing to take place?" Honoré deflects the confrontation by claiming "they lied to me—said they would not harm him!" (191). But in his heart Honoré knows that his silence was partly to blame. This is why, when Honoré first meets Frowenfeld by the graves of the immigrant's family, he notes that he has "some interest in two of these graves, sir, as I suppose—you will pardon my freedom—you have in the other four" (36). One of these graves is Bras-Coupé's, hence Honoré's financial metaphor: the "interest" of which he speaks is the interest one pays on a debt. The debt Honoré owes isn't shrinking, but accruing, and his silence aggravates rather than ameliorates this debt.

21. In "The Freedman's Case in Equity," Cable writes, "The amended Constitution holds him [the late Southern slave] up in his new political rights as well as a mere constitution can. On the other hand, certain enactments of Congress, trying to reach further, have lately been made void by the highest court of the nation" (2).

22. "By the 1890s," writes Allen Weinstein, "supporters of both bimetallism and the gold standard had become clearly identified with different class and sectional interest groups, and they defended their respective claims with far greater passion than displayed during the seventies" (358).

3. THE GOLD STANDARD OF THE PASSING NOVEL

1. M. Giulia Fabi exemplifies this trend when she writes, "In pre-Harlem Renaissance African-American fiction the representation of the passer's peculiar status is aimed at drawing attention to the fixity and constrictiveness of the

racialized black and white subject positions between which he or she has to choose rather than the fluidity of personal identity or the pleasures of 'experimenting with multiple subject positions'" (5).

2. Sundquist demonstrates how Homer Plessy's arrest was a staged act of civil disobedience and explains how this staging was prefigured by Twain's novel. See "Mark Twain and Homer Plessy."

3. Here, Chesnutt is riffing on a rhetorical technique popularized by racialists of the period, who likened race to specie. Take, for example, Robert Knox's 1850 theory of race, *The Races of Men*, in which the author comments, "With me, race, or hereditary descent, is everything; it stamps the man" (13).

4. In his true autobiography, *Along This Way*, Johnson celebrates the fact that most reviewers of *The Autobiography of an Ex-Colored Man* "accepted it as a human document," since he "had done the book with the intention of its being so taken" (238). Mar Gallego argues that the novel "'passes' for autobiography in order to revise and update all these traditions [the 'passing' genre, the motif of the 'tragic mulatto,' Du Boisian theory, and the sentimental novel] in an attempt to deconstruct the functioning parameters of the representation of both race and identity imposed by the dominant culture" (49).

5. This conflict is described by Richard Timberlake, who writes, "When this doctrine adopts real bills, in addition to real gold, as a supplemental guide to the creation of money, it loses its validity. Real gold is an effective anchor because its supplies are limited and its money price is fixed under the rules of the gold standard. But real bills may have any money price that bankers or central bankers attach to them, and their supplies are unlimited" (193).

6. Consuela Francis notes that this anxiety "stem[med] from the movement's architects slowly realizing that aesthetic achievement does not necessarily break through the reified conception of African American difference that whites bring to African American literature" (52). She goes on to write, "The success of this New Negro movement depended upon 'race co-operation,' the creation and articulation of a racial individuality that would give the black artist a place from which to speak. This racial individuality would allow black artists to contribute something new and significant to American culture. To do so, however, meant reifying and focusing on black difference, those qualities that most set African Americans apart from white America" (54).

7. Locke's tendency to state issues of racial discrimination in financial and/or monetary terms is clear in his essay "Negro Education Bids for Par" (1925). An extended economic metaphor in itself, the essay begins, "The stock of Negro education has a heavy traditional discount, and is chronically 'under the market.' Whatever the local variation, one can usually count upon a sag in both standard and facilities for the education of the Negro, section for section, program for program, below the top current level, so that to reach relative parity with surrounding systems of education, Negro education must somehow 'beat the market'" (567).

8. Houston Baker, Jr., paraphrases Locke: "You have confined me to the language of RACE . . . and I shall convert it into a weapon and creative instrument of massed, *national*, racial will" (*Modernism* 80).

9. As Jean Toomer's refusal to market himself as a black author demonstrates, this process is fraught with paradox, for New Negro cultural production is predicated upon the commodification of racial essentialism and the investment of readers in its significance (Lutz 169).

10. Kenneth Robert Janken, White's biographer, describes how White assisted others who shared his vision of such a cultural revolution. While White may not have founded the New Negro cultural movement, writes Janken, White "attempted to found a National Institute of Negro Letters, Music, and Art, and upon hearing that photography magnate George Eastman—who had endowed a conservatory in Rochester, New York, and had developed an interest in helping to found one for Negro music—White set out to convince him and other philanthropists of the efficacy of including in such a project drama and literature as well" (91).

11. Eichengreen argues that the Fed responded to the stock market rather than the other way around. He observes, for instance, that in 1928 the Fed sought to tighten domestic credit in order to put the brakes on the stock market boom (216). But he also notes that Federal Reserve Board members made only a halfhearted attempt at discouraging member banks from borrowing from the Fed and extending loans to brokers and speculators (217).

12. Huggins writes, "The creation of the 'New Negro' failed, but it was an American failure, having its counterparts in countless similar frustrated promotions" (303).

13. In "Racialization: The Genealogy and Critique of a Concept," Barot and Bird trace the term "racialization" to its origins. Curiously, deracialization seems to predate racialization by some nineteen years, deracialization having appeared in 1899 according to the *Oxford English Dictionary*.

## 4. BLACK IS . . . AN' BLACK AIN'T

1. In Littlefield's interpretation, Dorothy is a kind of "Miss Everyman," the Scarecrow stands in for midwestern farmers, the Tin Woodman represents the eastern workingman in the age of industrialization, and the Cowardly Lion is none other than William Jennings Bryan himself (52–53). Geer and Rochon agree that Baum's novel is a Populist allegory, but they disagree with Littlefield on which characters represent what historical figures. Central to their argument is "the belief that Baum used Dorothy to represent William Jennings Bryan" (60). Rockoff's treatment of the novel more closely resembles Littlefield's. He observes that "Dorothy represents America" itself, and he agrees with Littlefield that the Cowardly Lion stands in for Bryan in Baum's allegory (745, 748). Despite these minor differences of characterization, all of these scholars describe

the novel's monetary symbolism as part and parcel of what Gretchen Ritter has called "the imagined political universe of the Populists" (174).

2. In this allegorical reading the yellow brick road represents the gold standard. It may head in the right direction, but only silver and gold together will help Dorothy, the farmer's daughter, get back to where she belongs. It is worth noting that the hard times Dorothy's aunt and uncle in Kansas experience at the beginning of the novel are resolved when Dorothy makes her return from the Land of Oz—a leap made possible by her silver slippers.

3. Ranjit Dighe teases out the details of Littlefield's allegorical interpretation, and the additions historians have made to it over the last forty years, in his book *The Historian's "Wizard of Oz": Reading L. Frank Baum's Classic as a Political and Monetary Allegory*, which contains the text of the first edition of Baum's novel in its entirety. Unless otherwise noted, page number references in citations following quotes from Baum's text denote their location within Dighe's book. As for the Emerald City, Dighe describes it as "a glorious metaphor of how a fiat-money system works" (109n). Ever since the gold standard was abolished in 1933, he writes, "the government is no longer obligated to exchange gold or silver for dollars, so dollar bills today are only valuable because they are generally accepted as payment. If people suddenly decided that dollar bills were worthless pieces of paper, the dollar's value would evaporate, just as people in the Emerald City, if they removed their green glasses, would see that the City is not so green after all" (109n).

4. Note that Ellison is alluding specifically to the novel, and especially to the monetary props that are absent from the movie. Given the film's stature in the popular cultural imagination, it's not surprising that the book and its differences from the film have been largely forgotten. As a scholar of the American literary tradition, Ellison would have been mindful of the differences between the novel and the film.

5. Alan Nadel's *Invisible Criticism: Ralph Ellison and the American Canon* examines Ellison's allusions to Lewis Mumford's *The Golden Day*, Herman Melville's *Benito Cereno*, several of Ralph Waldo Emerson's essays, and Mark Twain's *Adventures of Huckleberry Finn*. Valerie Bonita Gray limits her examination of Ellison's allusive approach to Melville's *Benito Cereno* and *Moby-Dick* in her book, *"Invisible Man's" Literary Heritage: "Benito Cereno" and "Moby Dick."* Rudolf F. Dietze's *Ralph Ellison: The Genesis of an Artist* should be appended to this list, since four of its five chapters trace Ellison's allusions to Richard Wright, Fyodor Dostoyevsky, and T. S. Eliot, among others.

6. Chapter 4 of Busby's book, entitled "The Actor's Shadows: Ellison's Literary Antecedents," offers an exhaustive survey of *Invisible Man* criticism focused upon the novel's allusions. Busby also offers a comprehensive list of the philosophers, world authors, and popular cultural voices woven into the novel.

7. "Twentieth-Century Fiction and the Black Mask of Humanity" was writ-

ten in 1946 (prior to the publication of *Invisible Man*), but wasn't published until 1953.

8. Ras the Exhorter, who embodies the essentialist conception of racial difference (hence the pun on his name in the epigraph to this chapter, which was drawn from Ellison's original typescript), reinforces this connection later in the novel when he tells the narrator that the money the Brotherhood pays him "bleed black blood, mahn" (371).

9. When the narrator is driving Mr. Norton around the campus, he describes the trustee as having "a face pink like St. Nicholas', topped with a shock of silk white hair" (37). Later, after their adventure at the Golden Day, the narrator refers to Mr. Norton as "a small silken-haired, white-suited St. Nicholas" (107). The legend of St. Nicholas centers upon the bags of gold he gave to three daughters of a poor man so each could have a dowry and get married.

10. Aside from explicitly questioning faith in the inherent value of racial difference, this proclamation not only equates the loss of this faith with a stock market crash, but anticipates *the* stock market crash to which the narrator's own fall from proverbial grace (or blind faith) will be likened in the chapters ahead.

11. Burnside, one of the vets who feels the trustee's pulse, observes that "instead of beating, it *vibrates*" (78). The metaphoric connection between Mr. Norton's blood and gold that this illness undercuts, meanwhile, is rendered more explicitly in Ellison's original draft of the novel, in which the vet who feels the trustee's pulse remarks, "Your pulse, it vibrates. It's metallic!" (Ralph Ellison Papers).

12. The exact denomination that the fake coins emulate is spelled out in the original draft of the novel in which Tatlock says, "I got six of those five dollar gold pieces." Another participant in the battle royal replies, "Me too—Hey! these ain't no money!" (Ralph Ellison Papers).

13. Undoing the 1834 legislation that revised the dollar's gold content, FDR redefined the dollar as 13.71 grains of gold, down 59 percent from 23.22 grains.

14. The original draft of the novel is more straightforward, stating that the narrator "landed in college [d]uring the early days of the Depression" (Ralph Ellison Papers).

15. Jack notes that the bills the narrator receives along with his new paper identity "will pay your debts" (310). Here, Ellison is punning on the proclamation printed on all Federal Reserve Notes, "this note is legal tender for all debts, public and private." Note that the advance he gets from the Brotherhood is the exact same amount of money that Lucius Brockway got for thinking up the Liberty Paints slogan "If It's Optic White, It's the Right White," a perversion of "If you're white, you're right." No small amount of irony here, for the narrator, in his Brotherhood-prescribed role, will do the same kind of obfuscation and whitewashing as Brockway's paint/slogan.

16. A handwritten note of Ellison's included in the original draft of the novel draws a more explicit parallel between the bank and the narrator. Ellison

writes that the bank "is a symbol of himself. He is willing to grin for money. His breaking it betrays fear that this is what he will encounter in [the] Brotherhood. A foreshadowing" (Ralph Ellison Papers).

17. Note the monetary significance of the names of these two members of the Brotherhood: Jack is slang for money, while Tobitt is a homonym for "two bit."

18. The self-reflexive nature of the narrator's vision through the green spectacles is rendered intelligible when the narrator tries to quote from 1 Corinthians 13:12 and thinks, "'For now we see as through a glass darkly but then—but then—' I couldn't remember the rest" (491). The full quote, "For now we see through a glass, darkly; but then face to face: now I know in part; but then shall I know even as also I am known," is often translated as "For now we see *in a mirror*, dimly" (emphasis added). To look through the lenses, then, is to look in the mirror and see one's reflection.

19. Joseph T. Skerrett, Jr., argues that Ellison felt the anxiety of Wright's influence and therefore often downplayed the impact Wright's story had upon the underground themes of *Invisible Man*. According to Skerrett, Ellison exhibited this anxiety by citing Dostoyevsky's *Notes from the Underground* as the primary influence for the novel's prologue and epilogue instead of Wright's "The Man Who Lived Underground."

20. The building is Independence Hall, and it calls to mind the invisible man's job mixing Optic White paint to be used on a national monument (202).

21. Implicit in this demonstration is a denunciation of passing novels and strategic essentialism described in chapter 3. Again, pretending to agree is the same thing as agreeing, and the passing genre turns this agreement into an aesthetic not unlike Trueblood and his story of incest.

22. Ellison thereby prefigures Walter Benn Michaels's critique of early-twentieth-century pluralism, which unwittingly mapped racial difference onto nationalism in the process of grafting race onto culture.

23. William Walling summarizes the influence of the Black Arts Movement upon Ellison's reputation when he writes, "By 1968, it was clear, Ellison's position had become distinctly vulnerable from a separatist point of view" (127). Noting that Ellison was "one of the most consistently outspoken critics of the black arts movement," Walling chronicles the dismay of writers and critics like Julius Lester, Eldridge Cleaver, Hoyt Fuller, Larry Neal, and Addison Gayle, Jr., with Ellison's perceived role as a white apologist (128). This critical reception, notes Walling, reflected a growing hostility among black students of a younger generation. "By 1969," he writes, "the consequences of all this for Ellison's reputation were evident. Appearing as a speaker at Oberlin College in April, Ellison was attacked by the black students there for the manner in which he had treated Ras the Destroyer in *Invisible Man* . . . was accused of being an 'Uncle Tom' during the post-talk discussion, and was coolly informed by the students as a group that he did not have 'anything' to say to them" (128).

24. After he saw the pedestrian cinematic adaptation of Richard Wright's *Native Son* (1940) that starred Wright himself, Ellison vowed not to allow his novel to be debased by Hollywood. Accordingly, Ellison forbade even his literary executors from selling the rights to his novel to any filmmaker. So Sidney Lumet's desire to make a film version of Ellison's novel was thwarted from the beginning.

# BIBLIOGRAPHY

Adams, C. F., Jr. "The Currency Debate of 1873–74." *North American Review* May 1874: 111–66.

Adams, J. C., A. K. Miller, and Hugh Craig. "Reform of the Currency." *North American Review* Dec. 1896: 743–52.

Aiken, George L. *Uncle Tom's Cabin; or, Life among the Lowly. A Domestic Drama in Six Acts.* New York: Samuel French, 1858. *Uncle Tom's Cabin and American Culture.* Ed. Stephen Railton. 2005. 10 Mar. 2006 <http://www .iath.virginia.edu/utc/onstage/scripts/aikenhp.html>.

Ashworth, John. *Slavery, Capitalism, and Politics in the Antebellum Republic.* Vol. 1: Commerce and Compromise, 1820–1850. Cambridge: Cambridge UP, 1995.

Baker, Houston A., Jr. "A Forgotten Prototype: *The Autobiography of an Ex-Colored Man* and *Invisible Man*." *Virginia Quarterly Review* 49 (1973): 433–49.

———. *Modernism and the Harlem Renaissance.* Chicago: U of Chicago P, 1987.

*Bamboozled.* Dir. Spike Lee. 2000. DVD. New Line Home Entertainment, 2001.

Banton, Michael. *The Idea of Race.* Boulder: Westview Press, 1977.

Baraka, Amiri. "Primitive World: An Anti-Nuclear Jazz Musical." *The LeRoi Jones/Amiri Baraka Reader.* Ed. William J. Harris. New York: Thunder's Mouth, 1999. 400–49.

Barot, Rohit, and John Bird. "Racialization: The Genealogy and Critique of a Concept." *Ethnic and Racial Studies* 21 (2001): 601–18.

Barrett, Lindon. *Blackness and Value: Seeing Double.* Cambridge: Cambridge UP, 1999.

Baum, L. Frank. *The New Wizard of Oz.* Indianapolis: Bobbs-Merrill, 1903.

———. *The Wonderful Wizard of Oz.* 1900. Dighe 42–130.

Beard, Charles A. *An Economic Interpretation of the Constitution of the United States.* New York: Macmillan, 1913.

Bikle, Lucy Leffingwell Cable. *George Washington Cable: His Life and Letters.* New York: Charles Scribner's Sons, 1928.

Birdoff, Harry. *The World's Greatest Hit:* Uncle Tom's Cabin. New York: S. F. Vanni, 1947.

Bowers, E. "How Are You Green-Backs!" 1863. Sheet music: Minstrels: Bryant's Minstrels, Harvard Theatre Collection, Houghton Library, Harvard University.

Brown, William Wells. *Clotel; or, The President's Daughter: A Narrative of Slave Life in the United States*. London: Partridge and Oakey, 1853. Ed. Robert S. Levine. Boston: Bedford/St. Martin's, 2000.

Brownell, William C. "Cable's *The Grandissimes*." Rev. of *The Grandissimes* by George Washington Cable. *Nation* 9 Dec. 1880: 415–16. Rpt. in Turner, *Critical Essays* 17–21.

Bryan, William Jennings. "Has the Election Settled the Money Question?" *North American Review* Dec. 1896: 701–10.

Busby, Mark. *Ralph Ellison*. Twayne's United States Authors Series 582. Boston: G. K. Hall, 1991.

Cable, George Washington. "The Freedman's Case in Equity." *The Silent South*. 1885. Patterson Smith Reprint Series in Criminology, Law Enforcement, and Social Problems 57. Montclair, NJ: Patterson Smith, 1969. 1–39.

———. *The Grandissimes: A Story of Creole Life*. 1880. Introd. Michael Kreyling. New York: Penguin, 1988.

———. "My Politics." *The Negro Question: A Selection of Writings on Civil Rights in the South*. Ed. Arlin Turner. New York: Doubleday, 1958. 1–27.

Callahan, John F., ed. *The Collected Essays of Ralph Ellison*. New York: Modern Library-Random House, 1995.

Carpenter, Seth B., and William M. Rodgers III. "The Disparate Labor Market Impacts of Monetary Policy." *Labor History* 46 (2005): 57–77.

"Celebrate the Launch of the Kentucky Quarter." *The United States Mint*. 23 Sept. 2002. 9 Jan. 2006. <http://www.usmint.gov/mint_programs/50sq_program/states/KY/ index.cfm?action=KY_strike>.

Chesnutt, Charles W. *The House behind the Cedars*. 1900. Ridgewood: Gregg, 1968.

———. *The Marrow of Tradition*. 1901. *Charles W. Chesnutt: Stories, Novels, and Essays*. Ed. Werner Sollors. New York: Library of America, 2002. 463–718.

Christy, George. *Essence of Old Kentucky*. New York: Dick & Fitzgerald, 1852.

Cockrell, Dale. *Demons of Disorder: Early Blackface Minstrels and Their World*. Cambridge: Cambridge UP, 1997.

*CoinFacts.com*. 2005. Collector's Universe, Inc. 11 Jan. 2006 <http://www.coin facts.com/>.

"Conclusion of Mr. Benton's Speech; on Mr. Clay's Resolutions Relative to the Removal of the Deposites." *Workingman's Advocate* 8 Feb. 1834: 1.

Conway, H. J. *Uncle Tom's Cabin; or, Life among the Lowly. A drama in 5 parts founded on Mrs. H. B. Stowe's powerful and popular work of the same title, written for the Boston Museum*. [Unpublished, 1852.] *Uncle Tom's Cabin & American Culture*. Ed. Stephen Railton. 2005. 10 Mar. 2006 <http://www.iath.virginia.edu/utc/onstage/ scripts/conwayhp.html>.

Crawford, Arthur Whipple. *Monetary Management under the New Deal: The*

*Evolution of a Managed Currency System—Its Problems and Results.* Washington, D.C.: American Council on Public Affairs, 1940.

Crowther, Samuel. "Magic Money and Speculation." *Saturday Evening Post* 10 Mar. 1934: 8+.

*The Dark Side of the Rainbow.* 22 June 2005. 21 July 2005 <http://members.cox.net/stegokitty/ dsotr_pages/dsotr.htm>.

Dennison, Sam. *Scandalize My Name: Black Imagery in American Popular Music.* New York: Garland, 1982.

Dietze, Rudolf F. "Crainway and Son: Ralph Ellison's *Invisible Man* as Seen through the Perspective of Twain, Crane, and Hemingway." *Delta* 18 (1984): 25–46.

———. *Ralph Ellison: The Genesis of an Artist.* Band 70. Nurenberg: Verlag Hans Carl, 1982.

Dighe, Ranjit S., ed. *The Historian's "Wizard of Oz": Reading L. Frank Baum's Classic as a Political and Monetary Allegory.* Westport, CT: Praeger, 2002.

Earle, Jonathan H. *Jacksonian Antislavery and the Politics of Free Soil, 1824–1854.* Chapel Hill: U of North Carolina P, 2004.

"Effects of Unlimited Silver." *New York Tribune* 1 Jan. 1878: 5.

Eichengreen, Barry. *Golden Fetters: The Gold Standard and the Great Depression, 1919–1939.* NBER Series on Long-Term Factors in Economic Development. New York: Oxford UP, 1992.

Ellison, Ralph. "Change the Joke and Slip the Yoke." Callahan 100–12.

———. *Invisible Man.* 1952. 2nd Vintage International Edition. New York: Vintage-Random House, 1995.

———. National Book Award acceptance speech. 1 Sept. 2005. <http://www.nationalbook.org/nbaacceptspeech_rellison.html>.

———. Ralph Ellison Papers. Boxes 142–146, ms. Library of Congress, Washington, D.C.

———. "Society, Morality and the Novel." Callahan 694–725.

———. "To Albert Murray." 9 Aug. 1954. *Trading Twelves: The Selected Letters of Ralph Ellison and Albert Murray.* Ed. Albert Murray and John F. Callahan. New York: Modern Library-Random House, 2000. 78–81.

———. "Twentieth-Century Fiction and the Black Mask of Humanity." Callahan 81–99.

Emerson, Ralph Waldo. "Wealth." 1860. *The Complete Works of Ralph Waldo Emerson.* Vol. 6. 5 Feb. 2005. 1 Sept. 2005 <http://www.rwe.org/>.

Emmett, Dan. "Greenbacks! New Song for the Times." n.d. Sheet music: Minstrels: Emmett, Harvard Theatre Collection, Houghton Library, Harvard University.

Engle, Gary D. *This Grotesque Essence: Plays from the American Minstrel Stage.* Baton Rouge: Louisiana State UP, 1978.

Ernest, John. "Representing Chaos: William Craft's *Running a Thousand Miles for Freedom.*" *PMLA* 121 (2006): 469–83.

Fabi, M. Giulia. *Passing and the Rise of the African American Novel*. Urbana: U of Illinois P, 2001.

Fauset, Jessie Redmon. *Plum Bun: A Novel without a Moral*. 1928. Ed. Deborah McDowell. Black Women Writers Series. Boston: Beacon, 1990.

Fichtelberg, Joseph. *Critical Fictions: Sentiment and the American Market, 1780–1870*. Athens: U of Georgia P, 2003.

Foner, Eric. *Free Soil, Free Labor, Free Men: The Ideology of the Republican Party before the Civil War*. New York: Oxford UP, 1970.

Francis, Consuela. "(Re)Making a Difference: The Harlem Renaissance and the Anxiety of 1926." *Langston Hughes Review* 17 (2002): 49–59.

Fredrickson, George M. *The Black Image in the White Mind: The Debate on Afro-American Character and Destiny, 1817–1914*. New York: Harper and Row, 1971.

Friedman, Milton, and Anna Jacobson Schwartz. *A Monetary History of the United States, 1867–1960*. National Bureau of Economic Research Studies in Business Cycles 12. Princeton: Princeton UP, 1963.

Gagnon, C. "The Border Dispute and the 'Aroostook War.'" *The Upper St. John River Valley Communities*. 31 Jan. 2007. 4 June 2007 <http://www.up perstjohn.com/history/northeastborder.htm>.

Gallego, Mar. *Passing Novels in the Harlem Renaissance: Identity Politics and Textual Strategies*. Forum for European Contributions in African American Studies 8. Münster: Lit Verlag, 2003.

Garrett, Garet. "Concerning Money." *Saturday Evening Post* 3 Feb. 1934: 5+.

———. "Two Chapters in the Story of Gold." *Saturday Evening Post* 3 Mar. 1934: 8+.

Gates, Henry Louis, Jr. "Writing 'Race' and the Difference It Makes." *"Race," Writing, and Difference*. Spec. issue of *Critical Inquiry* 12 (1985): 1–20.

Geer, John G., and Thomas R. Rochon. "William Jennings Bryan on the Yellow Brick Road." *Journal of American Culture* 16.4 (1993): 59–63.

Gilroy, Paul. *Against Race: Imagining Political Culture beyond the Color Line*. Cambridge: Belknap-Harvard UP, 2000.

Goldberg, David Theo. *The Racial State*. Malden, MA: Blackwell, 2002.

Gossett, Thomas F. *Uncle Tom's Cabin and American Culture*. Dallas: Southern Methodist UP, 1985.

Gouge, William M. *A Short History of Paper Money and Banking in the United States, Including an Account of Provincial and Continental Paper Money*. Philadelphia: T. W. Ustick, 1833.

Gray, Valerie Bonita. *"Invisible Man"'s Literary Heritage: "Benito Cereno" and "Moby Dick."* Costerus 12. Amsterdam: Rodopi, 1978.

*Greenback Party History in Brief, 1875 to 1952*. Indianapolis: Greenback Party, 1952.

Gross, Ariela J. *What Blood Won't Tell: A History of Race on Trial in America*. Cambridge: Harvard UP, 2008.

Halévy, Elie. *The Growth of Philosophic Radicalism*. 1934. Trans. Mary Morris. London: Faber & Faber, 1949.

Harper, J. B. "New Jim Brown, 'Bout de Sputed Territory." *Jim Along Josey Roarer: An Entire New Collection of Negro Songs*. New York: Turner and Fisher, n.d.

Hartman, Saidiya V. *Scenes of Subjection: Terror, Slavery, and Self-Making in Nineteenth-Century America*. New York: Oxford UP, 1997.

Hoeller, Hildegard. "Racial Currency: Zora Neale Hurston's 'The Gilded Six-Bits' and the Gold-Standard Debate." *American Literature* 77 (2005): 761–85.

Howard, George C. "Uncle Tom's Religion." *Minstrel Songs*. Allen A. Brown Collection, Boston Public Library.

Huggins, Nathan Irvin. *Harlem Renaissance*. New York: Oxford UP, 1971.

Irish, John P. "The Silver Question." *Overland Monthly* May 1896: 561–73.

Jackson, Lawrence. *Ralph Ellison: Emergence of Genius*. New York: Wiley, 2002.

Jacobson, Matthew Frye. *Whiteness of a Different Color: European Immigrants and the Alchemy of Race*. Cambridge: Harvard UP, 1998.

Janken, Kenneth Robert. *White: The Biography of Walter White, Mr. NAACP*. New York: New Press, 2003.

"Jim Brown." *Jim Along Josey Roarer: An Entire New Collection of Negro Songs*. New York: Turner and Fisher, n.d.

"Jimmy Crow." n.d. Sheet music: Minstrels: T. D. Rice, Harvard Theatre Collection, Houghton Library, Harvard University.

Johnson, James Weldon. *Along This Way: The Autobiography of James Weldon Johnson*. 1933. New York: Viking, 1961.

———. *The Autobiography of an Ex-Colored Man*. 1912. Ed. William L. Andrews. New York: Penguin, 1990.

Knox, Robert. *The Races of Men: A Fragment*. Philadelphia: Lea and Blanchard, 1850. Miami: Mnemosyne, 1969.

Lane, C. D. "The Gold Miner and the Silver Question." *Overland Monthly* Nov. 1896: 585–88.

Larsen, Nella. *Passing*. 1929. New York: Negro Universities-Greenwood, 1969.

Lee, Kun Jong. "Ellison's Racial Variations on American Themes." *African American Review* 30 (1996): 421–40.

Levy, J. C. "Argentiae, or the Silver Problem." *Overland Monthly* Sept. 1896: 314–19.

Lewis, Barbara. "Daddy Blue: The Evolution of the Dark Dandy." *Inside the Minstrel Mask*. Ed. Annemarie Bean, James V. Hatch, and Brooks McNamara. Hanover, NH: Wesleyan UP, 1996. 257–72.

Lewis, David Levering. *When Harlem Was in Vogue*. New York: Penguin, 1997.

Lhamon, W. T., Jr. *Jump Jim Crow: Lost Plays, Lyrics, and Street Prose of the First Atlantic Popular Culture*. Cambridge: Harvard UP, 2003.

————. *Raising Cain: Blackface Performance from Jim Crow to Hip Hop*. Cambridge: Harvard UP, 1998.

Lima, Lázaro. *The Latino Body: Crisis Identities in American Literary and Cultural Memory*. Sexual Cultures Series. New York: New York UP, 2007.

Littlefield, Henry M. "The Wizard of Oz: Parable on Populism." *American Quarterly* 16 (1964): 47–58.

Locke, Alain. Foreword. Locke, *The New Negro* ix–xi.

————. "Negro Education Bids for Par." *Survey Graphic* 54 (1925): 567–70.

————. "The Negro's Contribution to American Art and Literature." *The American Negro*. Philadelphia: American Academy of Political and Social Science, 1928. Vol. 140 of *Annals of the American Academy of Political and Social Science*. 234–47.

————. "The New Negro." Locke, *The New Negro* 3–16.

————, ed. *The New Negro: An Interpretation*. 1925. Introd. Allan H. Spear. Series in American Studies. New York: Johnson Reprint, 1968.

————. *Race Contacts and Interracial Relations: Lectures on the Theory and Practice of Race*. Ed. Jeffrey C. Stewart. Moorland-Spingarn Series. Washington, D.C.: Howard UP, 1992.

Lott, Eric. *Love and Theft: Blackface Minstrelsy and the American Working Class*. Race and American Culture. New York: Oxford UP, 1995.

Lutz, Tom. *Cosmopolitan Vistas: American Regionalism and Literary Value*. Ithaca: Cornell UP, 2004.

MacDonnell, Francis. "'The Emerald City Was the New Deal': E. Y. Harburg and *The Wonderful Wizard of Oz*." *Journal of American Culture* 13.4 (1990): 71–75.

Mahar, William J. *Behind the Burnt Cork Mask: Early Blackface Minstrelsy and Antebellum American Popular Culture*. Music in American Life. Urbana: U of Illinois P, 1999.

Mason, Ernest D. "Alain Locke." *Dictionary of Literary Biography*. Ed. Trudier Harris. Vol. 51. Gale Research, 1987.

McCarthy, Timothy Patrick. "Legalizing Cultural Anxieties: *Plessy*, Race and Literary Representations of 'Passing' in James Weldon Johnson's *Autobiography of an Ex-Colored Man*." *Griot* 16.1 (1997): 1–10.

Meltzer, Allan H. *A History of the Federal Reserve*. Vol. 1. Chicago: U of Chicago P, 2003.

Melville, Herman. *The Confidence-Man: His Masquerade*. New York: Dix, Edwards and Co., 1857. *University of Virginia Library Digital Collections*. 21 Feb. 2009 <http://repo.lib.virginia.edu:18080/fedora/get/uva-lib:476181/uva-lib-bdef:100/getFullView>.

Menchaca, Martha. *Recovering History, Constructing Race: The Indian, Black, and White Roots of Mexican Americans*. Austin: U of Texas P, 2001.

Meyers, Marvin. *The Jacksonian Persuasion: Politics and Belief*. Stanford: Stanford UP, 1957.

Michaels, Walter Benn. *The Gold Standard and the Logic of Naturalism: American Literature at the Turn of the Century*. The New Historicism: Studies in Cultural Poetics 2. Berkeley: U of California P, 1987.

———. *Our America: Nativism, Modernism, and Pluralism*. Durham: Duke UP, 1995.

Mill, John Stuart. *Utilitarianism*. 2nd ed. 1863. Ed. George Sher. Indianapolis: Hackett, 2001.

Murji, Karim, and John Solomos, eds. *Racialization: Studies in Theory and Practice*. Oxford: Oxford UP, 2005.

Nadel, Alan. *Invisible Criticism: Ralph Ellison and the American Canon*. Iowa City: U of Iowa P, 1991.

Nathan, Hans. *Dan Emmett and the Rise of Early Negro Minstrelsy*. Norman: U of Oklahoma P, 1962.

———. "Two Inflation Songs of the Civil War." *Musical Quarterly* 29.2 (1943): 242–53.

Nugent, Walter T. K. *Money and American Society, 1865–1880*. New York: Free Press, 1968.

———. *The Money Question During Reconstruction*. New York: W. W. Norton, 1967.

O'Leary, Paul M. "The Coinage Legislation of 1834." *Journal of Political Economy* 45.1 (1937): 80–94.

O'Malley, Michael. "Specie and Species: Race and the Money Question in Nineteenth-Century America." *American Historical Review* 99 (1994): 369–95.

Omi, Michael, and Howard Winant. "Once More, with Feeling: Reflections on Racial Formation." *Comparative Racialization*. Spec. issue of *PMLA* 123 (2008): 1565–72.

———. *Racial Formation in the United States: From the 1960s to the 1990s*. 2nd ed. New York: Routledge, 1994.

"The Original Uncle Tom Tells How the Play Was First Produced." *Commercial Gazette* 27 May 1883. *Uncle Tom's Cabin & American Culture*. Ed. Stephen Railton. 2005. 4 June 2007 <http://www.iath.virginia.edu/utc/onstage/re vus/osar66at.html>.

Otter, Samuel. "Stowe and Race." *The Cambridge Companion to Harriet Beecher Stowe*. Ed. Cindy Weinstein. Cambridge: Cambridge UP, 2004. 15–38.

Pierson, Michael D. *Free Hearts and Free Homes: Gender and American Antislavery Politics*. Chapel Hill: U of North Carolina P, 2003.

*Plessy v. Ferguson*, 163 U.S. 537 (1896).

Poe, Edgar Allan. "The Gold-Bug." 1843. *The Collected Tales and Poems of Edgar Allan Poe*. New York: Modern Library-Random House, 1992. 42–70.

Poor, Henry V. *The Money Question: A Handbook for the Times*. New York: H. V. & H. W. Poor, 1896.

Reed, Ishmael. *Mumbo Jumbo*. New York: Scribner, 1972.

Remini, Robert V. *The Age of Jackson.* Columbia: U of South Carolina P, 1972.
————. *Andrew Jackson and the Bank War: A Study in the Growth of Presidential Power.* Norton Essays in American History. New York: W. W. Norton, 1967.
Rev. of *The Grandissimes* by George Washington Cable. *Atlantic Monthly* Dec. 1880: 829–31. Rpt. in Turner, *Critical Essays* 13–15.
Rice, Thomas Dartmouth. "Jim Crow." n.d. Sheet music: Minstrels: T. D. Rice, Harvard Theatre Collection, Houghton Library, Harvard University.
Richards, Jason. "Imitation Nation: Blackface Minstrelsy and the Making of African American Selfhood in *Uncle Tom's Cabin.*" *Novel* 39.2 (2006): 204–20.
Richards, Leonard L. *Shays's Rebellion: The American Revolution's Final Battle.* Philadelphia: U of Pennsylvania P, 2002.
Richardson, James D., ed. *A Compilation of the Messages and Papers of the Presidents, 1789–1897.* Vol. 2. Washington, D.C.: Government Printing Office, 1896.
Ritter, Gretchen. "Silver Slippers and a Golden Cap: L. Frank Baum's *The Wonderful Wizard of Oz* and Historical Memory in American Politics." *Journal of American Studies* 31 (1997): 171–202.
"The Rival Circuses." *Overland Monthly* Sept. 1896: 372.
Robinson, Cedric J. *Black Movements in America.* New York: Routledge, 1997.
Rockoff, Hugh. "The 'Wizard of Oz' as a Monetary Allegory." *Journal of Political Economy* 98 (1990): 739–60.
Roediger, David R. *The Wages of Whiteness: Race and the Making of the American Working Class.* Rev. ed. Haymarket Series. London: Verso, 1999.
Rogin, Michael. *Blackface, White Noise: Jewish Immigrants in the Hollywood Melting Pot.* Berkeley: U of California P, 1996.
Rubin, Louis D., Jr. *George W. Cable: The Life and Times of a Southern Heretic.* New York: Pegasus, 1969.
Ryan, Susan M. "Misgivings: Melville, Race, and the Ambiguities of Benevolence." *American Literary History* 12 (2000): 685–712.
St. Louis, Brett. "Racialization in the 'Zone of Ambiguity.'" Murji and Solomos 29–50.
Saxton, Alexander. "Blackface Minstrelsy and Jacksonian Ideology." *American Quarterly* 27 (1975): 3–28.
Schleslinger, Arthur M., Jr. *The Age of Jackson.* Boston: Little, Brown and Co., 1945.
Schuyler, George S. *Black No More: Being an Account of the Strange and Wonderful Workings of Science in the Land of the Free, A. D. 1933–1940.* New York: Macaulay, 1931.
Shell, Marc. *Money, Language, and Thought: Literary and Philosophic Economies from the Medieval to the Modern Era.* Berkeley: U of California P, 1982.
"The Silver Dollar." *Harper's Weekly* 23 June 1877: 479.
"The Silver Heresy." *New York Tribune* 3 Jan. 1878: 1.

Skerrett, Joseph T., Jr. "The Wright Interpretation: Ralph Ellison and the Anxiety of Influence." *Massachusetts Review* 21 (1980): 196–212.

Smith, Barbara Herrnstein. *Contingencies of Value: Alternative Perspectives for Critical Theory*. Cambridge: Harvard UP, 1988.

Smith, John. "Jumbo Jum." 1840. Sheet Music: Minstrels, Harvard Theatre Collection, Houghton Library, Harvard University.

"A Sound Currency." *Workingman's Advocate* 8 Mar. 1834: 1.

"Specie Payments." *Harper's Weekly* 18 Dec. 1869: 802–3.

Stephens, Robert O. "Cable's Bras-Coupé and Merimee's Tamango: The Case of the Missing Arm." *Mississippi Quarterly* 35 (1982): 387–405.

Stowe, Harriet Beecher. *A Key to Uncle Tom's Cabin; Presenting the Original Facts and Documents upon Which the Story Is Founded, Together with Corroborative Statements Verifying the Truth of the Work*. Boston: John P. Jewett, 1853.

———. *Uncle Tom's Cabin; or, Life among the Lowly*. 1852. Ed. Elizabeth Ammons. New York: W. W. Norton, 1994.

Sumner, William G. *A History of American Currency*. New York: Henry Holt, 1874.

Sundquist, Eric J. *The Hammers of Creation: Folk Culture in Modern African-American Fiction*. Mercer University Lamar Memorial Lectures 35. Athens: U of Georgia P, 1992.

———. "Mark Twain and Homer Plessy." *Mark Twain's "Pudd'nhead Wilson": Race, Conflict, and Culture*. Ed. Susan Gillman and Forrest G. Robinson. Durham: Duke UP, 1990. 46–72.

Timberlake, Richard H. *Monetary Policy in the United States: An Intellectual and Institutional History*. Chicago: U of Chicago P, 1993.

Tipping, Schölin. "'The Sinking Plantation-House': Cable's Narrative Method in *The Grandissimes*." *Essays in Poetics* 13.1 (1988): 63–80.

"Topics of the Time." *Scribner's Monthly* Nov. 1878: 146–49. *Making of America*. Cornell U Lib., Ithaca. 19 June 2003 <http://cdl.library.cornell.edu/moa/moa_search.html>.

"Topics of the Time." *Scribner's Monthly* Oct. 1879: 935–39. *Making of America*. Cornell U Lib., Ithaca. 19 June 2003 <http://cdl.library.cornell.edu/moa/moa_search.html>.

Turner, Arlin, ed. *Critical Essays on George W. Cable*. Boston: G. K. Hall, 1980.

Turner, Arlin. *George W. Cable: A Biography*. Durham: Duke UP, 1956.

Twain, Mark. *Pudd'nhead Wilson; And, Those Extraordinary Twins*. Ed. Sidney E. Berger. New York: W. W. Norton, 2005.

Unger, Irwin. *The Greenback Era: A Social and Political History of American Finance, 1865–1879*. Princeton: Princeton UP, 1964.

United States Federal Reserve. *Federal Reserve Board Open Market Operations*. 28 Mar. 2006. 19 Apr. 2006 <http://www.federalreserve.gov/fomc/fundsrate.htm>.

Valentine, John J. "The Natural Law of Money." *Overland Monthly* July 1896: 121–23.

Wald, Gayle. "The Satire of Race in James Weldon Johnson's *Autobiography of an Ex-Colored Man*." *Cross-Addressing: Resistance Literature and Cultural Borders*. Ed. John C. Hawley. SUNY Series in Postmodern Culture. Albany: State U of New York P, 1996. 139–55.

Walling, William. "'Art' and 'Protest': Ralph Ellison's *Invisible Man* Twenty Years After." *Phylon* 34 (1973): 120–34.

Weinstein, Allen. *Prelude to Populism: Origins of the Silver Issue, 1867–1878*. New Haven: Yale UP, 1970.

Wells, David A. *Robinson Crusoe's Money; or The Remarkable Financial Fortunes and Misfortunes of a Remote Island Community*. New York: Harper & Brothers, 1876.

"Where There's Life, There's Hope." *Life* Jan. 1934: 26.

White, Walter. *Flight*. 1926. Voices of the South. Baton Rouge: Louisiana State UP, 1998.

Wilentz, Sean. *Andrew Jackson*. The American Presidents. New York: Times Books, 2005.

Willis, H. Parker. "The Failure of the Federal Reserve." *North American Review* May 1929: 547.

Winant, Howard. *The New Politics of Race: Globalism, Difference, Justice*. Minneapolis: U of Minnesota P, 2004.

———. "Whiteness at Century's End." *The Making and Unmaking of Whiteness*. Ed. Birgit Brander Rasmussen, Eric Klinenberg, Irene J. Nexica, and Matt Wray. Durham: Duke UP, 2001. 5 Feb. 2006 <http://www.soc.ucsb.edu/faculty/winant/ White_Racial_Projects.html>.

Wittke, Carl. *Tambo and Bones: A History of the American Minstrel Stage*. New York: Greenwood, 1968.

*The Wiz*. Screenplay by Joel Schumacher. Dir. Sidney Lumet. Perf. Diana Ross, Michael Jackson, Nipsey Russell, and Ted Ross. 1978. DVD. Universal, 1999.

Woodmansee, Martha, and Mark Osteen, eds. *The New Economic Criticism: Studies at the Intersection of Literature and Economics*. Economics as Social Theory. London: Routledge, 1999.

Wright, Richard. "The Man Who Lived Underground." *Eight Men: Stories by Richard Wright*. Ed. David Bradley. New York: Thunder's Mouth, 1987. 27–92.

Zwarg, Christina. "Fathering and Blackface in *Uncle Tom's Cabin*." *Novel* 22.3 (Spring 1989): 1–15.

# INDEX